DYNAMICS

Credits:

Content Developers: Michiel Duvekot, Lee Graft, Scyalla Magloir, John Patton

Copy Editor: Erica Fyvie

Technical Editors: Lenni Rodrigues, David Haapalehto

Cover Design: Louis Fishauf

Cover Image: Leon Vymenets

Production Manager: Carla Sharkey

Product Manager: Danielle Lamothe

Indexing: Bob Gundu

DVD Production: Roark Andrade, Julio Lopez

A special thanks goes out to:

Brian Cho, Shawn Dunn, Deion Green, Ken Ibrahim, Rachael Jackson, Robert MacGregor, Roland Reyer, Jason Schleifer, Michael Stamler, Marcus Tateishi, Flavio Trevisan.

Maya Dynamics

TABLE OF CONTENTS

CONTENTS

HOW TO USE THIS BOOK

Learning Maya 6 | Dynamics is your key to unlocking the power of Maya's Dynamics engine. Learn to master complex motion in Maya such as smoke, rain, fire, or colliding objects and add realism to your animations. This book is designed to help you comprehend Maya Dynamics regardless of your current skill level.

However, before you start this book, you should already have some knowledge of working in Maya. As an added bonus, we have included the Maya Beginner's Guide | Dynamics video on the accompanying DVD-ROM, where you will complete six easy-to-follow, step-by-step exercises to get you up and running with Maya Dynamics right away!

Theoretical discussions

Each section of this book is introduced by a theoretical discussion explaining the concepts at play when working with various features. These sections will help you understand why and how Maya works so that you are better equipped to solve problems as your skills improve.

Project-based tutorials

Each chapter includes step-by-step tutorials to help you improve your skills when working with tools and features in Maya. Complete the full project for a broader understanding of the workflows or focus on specific tools to understand how they work.

Instructor overviews

View the instructor overviews provided on the DVD-ROM for additional discussions and demonstrations to compliment the lessons in this book. Instructor overviews are provided by Alias Certified Instructors and are intended to act as your virtual trainer.

Index

Expert users may skip to the index in order find quick answers and solutions to production challenges without working through every lesson.

Updates to this book

In an effort to ensure your continued success through the lessons in this book, please visit our web site for the latest updates available:

www.alias.com/maya/learningtools_updates/

Installing tutorial files

To install the tutorial scene files, copy the *support_files* directory from the DVD-ROM found at the back of this book onto your local hard drive.

Maya Dynamics

WHAT IS MAYA DYNAMICS?

Dynamics in Maya uses rules of physics to let you simulate natural forces in your animation. Effects with complex motion such as smoke, rain, fire, or colliding objects lend themselves well to dynamically controlled animation. This animation is typically achieved by creating elements in a scene that react to the forces applied to them. By creating an environment of fields, expressions, goals, etc., the animator has artistic control over the affected objects, balancing the need for realism and animation requirements.

Maya Dynamics is the animation of rigid bodies, soft bodies, and particles, the use of dynamic constraints, and the rendering strategies for hardware and software particle types.

A volcanic eruption

The following sections provide a very brief overview of some of the key topics discussed in this book:

Rigid bodies

The rigid body system in Maya provides animation of geometric objects in a dynamically controlled, collision-based system.

- **Active and Passive Rigid Bodies** - Active and Passive Rigid Bodies are created to collide and react with one another in a realistic manner. Active objects typically fall, move, spin, and collide with passive objects.
- **Rigid body constraints** - Rigid body constraints allow dynamic objects to be constrained or constrain each other. Spring, hinge, pin, etc. are some of the constraint types that will be explored.

Particles

Particles are objects that have no size or volume. They are reference points which are displayed, selected, animated, and rendered differently than other objects in Maya.

- **Particle object and Array attributes** - Like other nodes in Maya, particles can be thought of as an object with a collective transform. They also contain attributes that control the individual particles using Array attributes. The individual particle behavior can be controlled with ramps, scripts, and expressions.
- **Fields** - Fields such as gravity, turbulence, air, and others are used to easily move particles around your scene without the use of MEL and expressions.
- **Particle expressions** - Particle expressions are a powerful and almost limitless method of controlling particle parameters. Particle expressions share the MEL syntax and methodology. Functions such as linstep(), sin(), and rand() provide mathematical control over particle appearance and motion.
- **Particle collisions** - Particle collision events provide a method for creating and killing particles when they collide with geometry. Particle collision event procedures can be used to trigger specific MEL-scripted commands at collision time.
- **XEmit function** - The emit function allows the user to create and position particles based on information directly derived from MEL and expressions. It requires an ample amount of MEL knowledge as more complicated usage of the emit function can get MEL-intensive.

Clip effects

Clip effects provide you with powerful and flexible tools for creating common dynamic effects. These are typically MEL scripts and expressions that automate the setup of the effect for the user. They also provide an excellent set of MEL and expression examples.

- **Fire** - This clip effect will light an object on fire for both hardware and software rendering.
- **Smoke** - The smoke clip effect makes use of hardware sprites and is a good example of how to setup hardware sprites.
- **Fireworks** - The fireworks effect allows you to make fireworks that are setup for software rendering quickly and easily.
- **Lightning** - The lighting clip effect lets you create an electrical arc between two or more objects.
- **Shatter** - The shatter clip effect lets you break up objects into parts you can use for dynamic simulations.
- **Curve Flow** - The Curve Flow clip effect allows you to select a curve as a motion path for particles.
- **Surface Flow** - The Surface Flow clip effect allows you to use a surface as a path for particles.

Particle instancing

With particle instancing, you can use particles to control the position and motion of instanced geometry.

- **Animated instance** - Particle instancing is only part of the functionality. You can instance a keyframed object to particles in the scene.
- **Cycled instance** - With the Particle Instancer, you can cycle through a sequence of snapshot objects to create the instanced motion.
- **Software sprites** - The Particle Instancer also provides aim control of the instanced object. If this instanced object is a textured plane, it can be aimed at the camera creating a software renderable sprite method.

Goals

Goals are a very powerful method of animating particles. Goals are a destination point that a particle wants to achieve. Particles can have multiple goal objects and per particle attributes designed specifically for goal-based interaction.

- **Goal Weight and Smoothness** - Goal Weight and Smoothness can be animated to provide particle movement that would be otherwise difficult to create with fields or expressions.
- **Per Particle Goal attributes** - Goal attributes such as parentU and goalPP provide individual particle control. With the use of the parentId attribute, these values can be transferred from one particle to another.

Soft bodies

Animating geometry for fluid-like motion or with dynamic response is accomplished with soft body particles.

- **Soft bodies** - Soft bodies are geometry that have particles controlling the position and movement of the CV's or poly vertices of the objects.
- **Goals** - Goals are a fundamental part of controlling soft bodies. The Goal Weight controls the deviation of the soft body from its goal object.
- **Springs** - Although springs can be applied to any particle, even to dynamic geometry, they are especially suited to binding soft body components together. Spring parameters such as Stiffness, Rest Length, and Damping can be controlled on a per object or per spring basis in Maya.

Particle rendering

What good is all this particle animation if you cannot render it out to contribute to the final shot?

- **Hardware rendering** - Hardware rendering of particles provides a quick method of image creation. Typically, these images are then taken to the compositor who sweetens and integrates them with the rest of the scene elements.
- **Software rendering** - Software rendering allows for scene integration of particles and rendered objects. Volumetric particle rendering is also created with software rendered particle types. Shadowing, glows, and other lighting effects are also combined.
- **Compositing** - Without compositing, much of this process would not be possible. Dynamics should always be viewed as another contributor to the elements that will make up the final image.

THE DEPENDENCY GRAPH

While creating dynamics, it is a good idea to have a basic knowledge of how Maya's system architecture works. Maya's system architecture uses a procedural paradigm that lets you integrate traditional keyframe animation, inverse kinematics, dynamics, and scripting on top of a node-based architecture that is called the **Dependency graph**. If you wanted to reduce this graph to its bare essentials, you could describe it as *nodes with attributes that are connected*. This node-based architecture gives Maya its flexible procedural qualities.

Below is a diagram showing a primitive sphere's Dependency graph as shown in the Hypergraph. A procedural input node defines the shape of the sphere by connecting attributes on each node. This system is much like a production line. You can think of each node as contributing or performing some operation on the data that is passing through it.

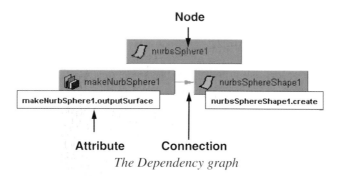

The Dependency graph

Nodes

Every element in Maya, whether it's a curve, surface, deformer, light, texture, expression, modeling operation, or animation curve, is described by either a single node or a series of connected nodes.

A *node* is a generic object type in Maya. Different nodes are designed with specific attributes so that each node can accomplish a specific task. Nodes define all object types in Maya including geometry, shading, and lighting. Below are three typical node types as they appear on a primitive sphere:

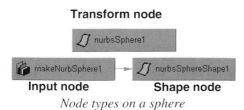

Node types on a sphere

- **Transform node** - Transform nodes contain positioning information for your objects. When you move, rotate, or scale a sphere, this is the node you are affecting.
- **Input node** - The input node represents options that drive the creation of your sphere's shape such as Radius or endSweep.
- **Shape node** - The Shape node contains all the component information that represents the actual look of the sphere.

Maya's UI presents these nodes to you in many ways. Below is an image of the Channel Box where you can edit and animate node attributes:

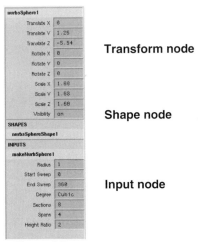

Channel Box

Attributes

Each node is defined by a series of attributes that relate to what the node is designed to accomplish. In the case of a Transform node, Translate X is an attribute. In the case of a shader node, Color Red is an attribute. It is possible for you to assign values to the attributes. You can work with attributes in a number of user interface windows including the Attribute Editor, the Channel Box and the Spread Sheet Editor.

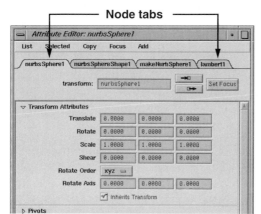

The Attribute Editor

One important feature in Maya is that you can animate virtually every attribute on any node. This helps give Maya its animation power.

Connections

Nodes don't exist in isolation. A finished animation results when you begin making connections between attributes on different nodes. These connections are also known as dependencies. In the case of modeling, these connections are sometimes referred to as construction history. Most of these connections are created automatically by the Maya user interface as a result of using commands or tools. If you desire, you can also build and edit these connections explicitly using the Connection Editor, by entering MEL commands, or by writing MEL-based expressions.

Hierarchies

When you are building scenes in Maya, you can build dependency connections to link node attributes. When working with Transform nodes or joint nodes, you can also build hierarchies which create a different kind of relationship between your objects.

In a hierarchy, one Transform node is *parented* to another. When Maya works with these nodes, Maya looks first at the top node, or *root* node, then down the hierarchy. Therefore, motion from the upper nodes is transferred down into the lower nodes. In the diagram below, if the *group1* node is rotated, then the two lower nodes will rotate with it. If the *nurbsCone* node is rotated, the upper nodes are not affected.

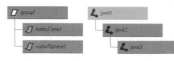

Object and joint hierarchy nodes

Joint hierarchies are used when you are building characters. When you create joints, the joint pivots act as limb joints while bones are drawn between them to help visualize the joint chain. By default, these hierarchies work just like object hierarchies. Rotating one node rotates all of the lower nodes at the same time.

When you are working with characters, you will use *inverse kinematics* to reverse the flow of the hierarchy.

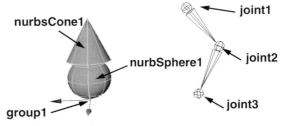

Object and joint hierarchies

The Hypergraph

In Maya, you can visualize hierarchies and dependencies using the Hypergraph. The following steps demonstrate how to work with various node types in the Hypergraph:

Working with hierarchies and dependencies

If you understand the idea of *nodes with attributes that are connected,* then you will understand the Dependency graph. You can see what this means in Maya by building a simple primitive sphere.

1 Setup your view panels

To view nodes and connections in a diagram format, the Hypergraph is required along with a Perspective view.

- Select **Panels** → **Layouts** → **Two Panes Side by Side**.
- Setup a Perspective view in the first panel and a Hypergraph view in the second panel.
- Dolly into the Perspective view to get closer to the grid.

2 Create a primitive sphere

- Go to the Modeling menu set.

- Select **Create** → **NURBS Primitives** → **Sphere**.

- Press **5** to turn on smooth shading and **3** to increase the surface smoothness of the sphere.

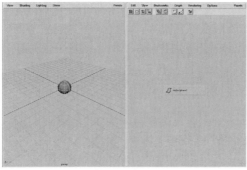

New sphere

3 View the Shape node

In the Hypergraph, you are currently looking at the scene view. The scene view is focused on *Transform nodes*. This node type lets you set the position and orientation of your objects.

Right now, only a *nurbsSphere* node is visible. In actual fact, there are two nodes in this hierarchy but the second is hidden by default. At the bottom of most hierarchies, you will find a *Shape node* which contains the information about the object itself.

- In the Hypergraph, select **Options** → **Display** → **Shape Nodes**.

You can now see the *Transform node* which is, in effect, the positioning node and the *Shape node* which contains information about the actual surface of the sphere. The Transform node defines the position of the shape below it.

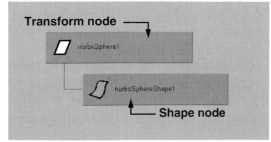

Transform and Shape nodes

- In the Hypergraph, select **Options** → **Display** → **Shape Nodes** to turn these **Off**.

  You will notice that when these nodes are expanded, the Shape node and the Transform node have different icons. When collapsed, the Transform node takes on the Shape node's icon to help you understand what it going on underneath.

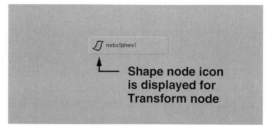

Transform node on its own

4 View the dependencies

To view the dependencies that exist with a primitive sphere, you need to take a look at the Input and Output Connections.

- Click on the sphere with the **RMB** and select **Inputs** → **Make Nurb Sphere** from the marking menu.

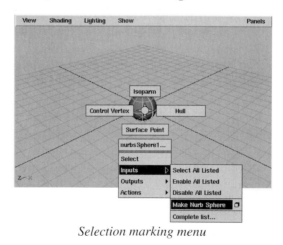

Selection marking menu

Note: You can also select the input node by choosing it in the Channel Box.

- In the Hypergraph, click the **Input and Output Connections** button.

The original Transform node is now separated from the Shape node. While the Transform node has a hierarchical relationship to the Shape node, their attributes are not dependent on each other.

The input node called *makeNurbSphere* is a result of the original creation of the sphere. The options set in the Sphere Tool's option window have been placed into a node that feeds into the Shape node. The Shape node is dependent on the input node. If you change values in the input node, then the shape of the sphere changes.

5 Edit the attributes in the Channel Box

In the Channel Box, you can edit attributes belonging to all of the node types. This lets you affect both hierarchical relationships and dependencies.

If you edit an attribute belonging to the *makeNurbSphere* node, then the shape of the sphere will be affected. If you change an attribute belonging to the *nurbsSphere* Transform node, then the positioning will be changed. Using the Channel Box will help you work with the nodes.

- For the Transform node, change the **Rotate Y** value to **45**.

- For the input node, change the **Radius** to **3**.

  You can set attribute values to affect either the scene hierarchy or the Dependency graph.

Animating the sphere

When you animate in Maya, you are changing the value of an attribute over time. Using keys, you set these values at important points in time, then use tangent properties to determine how the attribute value changes between the keys. The key and tangent information is placed in a separate animation curve node that is then connected to the animated attribute.

1 Select the sphere

- In the Hypergraph, click on the **Scene Hierarchy** button.

- **Select** the *nurbsSphere* Transform node.

2 Return the sphere to the origin

Since you earlier moved the sphere along the three axes, it's a good time to set it back to the origin.

- In the Channel Box, change the **Rotate Y** attribute to **0**.

3 Animate the sphere's rotation

- In the Time Slider, set the playback range to **120** frames.
- In the Time Slider, go to frame **1**.
- Click on the **Rotate Y** channel name in the Channel Box.
- **RMB-click** and select **Key Selected** from the pop-up menu.

  This sets a key at the chosen time.
- In the Time Slider, go to frame **120**.
- In the Channel Box, change the **Rotate Y** attribute to **720**.
- **RMB-click** and select **Key selected** from the pop-up menu.
- Playback the results.

  The sphere is now spinning.

4 View the Hypergraph dependencies

- In the Hypergraph, click the **Input and Output Connections** button.

  You see that an animation curve node has been created and connected to the Transform node. The Transform node is now shown as a trapezoid to indicate that it is connected to the animation curve node. If you click on the connection arrow, you will see that the connection is to Rotate Y.

  If you select the animation curve node and open the Attribute Editor, you will see that each key has been recorded along with value, time, and tangent information. You can actually edit this information here, or use the Graph Editor where you get more visual feedback.

Connected animation curve node

Parenting in the Hypergraph

So far, you have worked a lot with the dependency connections but not with the scene hierarchy. In a hierarchy, you always work with Transform nodes. You can make one Transform node the parent of another node, thereby creating a child which must follow the parent.

You will build a hierarchy of spheres that are rotating like planets around the sun. This example is a helpful way to understand how scene hierarchies work:

1 Create a new sphere

- In the Hypergraph, click on the **Scene Hierarchy** button.
- Go to the Modeling menu set.
- Select **Create** → **NURBS Primitives** → **Sphere**.
- **Move** the sphere along the Z-axis until it sits in front of the first sphere.
- Press **3** to increase the smoothness of the sphere.
- Go to the **Hypershade** menu.
- Apply a checker shader to both spheres.

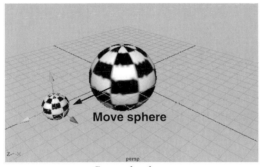

Second sphere

2 Parent the sphere to the first sphere

- In the Hypergraph, **MMB-drag** the node icon for the second sphere onto the first sphere. They are now parented together.
- Playback the scene.

  The second sphere rotates along with the first sphere. It has inherited the motion of the original sphere.

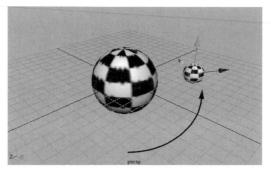

Rotating hierarchy

SUMMARY

The material in this book is presented in a progressive manner to take you through an entire range of tools and techniques that are available using Maya's dynamics system.

After successfully completing the exercises in this book you will:

- Understand how dynamics in Maya work so you can create your own effects;

- Know how to work with rigid bodies and dynamic constraints;

- Be able to control particles with fields, ramps, and expressions;

- Understand hardware and software rendering techniques;

- Learn how to use particles to control the position and motion of instanced geometry;

- Be able to optimize and troubleshoot scenes involving dynamics;

- Know how to dynamically animate NURBS and polygonal surfaces using soft bodies;

- Understand how particle collisions work.

1 Rigid Body Dynamics

This chapter introduces the fundamental tools and techniques required to achieve realistic "solid" collisions in Maya using rigid bodies.

In this chapter you will learn about the following:

- How to create rigid bodies;
- Identifying the differences between Active and Passive Rigid Bodies;
- How to create and connect fields to rigid bodies;
- How to work with the rigid body solver and its attributes;
- How to combine keyframing with rigid body dynamics.

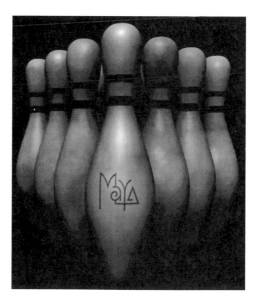

Bowling pins

WHAT IS A RIGID BODY?

Rigid bodies within the context of Maya are defined as any object whose surface does not deform when a collision occurs. Common examples in nature would be billiard balls, floors and ceilings, or a bowling ball. Of course, in the real world these surfaces do actually deform to a very small extent when a collision occurs. Within Maya, we overlook this minimal deformation and consider an object as either rigid or not rigid to simplify the process.

In Maya, any NURBS or polygonal surface can contain rigid body properties. Curves, particles, and lattices, for example, cannot become rigid bodies since they contain no surface information. Surfaces, however, that are made from curves, particles or lattices, for example, can be rigid bodies.

Soft bodies are NURBS or polygonal surfaces that have particle-like control of their respective CV's or poly vertices. Soft bodies will be explored in later lessons.

Active vs. Passive Rigid Bodies

Maya's rigid bodies are divided into two categories: *active* and *passive*. There are important distinctions between these two types of rigid bodies.

	ACTIVE	PASSIVE
Can be keyframed	No	Yes
Responds to collisions	Yes	No
Causes collisions	Yes	Yes
Affected by fields	Yes	No

A comparison of Active vs. Passive Rigid Bodies

The Soft/Rigid Bodies menu

The Soft/Rigid Bodies menu is used to create rigid and soft bodies, create dynamic constraints, and keyframe the active and passive state of objects.

Soft/Rigid Bodies menu

Important rigidBody nodes

The rigid body command you choose will create several new important nodes and attributes for each selected object. These nodes (and their associated attributes) can be viewed in the Channel Box, Hypergraph, Outliner, or Attribute Editor. In the Channel Box, you will notice the following nodes are created for each selected object:

rigidBody - The *rigidBody* node is located under the **SHAPES** section for each selected rigid body object in the Channel Box.

To view and select a *rigidBody* node from the Outliner, you may first need to show shapes by selecting **Outliner → Display → Shapes**. The *rigidBody* node will appear as a child of the object's Transform node.

The attributes within this node contain information that determines the active/passive status of the rigid body and various controls relating to the properties of each specific rigid body object.

rigidSolver - The *rigidSolver* node provides control over the evaluation of the rigid body dynamics. This node is listed under both the **INPUTS** and **OUTPUTS** sections within the Channel Box for the selected item. By default, one *rigidSolver* node is used to control the evaluation of all rigid bodies in the scene.

time - The *time* node determines when the rigidSolver's evaluations will take place. This is useful if you wish to have multiple simulations within the same scene running based on different time parameters.

A bowling alley

This example incorporates the use of Active and Passive Rigid Bodies and is intended to familiarize you with the process of setting up a simple rigid body simulation in Maya.

The bowling alley

1 Set project and load the file

If you haven't already set your project, do it now as follows:

- Select **File** → **Project** → **Set...**
- Choose the Dynamics project.

Note: The data files and installation instructions are on the DVD-ROM that accompanies this book. All textures associated with the data in this book are found in the *source images* directory of the Dynamics project. Since Maya stores both absolute and relative texture pathnames, you may occasionally need to reload or browse and reset the new texture path as it exists on your computer.

- Select **File** → **Open Scene...**
- Select the file named *bowling.mb*.

2 Create the Active Rigid Bodies

- Use the Outliner to select *pin1 to pin10*.
- **Ctrl-click** *bowlingBall* to the selection.
- Select **Soft/Rigid Bodies** → **Create Active Rigid Body - ❑**.
- In the Options window, select **Edit** → **Reset Settings** to set the options to the default state.
- Press **Create**.

3 Create the Passive Rigid Bodies

- Use the Outliner to select the following objects:

    bowlingLane, leftGutter, rightGutter, innerCage, backCage.

Note: *InnerCage* and *backCage* are parented to *fullCage*. You will not be needing the entire cage for the dynamic simulation.

- Select **Soft/Rigid Bodies** → **Create Passive Rigid Body - □**.
- In the Options window, select **Edit** → **Reset Settings** to set the options to the default state.
- Press **Create**.

4 Set rigidBody attributes for the bowling ball

- Select *bowlingBall*.
- Locate the *rigidBody* node for this object in the **SHAPES** section of the Channel Box.
- Set the following attribute values for the *rigidBody* node:

    InitialVelocityZ to **-55**;

    InitialSpinX to **-900**;

    Mass to **400**;

    Bounciness to **0**;

    standIn to **sphere**;

    applyForcesAt to **verticiesOrCvs**.

5 Set rigidBody attributes for the bowling pins

- Select all of the bowling pins.
- Enter the following attribute values for the *rigidBody* nodes:

    Mass to **35**;

    Bounciness to **0.5**;

    Static Friction to **0.05**;

    Dynamic Friction to **0.05**;

    applyForcesAt to **verticiesOrCvs**.

We'll discuss the specific definition of these attributes in a later chapter. For now, we just want to get some collisions happening.

Note: When multiple items are selected, (denoted by **...** in the name field of the Channel Box) it is only necessary to enter the attribute values for the first selected object. The change will be made to all selected items that contain the attribute being edited.

6 Turn on dynamic labels

In some cases when dealing with complex scenes containing large numbers of rigid bodies, it is difficult to keep track of which rigid bodies are passive and active. When set to **On**, the **displayLabel** attribute will display a small label next to each rigid body in the viewport indicating if it is an Active or Passive Rigid Body.

Note: Other dynamic components such as dynamic constraints (discussed later), also have labels associated with them.

- Select any *rigidBody* object in the scene.
- Click on the *rigidSolver* node near the bottom of the Channel Box.
- Set the **displayLabel** attribute to **On**.
- Rewind to display the dynamic labels.

   The labels are placed at the object's center of mass which is represented by a small X on each object.

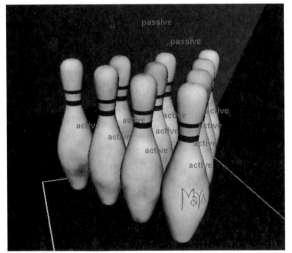

Displaying rigid body labels at the object's center of mass

7 Create a gravity node

- Click in the viewport to deselect any currently selected objects.
- From the Dynamics menu select **Fields → Gravity - ❑**.
- In the Gravity Options window select **Edit → Reset Settings**.
- Press **Create**.

8 Connect the objects to gravity

- Select all 10 pins and the *bowlingBall*.
- Select the gravity field last.
- Select **Fields** → **Affect Selected Object(s)**.

Tip: The same results could have been achieved by selecting the pins and ball, then choosing **Fields** → **Gravity**. This process would automatically connect the selected items to the chosen field.

A word about selection

If you are doing your selection in the Hypergraph, you will find that **Shift-selecting** is required. If you are doing your selection in the Outliner, then **Ctrl-selection** will give you an individual selection. **Shift-selection** in the Outliner gives you a selection of the objects that lie between the first selection and the second selection. You can also **LMB-drag** to select objects and attributes in various places in Maya.

Going forward, it is assumed that selection behavior and preferred selection technique is at your discretion. The Outliner and the Hypergraph have their inherent strengths for organization and object manipulation. You can choose to use the one you are most comfortable with for the task at hand.

9 Test the results

- Rewind and then playback the scene.

    The bowling ball is projected along the Z-axis while spinning on its local X-axis. The ball collides with the pins and the pins collide with each other and the barriers of the bowling alley. Notice that the barriers remain stationary.

Caching

Caching allows Maya to evaluate calculations once per frame and store the results of those calculations in memory (RAM) where they can be accessed during subsequent playback at much faster speeds. In addition to providing improved performance, caching allows you to scroll through the animation without problems.

When caching is enabled, Maya will continue to use the cached version of the data as the "master" until the cache has been deleted. For this reason, any modifications made to the simulation after caching the data will not exist in the currently cached version of the playback, since those changes were not part of the original calculations that were computed during the cache run-up.

It is best to tweak values and then cache the scene. Once you have evaluated those changes and wish to make more, delete the cache, make the new changes, then re-cache the scene again.

Note: The first playback cycle where Maya records the calculations into RAM is commonly referred to as a "run-up".

---

1 Cache the playback

- In the timeline, set the playback range to start at frame **1** and end at frame **100**.
- Select *bowlingBall*.
- Click on the *rigidSolver* node in the Channel Box and set the following:

      cacheData to **1**.

   A value of **1** corresponds to **On**, a value of **0** corresponds to **Off**.

Note: You can also enable or disable caching by selecting **Solvers** → **Memory Caching** → **Enable (or Disable)**.

- Rewind and then playback the scene.

   You can scrub in the timeline after the simulation has played through once.

2 Delete the cache

- Select **Solvers** → **Memory Caching** → **Delete** to clear the previously cached data from memory.

3 Modify the attribute values

- Experiment with the values used for InitialVelocityZ, InitialSpinX, Mass, and Bounciness to see how the simulation results differ.
- Re-cache the scene so you can see the result playback in real time.
- Repeat this process until you've achieved the desired motion.

Combining keyframes with dynamics

In some cases, relying solely on the influence of fields, InitialVelocity, InitialSpin, and other dynamic attributes to animate objects may not provide the level of control required. In these cases, it is useful to combine keyframing techniques with dynamic techniques to tune the motion of the animation. We'll discuss how to ignore dynamics while an object is controlled by keyframes, and how to combine keyframes and dynamics.

1 Load the file

- Select **File → Open Scene...**
- Select *keyedDynamics.mb.*

When you playback the scene, you will notice the ball has an initial velocity in the direction of the negative Z-axis which propels it into the pins as in the previous file.

2 Group the bowlingBall

Creating a group on the *bowlingBall* provides a second transform with which to apply hierarchical animation. In this case, you will use a motion path.

- Rewind to frame **1**.
- Select *bowlingBall.*
- Select **Edit → Group -** ❑.
- In the Group Options window, set **Group Pivot** to **Center**.

The Group Options window

- Rename the new group to *ballTranslate.*
- Rename *bowlingBall* to *ballRotate.*

  ballTranslate will handle the translation of the ball along the motion path. *ballRotate* is where you will keyframe rotation and use dynamics to control the motion of the ball after the motionpath animation has been completed.

The hierarchy of the ball should appear as shown below:

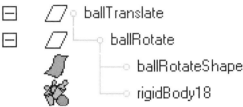

Hierarchy of ballTranslate in the Outliner with Display Shapes turned On

3 Move ballTranslate's pivot to its base

It is important to move the pivot point of *ballTranslate* to the base of the bowling ball so it is attached to the motion path at the base instead of the center of the ball.

- Select *ballTranslate* and press **W** to enable the **Move Tool**.

- Press **Insert** on the keyboard to switch to pivot mode. On a Macintosh computer, press **home**.

- Move the pivot point manipulator to the base of the ball. Hold the **C** key to use curve snap. When done, press **Insert** again.

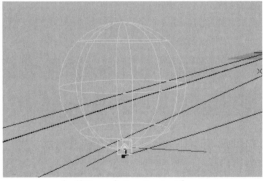

ballTranslate pivot at base

You can check the exact position of the pivot in the Attribute Editor. If you want to set it precisely, you can edit the **Y** value for the **Local Rotate** and **Local Scale** here.

Local Space			
Local Rotate Pivot	1.0390	0.0000	56.5622
Local Scale Pivot	1.0390	0.0000	56.5622
World Space			
World Rotate Pivot	1.0390	0.0000	56.5622
World Scale Pivot	1.0390	0.0000	56.5622

The position of the pivot

4 Turn Off the State of the rigidSolver

You'll be setting up animation now and we do not want the dynamics to interfere with the keyframed animation for now. A quick way to do this is to set the state of the rigidSolver to **Off**.

- Select the ball's *rigidBody* node from the Outliner.
- Open the Attribute Editor and select the **rigidSolver** tab.
- Turn off **State**.

rigidBody18	time1	rigidSolver

rigidSolver: rigidSolver

Rigid Solver Attributes	
Step Size	0.020
Collision Tolerance	0.020
Scale Velocity	1.000
Start Time	1.000
Current Time	1.000

Rigid Solver Methods
Solver Method: Runge Kutta

Rigid Solver States
- ☐ State
- ☑ Friction
- ☑ Bounciness
- ☑ Contact Motion
- ☐ Contact Data

The State of the rigidSolver

5 Attach the ball to the motion path

- Set the playback frame range from **1** to **60**.
- The current frame should be **1**.
- **Select** *ballTranslate* then, **Shift-select** *ballCurve*.

- Select **Animate** → **Motion Paths** → **Attach to Motion Path -** ⊡.

Set the following options:

> **Time Range** to **Time Slider**;
>
> **Follow** to **On**;
>
> **Front Axis** to **Z**;
>
> **Up Axis** to **Y**;
>
> **World Up Type** to **Scene Up.**

- Press **Attach** to attach *ballTranslate* to the motion path.

6 Set Playback Range

- Set the playback frame range to start at frame **1** and end at frame **200,** and then playback the scene.

Keyframe the ball rotation

The ball now moves along the curve, but it no longer rotates, until frame 60, when the ball becomes an Active Rigid Body again. You'll need to put some spin on the ball by keyframing the rotation of the *ballRotate* node.

1 Keyframe ballRotate

- Go to frame **1**.
- Select *ballRotate* node.
- Open the Channel Box.
- Set a keyframe on the **Rotate X** channel of *ballRotate*.
- Advance to frame **10**.
- Enter a value of **360** for the **Rotate X** attribute of *ballRotate*.
- Set another keyframe for that attribute.

2 Cycle the Rotate X animation curve

The cycling option in the Graph Editor causes the rotation that was just set up to repeat in 10 frame increments throughout the animation. Therefore, the same rotation motion that occurred on frames 1-10 will also occur on frames 11-20, 21-30, and so on.

- Open the Graph Editor by selecting **Window** → **Saved Layouts** → **Persp/Graph/Outliner**.
- Locate and select the **Rotate X** curve in the Graph Editor.
- Press **F** to frame selected.

- With the same curve still selected, choose **Curves** → **Post Infinity** → **Cycle with Offset**.

- Select **View** → **Infinity** to **On**.

  This displays the cycled curve data in the Graph Editor. This option can be left on or toggled to **Off** again to avoid clutter in the Graph Editor.

Combine keyframing and dynamics

1 Keyframe the active/passive state of the ball

In order for the ball to be either active or passive at different frames in the animation, you will keyframe its active state attribute using special menus.

- Rewind to frame **1**.

- Locate the *rigidBody* node for *ballRotate* in the Channel Box.

- Select **Soft/Rigid Bodies** → **Set Passive Key** to key this as a passive body.

- Advance to frame **60**.

- Select **Soft/Rigid Bodies** → **Set Active Key** to key this as an active body.

Note: Keying the active/passive state using these menus is the most reliable method. Sometimes setting the active/passive keyframe a frame or two before the motion path ends helps to prevent problems with order of evaluation.

---

2 Turn On the state of the rigidSolver

Now that you have completed the keyframe animation, you can enable dynamics again.

- With the *rigidBody* still selected, look under the **INPUTS** section in the Channel Box and click on *rigidSolver*.

- Type **1** in the **state** field to turn **On** state.

3 Keyframing the Ignore attribute

Since no substantial collisions occur in this animation until many frames into the simulation, Maya can ignore the computation of the pins until near the time of collision to speed up playback.

- Verify playback start range is at **1**.

- Select all **10** bowling pins.
- In the Channel Box go to the **SHAPES** section and **RMB** to keyframe the **Ignore** attribute of the *rigidBody* nodes as follows:

  Keyframe **Ignore** at frame **1** to **On**;

  Keyframe **Ignore** at frame **50** to **Off**.

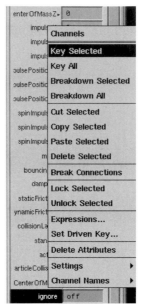

Using the RMB in the Channel Box to keyframe

4 Test the scene

- Playback the animation.

  The ball translates and rotates along the motion path as a Passive Rigid Body. It continues moving and rotating after the motion path animation has completed as an Active Rigid Body. This continued motion is the combined result of the gravity field, motion inherited from the path animation, and keyframed rotation.

TIPS AND TRAPS

The following are some additional tips to consider for this exercise and for rigid bodies in general:

- The **Ignore** attribute may cause some problems if it is keyframed **On** or **Off** at the same time some other important operation (such as the active state) is keyframed. To fix this, keyframe **Ignore** one frame before the other important action.

- Keyframing the **Ignore** flag while the simulation is cached (or vice-versa) may cause some unexpected behavior. Choose one or the other but avoid doing both simultaneously or the simulation may produce unexpected results (offsetting of objects' positions or objects spinning off into space at the wrong time, etc.)

- Avoid keyframing the active attribute using the Channel Box on any objects containing hierarchies. Instead, use the Set Active or Set Passive menu options under the Soft/Rigid Bodies menu.

- If the ball bounces along the bowling alley, set **Bounciness** to **0** on the ball and the alley and increase the mass of the ball. Also, make sure **Apply Force At** is set to **verticesOrCVs** for the pins.

- If the ball doesn't follow the path correctly, make sure the pivot point of *ballTranslate* is at the base of the ball. If the ball appears to follow the basic shape of the path but is offset in space, this is likely the cause.

- If you playback the scene after the ball is attached to the motion path, the ball may offset itself from the *ballCurve*. To avoid this behavior, restart the scene. After the **Ignore** attribute has been keyframed, select the *rigidSolver* node in the Channel Box and set the attribute **State** to **Off**. After the active/passive state of the ball has been keyframed, select the *rigidSolver* node and set the **State** attribute to **On**.

- Verify that your **undo queue** in the **Preferences** are set to **infinite** or to a high number. Realize that undo doesn't always work as reliably with dynamics due to the way dynamic simulations are being computed in the software. In general, when working with dynamics, you must work methodically and think about each step before progressing. Also, avoid scrubbing playback in the timeline if your scene is not cached.

- Changing the **Mass** attribute of an object will not affect how it falls under the force of gravity. However, it will affect how much force is exerted when a collision occurs. Also, changing the mass will affect how a non-gravity field (i.e. turbulence) will move the object around in the scene.

- The file *friction.mb* has rigid body books that slide down a table. You can use this file to get a clear idea of how the **Static** and **Dynamic Friction** attributes work.

These attributes provide general changes and are not precision controls. Valid values normally range from 0 to 1 although you can use higher values. Static friction controls a "threshold" as to how high the table will need to angle before the book begins to slide. Dynamic friction controls the "slipperiness" (energy loss) of the book once it is in motion along the table surface. Values closer to 1 correspond to more energy lost or more stickiness in the collision. It is important to remember that the friction values on the books *and* the table need to be taken into consideration since both contribute to the final simulation. Try adjusting the static and dynamic friction attributes for the books and the table and compare the different results.

The long arrows displayed from the *rigidBodies* in this file during playback show the direction of the velocity of the traveling *rigidBody*. This is a display feature on the *rigidSolver* node (*displayVelocity*) that can be turned on and off.

The **scaleVelocity** attribute (also on the *rigidSolver*) simply scales the length of this arrow and has no control of the motion of the objects on the solver.

- Can a rigid body be deformed? By definition a rigidBody is rigid which means non-deformable. In Maya you can apply a deformer to a rigid body, however, the collision calculations will be based on the shape of the original, non-deformed object (also known as the intermediate object). This will not likely be the effect you are after. One exception to this rule is particle collisions. You can make particles collide with deforming geometry and deforming rigid bodies. Particle collisions are discussed in greater detail later in this book.

- There are a couple of hotkeys included in the preferences of the Dynamics data. Pressing the **!** hotkey will cycle your background color from light grey to dark-grey to black. pressing the **@** hotkey will toggle the persp camera's Resolution Gate on and off.

Building a house of cards

Use what you've learned here to build a house of cards on a table. Apply fields to the cards to make them collide with each other and the table.

Remember that the normal orientation of a surface is very important in rigid body collisions. If you build the cards as a single-sided polygonal surface, you will find that some cards will not collide correctly. You can fix this quickly by selecting all the rigid body objects and selecting **Edit Polygons** →

Extrude Face, then extruding a little along the Z-axis. You do this even after you have created the rigid bodies.

SUMMARY

You now have a basic understanding of how Maya's rigid body dynamics system works. Rigid bodies are objects in Maya that can cause and respond to collisions. Active Rigid Bodies cause and respond to collisions and fields and cannot be keyframed. Passive Rigid Bodies cause, but do not respond, to collisions, and do not respond to fields, but can be keyframed.

RigidBodies are controlled by the *rigidSolver* and the *time* node. Important attributes of the *rigidBody* and the *rigidSolver* can be adjusted in the Channel Box. It is possible to keyframe the active/passive state of the *rigidBody* to combine keyframing and dynamic animation together.

In upcoming chapters, we will discuss the various rigid body attributes and solver attributes in greater detail so you understand their specific function better. The upcoming chapters will also focus more on tuning and optimizing the simulation.

You should now be able to:

- Create Active and Passive Rigid Bodies;
- Use keyframes, motion paths, and fields to control rigid body motion;
- Keyframe the active/passive state of a rigid body;
- Use the Ignore attribute and caching to speed playback;
- Use cycling in the Graph Editor;
- Recognize and understand important *rigidBody* nodes such as *time*, *rigidSolver*, and *rigidBody*.

2 **Rigid Body Constraints**

This chapter focuses on working with Maya's rigid body constraints. The three examples are a hanging wind chime, a medieval catapult, and an example pod engine setup.

In this chapter you will learn about the following:

- About constraint types;
- Animating constraint parameters;
- Parenting constraints;
- Application with dynamic and non-dynamic constraints;
- Rigid body groups.

A wind chime

DYNAMIC CONSTRAINT TYPES

Rigid body constraints are created using **Soft/Rigid Bodies** →**Create Constraint**. There are six dynamic constraint types divided into two categories:

Dual body constraints - The *dual body* constraints allow for constraining of a rigid body to a point in space or to another rigid body.

- Pin
- Hinge (and rotateHinge)
- Spring

Single body constraints -The single body constraints allow for the constraint of a rigid body to only a point in space or, in the case of the Barrier, to a plane in space.

- Nail
- Barrier

Constraint descriptions:

Pin constrains two Active Rigid Bodies to each other, or an Active and a Passive Rigid Body to each other. It does not allow for constraint to a point in space. The pinning point or pivot is adjustable and can be keyframed on and off.

Hinge constrains an Active Rigid Body to another active or Passive Rigid Body with a user defined pivot orientation. This pivot constrains the motion to one axis. It can also constrain a rigid body to a point in space.

directionalHinge works just like a hinge constraint. The difference is that the orientation of the hinge axis will change depending on the motion of the object(s) that it is connected to. So, if you rotate an object that has a directionalHinge attached, the constraint will orient its axis to match. To use a directionalHinge, create a constraint, then set its constraint type to directionalHinge in the Attribute Editor.

Spring constrains an active or a Passive Rigid Body to another Active Rigid Body or a point in space. The spring constraint contains attributes that control the elastic properties, **Stiffness, Restlength,** and **Damping**.

Nail constrains an Active Rigid Body to a point in space. This point can be grouped and translated under another object as a child.

Barrier creates a planar boundary that an Active Rigid Body cannot pass through.

Auto Creating

When you select an object to be dynamically constrained to a point or another object, Maya will automatically turn the necessary objects into rigid bodies if they are not rigid bodies already. This feature is controlled by the **Auto Create Rigid Body** flag in the **Dynamics** section of the **Window** → **Settings/Preferences** → **Preferences...**

Constraint examples

The scene file *constraint_examples.mb* contains a sample application of each constraint type.

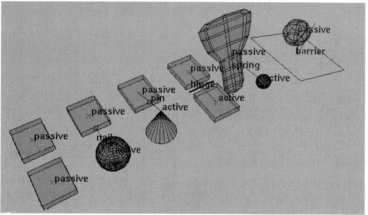

Constraint examples scene

A wind chime

In this exercise, you will hook up the provided geometry into a free hanging kinetic wind chime.

1 Open a file

- Open the file *chime_start.mb*.

  This file consists of five cylindrical poles (with caps). Each will hang from an upper support structure. There is also a middle gong object and a wind flap. The entire structure will hang from a ring at the top.

The chime_start file

2 Create Active Rigid Bodies

- Select all five chimes and make them into Active Rigid Bodies with the following settings:

  Mass to **1**;

  Bounciness to **0.6**;

  Damping to **0.25**;

  Static and **Dynamic Friction** to **0.2**;

  standIn to **none**;

  Active to **On**;

  Apply Forces At to **boundingBox**.

- Select *flapRingShape* and make it an Active Rigid Body with the settings below. Make sure you are selecting *flapRingShape* and not the *flapRing*. You may need to make sure **Display** → **Shapes** is on in the Outliner. Set the following:

  Mass to **5**;

  Bounciness to **0.6**;

  Damping to **0.9**;

  Static and **Dynamic Friction** to **0.2**;

  standIn to **sphere**;

  Active to **On**;

  Apply Forces At to **boundingBox**.

- Select *topRing* and make it an Active Rigid Body with the following settings:

    Mass to **1**;

    Bounciness to **0.6**;

    Static and **Dynamic Friction** to **0.2**;

    standIn to **Cube**;

    Active to **On**;

    Apply Forces At to **boundingBox**.

3 Create a nail constraint to support the entire structure

Now that the rigid body properties are set, you will start adding in the constraints.

A nail constraint will let you hang the sculpture from a point in space.

- Select *topRing*.

- Select **Soft/Rigid Bodies** → **Create Constraint -** ❑ and set the following:

    Constraint Type to **Nail**.

- Press **Create**.

- Translate the *rigidNailConstraint* pivot to the bottom of the *hangingRing* object.

- Parent the nail constraint to the *hangingRing* object so that you can later move the entire wind chime by moving the *hangingRing* object if desired.

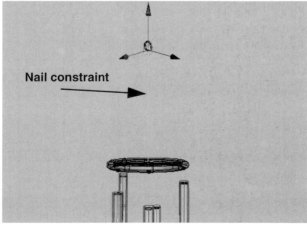

Nail constraint

Move the nail constraint point to the hangingRing's position

4 Create nail constraints for the hanging chimes

Since each chime is hanging from a point in space, nail constraints will be used. Pins could be used if you wanted the weight of each chime to influence the rotation of the *topRing* object. To avoid playing a balancing act and to keep things simple for right now, use *nail* constraints.

A nail will be created for each *chime*, then parented to a small *chimeAttach* object (in the *topRing* hierarchy):

- Use the Outliner to select the *chime*.
- Select **Soft/Rigid Bodies** → **Create Constraint** - ❏ and set the following:

  Constraint Type to **Nail**.
- Press **Create**.
- Translate *rigidNailConstraint* pivot up in **Y** so it is within the *chimeAttach* object.
- Parent the *rigidNailConstraint* to *chimeAttach.*

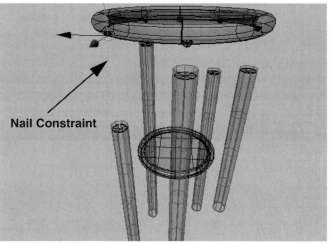

Move the nail constraint pivot to the hanging point

5 Repeat for the remaining chimes

Now add nails for the remaining four chimes:

- Select *chime1* and create a nail constraint.
- Move the nail up and parent it to *chimeAttach1*.
- Repeat the process for *chime2*, *chime3* and *chime4* and their respective *chimeAttach* objects.

Tip: You can use the **g** hotkey to repeat the last command. In this example, it is useful for repeatedly creating the nail constraints.

6 Adjust center of mass for each chime

Currently, each nail hangs from the center of the chime. Ideally, the chime should hang closer to the top of the chime as though a string was attached to the top of the chime. You can easily move the **centerOfMassY** attribute on each rigid body to accomplish this. There is no manipulator for centerOfMass so you need to use the Channel Box.

- Select a chime object.
- Highlight **centerOfMassY** in the Channel Box for the rigid body.
- **MMB-drag** in the viewport to change the value. You'll see the length of the nail constraint change. Move the center of mass to the *chimeCap* at the top of each chime.

Tip: Pressing **Ctrl** while you **MMB-drag** in the viewport changes the Channel Box attribute values in smaller increments.

- Repeat for the remaining chimes.

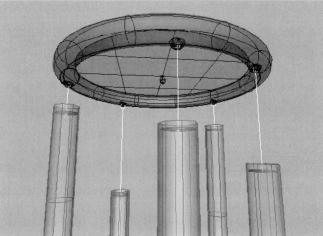

Center of mass(x) for each chime moved near chimeCaps

7 Create a pin constraint for the center gong object and flap

The wind flap at the bottom should blow in the wind and also influence the gong ring it is attached to. The gong should also influence the wind flap. Since both objects will have influence on each other, you will use a pin constraint.

- Select *flapRing* and *gong*.
- Select **Soft/Rigid Bodies** → **Create Constraint - □**.

  Set the following:

  Constraint Type to **Pin**.

  Notice that the pin constraint is created between the two object's center of mass.

Once the constraint is created, you can move the constraint pivot to the desired location. Moving it up just beneath the gong object will give the wind flap object more influence than the ring.

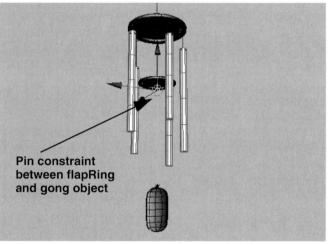

Contraint pivot in desired location

8 Create a pin between topRing and gong

To get the *gong* to hang from *topRing*, add a pin constraint between the *gong* and *topRing* and position it just under the *topRing* object.

- Select *gong* and *topRing* to create a pin constraint.
- Move the pin constraint just slightly beneath the *topRing's* planar surface.

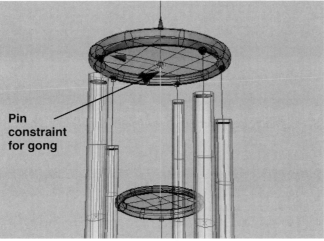

Pin contraint added

9 Connect existing fields to the various objects

This scene contains a gravity, turbulence, and radial field. These fields have some preset values that will blow the wind chimes and flap around.

- In the Outliner, **Ctrl+select** all the *chimes* and the *gong*.
- Individually, **Ctrl+select** *gravityField1*, *radialField1* and *turbulenceField1* which are under the *fields* group.
- Select **Fields** → **Affect Selected Object(s)**.
- Select the *flapRing*, **Control Select** *gravityField1* and *airField1*.
- Select **Fields** → **Affect Selected Objects(s)**.

10 Playback

- Playback about **200** frames to watch the simulation play.

11 Adjust the mass of the wind chime pieces with the Spread Sheet

Keep in mind that the mass of all rigid body pieces directly affects the motion of the simulation. The Attribute Spread Sheet is a great way to compare values of many objects and quickly make changes.

- Select the rigid body objects of the wind chime by selecting **Edit** → **Select All by Type** → **Rigid Bodies**.
- Select **Window** → **General Editors** → **Attribute Spread Sheet...**

- Click the **Shape Keyable** tab in the spreadsheet to locate the *rigidBody* nodes. You may have to scroll down to see the *rigidBody* nodes and their attributes.

  If you want to select the *rigidBody* only, you can use this MEL command

  ```
  select `ls -typ "rigidBody"`;
  ```
  This command will select all nodes that are of type *rigidBody*.

- Locate the **Mass** attributes of the selected objects and adjust as desired.

	Spin Impulse Y	Spin Impulse Z	Mass	Bounciness	Damping	Static Friction	Dynamic Friction
rigidBody1	0	0	1	0.6	0	0.2	0.2
rigidBody2	0	0	1	0.6	0	0.2	0.2
rigidBody3	0	0	1	0.6	0	0.2	0.2
rigidBody4	0	0	1	0.6	0	0.2	0.2
rigidBody5	0	0	1	0.6	0	0.2	0.2
rigidBody6	0	0	5	0.6	0	0.2	0.2
rigidBody7	0	0	1	0.6	0	0.2	0.2
rigidBody8	0	0	1	0.6	0	0.2	0.2

Attribute Spread Sheet

Tip: You can **drag-select** multiple cells in single or multiple columns to make simultaneous value changes. You can **Ctrl-shift** select cells. Entire rows or columns can be selected by clicking on the row or column title.

12 Add InitialSpin to animate the piece (optional)

Experiment with **Impulse**, **Spin Impulse**, and **InitialVelocity**. These attributes exist on Passive and Active Rigid Bodies but only have an effect with Active Rigid Bodies.

Impulse - A force that gets applied to a rigid body on every frame of the simulation. These can be useful if you always want to keep something moving in a given direction and you want that force to be reapplied continuously. Impulses are rarely used but can come in handy.

Spin Impulse - Adds a force to each frame that will cause the object to spin around the specified axis.

InitialSpin - Adds a force at the first frame of the simulation to cause spinning around the defined X,Y, or Z-axis of the Active Rigid Body.

For this example, you might try adding some InitialSpinY to the *flapRing*.

Creating the strings (optional)

In the file *chime_done.mb* you'll see that each of the objects is hanging from a geometric string object. There is a display layer called "cords" that contains this geometry. The dynamic constraints do not render. Therefore, lofted surfaces were created between the attached objects to represent strings.

To do this, a tiny circular isoparm was duplicated in the center of each *chimeCap*. Then that curve was projected (**Edit NURBS → Project Curve On Surface**) in the top view up onto each *chimeAttach* object.

The history was deleted on the *chimeAttach* projection curve. A loft (**Surfaces → Loft**) was then created between the original duplicated *chimeCap* isoparm and the projected curve above.

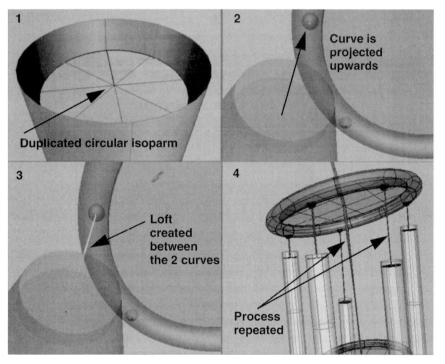

Construction history is kept so the loft will redraw as the chimes move around. This works as a simple and quick approach. For more realism, soft bodies (covered in later chapters) could be used to create the cords.

Other related data files

- The file *chime_done.mb* is a finished working version of this file.

- The file *chime_doneBaked.mb* is a renderable version of this file.

- The *chimes.mpg* movie shows you a sample render of this scene file.

- There are also extra example files (*mobile_geometry.mb*, *mobile_balanced.mb*) that demonstrate a similar file that requires more effort in balancing and understanding mass and center of mass.

Related exercises

- Animate the translation of the hanging ring object to see how it affects the other rigid bodies in the scene.

- Use the method described above to create a string object between *chime4* and *chime4Attach* in the *chime_start.mb* file.

- Adjust field positions and attributes, and experiment with rigid body attribute settings.

Medieval destruction

In this exercise, you will construct a catapult using the hinge and spring constraints. You will also use two orient constraints that are non-dynamic. There are many ways this example could be setup; this is just one example that is used to show you some different ideas.

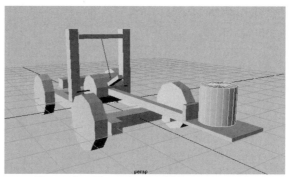

Catapult with spring and hinge constraint

1 Open scene file

- Open the file *catapult.mb.*

This file contains the catapult geometry. Note the following inventory of objects:

overhead - static anchor for spring constraint;

lever - armature anchor for spring constraint;

frame - geometry of catapult frame;

wheels - geometry of catapult wheels;

boom - armature arm;

boomWheel - armature fulcrum.

2 Spring constrain the lever to the overhead

Use the spring constraint to pull the armature towards the overhead anchor which will remain stationary.

- **Shift-select** *lever* and *overhead* objects.
- Select **Soft/Rigid Bodies** → **Create Constraint** - □. Set the following:

   Constraint Type to **Spring**.

- Press **Create**.

   This converts *lever* and *overhead* to Active Rigid Bodies and builds a spring constraint between them.

3 Change the overhead object to a Passive Rigid Body (make sure caching is off)

- Select the *overhead* object.
- In the Channel Box for the **Active** attribute enter, **0** or **Off**.
- In the Channel Box, make sure the **cacheData** attribute for the *rigidBodySolver* node is set to **Off.**

   If caching is on accidentally, there can be some strange object offsetting or rewind problems that will occur later. To help avoid these problems in this example, avoid scrubbing and excessive undoing.

4 Orient constrain the boomWheel to the lever

The lever object will rotate the *boomWheel* object so you must orient constrain the *boomWheel* to the *lever*.

- Select the *lever* first then the *boomWheel* object.
- Go to the Animation menu set.
- Select **Constrain** → **Orient**.

   This will create a *boomWheel_orientConstraint* under the *boomWheel* object.

Note: Be careful not to confuse the animation constraints with the dynamic rigid body constraints.

---

5 Hinge constrain the lever object

To get the *lever* to only rotate about the same axis as the *boomWheel*, you will use a hinge constraint on the lever and then move the hinge to the center of the *boomWheel*.

- Select the *lever* object.
- Select **Soft/Rigid Bodies** → **Create Constraint** - ❑. Set the following:
  Constraint Type to **Hinge**.
- Press **Create**.

6 Reposition the hinge

- Select the hinge object and rotate it so that it is parallel with the X-axis of the *boomWheel*.

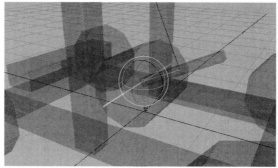

Hinge constraint orientation

- Translate the hinge to the center of the *boomWheel*.

You should use an Orthographic view to align this accurately.

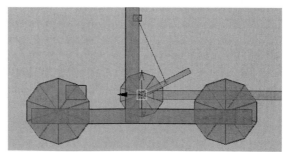

Hinge constraint position

7 Test the setup at this point

- Select the *rigidSpring_Constraint*.

- In the Channel Box or Attribute Editor, enter a value into the **SpringRestLength** attribute that is half of its current value.

  This will force the spring to try to assume this new length, thus pulling the *lever* towards the *overhead* object.

  A quick way to change a value to half of its original value is to type `/=2` in the Channel Box.

8 Attach the boom to the boomWheel

You should have the *boomWheel* rotating correctly. You want the *boom* and its launcher to follow this rotation. To do this you will apply another orient constraint between the *boomWheel* and the *boom*.

- Select the *boomWheel* first, then the *boom* object.
- Select **Constrain → Orient**.

  The *boom* is now orient constrained to the *boomWheel.*

  The *boom* also contains, as children, the geometry that will hold the projectile. It is named *launcherPad*.

9 Make the launcherPad into a Passive Rigid Body group

- Select the *launcherPad* group which contains the launcher geometry (stop, pad).
- Make this group a Passive Rigid Body group by selecting **Soft/Rigid Bodies → Create Passive Rigid Body**.

Note: You can make a hierarchy of objects into a single rigid body group by selecting the group and performing the create rigid body command. This works as long as there are no existing rigid bodies in this hierarchy.

---

10 Create a bomb

- Create a piece of geometry and place it on the *launcherPad* with a tiny little bit of clearance between the bomb and launch pad.
- Turn this object into an Active Rigid Body by applying a gravity field to it.
- Playback the scene.

11 Tune the throw

To tune the throw, you will change the spring constraint attributes:

> **Spring Stiffness** to **200**;
>
> **Spring Damping** to **5**;
>
> **Spring Rest Length** to **1**.

For the *springRestLength* you have already tried a value that is one half its initial value. Other values will change the action but it is generally a good idea to keep this value constant and use the other values of **SpringStiffness** and **Damping** to control the catapult strength and recoil.

Damping and **Friction** settings on the *launcherPad* and the *bomb* will also play a part in the simulation. Try **Friction** of **3** and **Damping** of **1** on both the *bomb* and *launcherPad* to get started.

Friction controls how much resistance occurs between surfaces. Damping can be thought of as air density.

Related exercises

Create more realism for the catapult:

- Keyframe rigid body dynamic attributes to settle the recoil of the armature.

  Hint: *rigidSpringConstraint1.damping*.

- Stop armature from going through the overhead geometry.

  Hint: Use a hidden rigid body object.

Pod Engines

In this more complex example, you will learn how to control high resolution geometry via lower resolution rigid bodies. You will setup a network of constraints between hidden control objects that control higher resolution geometry. In part two of this example, you will learn how to put a complex rigid body setup onto a motion path for animation.

Pod engines controlled by rigid constraints

1 Open scene file

- Open the file *pods_start.mb*.

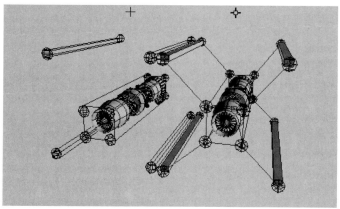

Starting scene file with one pod setup

This file contains two pod engines. The engine on the right is already setup and will be used as reference for you to setup the engine on the left.

Also note the display layers in the scene. You can use these to help organize the scene. Several items are set as references so they are visible in shaded mode but not selectable.

2 Create Passive Rigid Bodies with no collisions

- Use the display layers to hide *engine1, engine2,* and *controls2*.

- Individually, select the eight spheres at the ends of the *controlArmsGroup*.

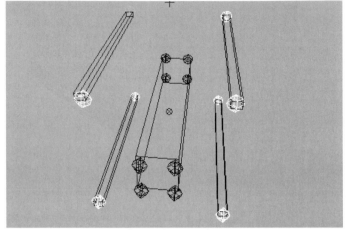

Geometry for anchoring the constraints

- Select **Soft/Rigid Bodies** → **Create Passive Rigid Body**.
- With all of the newly created Passive Rigid Bodies still selected, set the following attributes in the Channel Box.

Tip: If you accidentally deselected them, you can set your pick mask to select only rigid bodies, then drag select over the spheres to select the *rigidBody* nodes.

Mass to **1**;

Bounciness to **0.4**;

Damping to **0.8**;

Frictions to **0.6**;

StandIn to **None**;

Active to **Off**;

Collisions to **Off** (very important);

Apply Forces At to **boundingBox**.

3 Create Active Rigid Bodies with no collisions

- Individually **Shift-select** the eight spheres surrounding the box and also select the box.

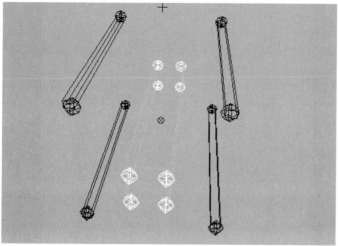

Spheres and surrounding box selected

- Select **Soft/Rigid Bodies → Create Active Rigid Body**.
- With these newly created Active Rigid Bodies still selected, set the following attributes in the Channel Box:

    Mass to **1**;

    Bounciness to **0.4**;

    Damping to **0.8**;

    Frictions to **0.6**;

    StandIn to **None**;

    Active to **On**;

    Collisions to **Off** (very important);

    Apply Forces At to **boundingBox**.

4 Create spring constraints

- Make the *controls2* display layer visible but keep it set to reference (R mode). Use the objects in *control2* as a guide so you can see how to configure the constraints for *control1*.
- Select the upper left front sphere on the control arm and the upper left front sphere of the main box as shown below.

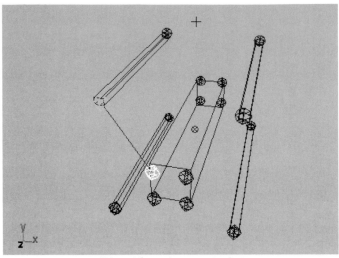

Rig with spring constraint

- Select **Soft/Rigid Bodies** → **Create Constraint - ❐**.

  Set the following:

    Constraint Type to **Spring**;

    Stiffness to **200**;

    Damping to **10**;

    Spring Rest Length to **On** and set to **3.0**.

5 Repeat springs for remaining pairs of spheres

Create the same spring constraint for the remaining pairs of spheres:

- Select the upper right front sphere on the control arm and the upper front right sphere of the main box.

- Press **g** to redo the last action.

  This will create another spring constraint. If you've done some other action or if it doesn't work, you can always create the spring constraint from the menu.

- Repeat all around the structure until you have a spring setup that looks like your reference on display layer *control2* and in the image below.

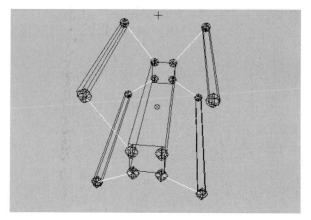

Rig with four spring constraints

6 Create pin constraints

Now you'll create pin constraints between the box object and each sphere at the corner of the box. This is done to keep the box from rotating out of control.

- Select the upper left box ball, **Shift-select** the box.

- Select **Soft/Rigid Bodies** → **Create Constraint -** ⊓. Set the following:

  Constraint Type to **Pin**.

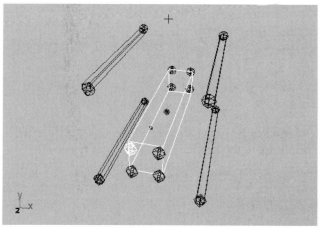

Rig with pin constraint for attachment

- Leave the pin where it was created; you'll move it into place later.

- Repeat the process for the remaining seven spheres around the box.

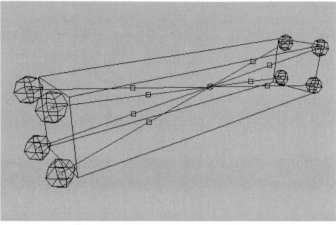

Pin constraints prior to positioning

7 Move the pins into place

Now you will move each pin to the center of each box sphere:

- Set your pick mask so you only select rigid constraints.
- Use your front and side Orthographic camera views to align the constraints so they are positioned at the corners of the box (the centers of each sphere) as shown below. Again, use the *controls2* display layer for reference if you need it.

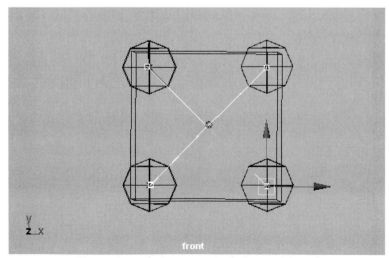

Front view of pin constraint being positioned

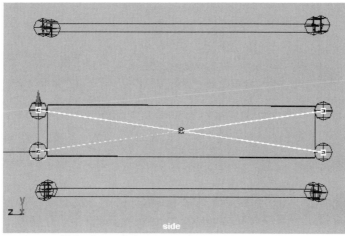

Side view of pin constraint positioning

8 Connect fields

- Select all seventeen rigid bodies you created (two sets of eight spheres and the main box).

- **Ctrl+select** the *gravityField1* and *turbulenceField1* objects under the *engineOne* hierarchy.

- Select **Fields** → **Affect Selected Object(s)**.

Animating the pods along a path

1 Open File

- Continue to use the file you're working with or open the file *pods_pathStart.mb*.

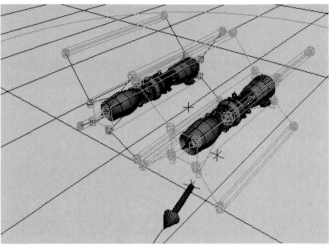

Scene file of pods_pathStart.mb

2 Group all constraints and parent into rig, update display layer

- Use the Outliner to select all the spring and pin constraint nodes that were created for *engineOne*.

- Add these items to the *controls1* display layer.

- Now group them using **Edit → Group**.

- Rename the group *constraints.*

- Drag the *constraints* group onto the *engineOne* group in the Outliner.

3 Attach the arrow object to a motion path

- Select *Arrow* and **Ctrl+select** *mainCurve.*

- Select **Animate → Motion Paths → Attach to Motion Path - ❏**. Set the following:

    Time Range to **Start/End**;

    Start Time to **30**;

    End time to **230**;

    Follow to **On**;

    Front Axis to **Z**, **Up Axis** to **Y**;

    World Up Type to **Scene Up**;

    Bank to **On**;

    Bank Scale/Limit to **1** and **90**, respectively.

When you playback, the arrow follows along the path. Don't
change the shape of the path unless you are at frame 1. This can
cause problems that are difficult to recover from.

4 Parent both controlArms under the mainControl locator

- Use the Outliner to **MMB-drag+drop** *controlArmsGroup* and
  controlArmsGroup1 onto *mainControl*.

Hierarchy as viewed in the Outliner

5 Point and orient constrain mainControl to Arrow object

By using point and orient constraints, the control arms (which are non-
dynamic objects), will follow along with the motion path object. The
constraints will drag all the dynamic objects along for the ride.

- Select *Arrow* and **Ctrl+select** *mainControl*.

- Select **Constrain → Point**.

- Select *Arrow* and **Ctrl+select** *mainControl*.

- Select **Constrain → Orient**.

6 Playback twice, ignore error message

- Playback the animation, troubleshoot if necessary.

  There is a lot going on here, including several layers of
  hierarchy, point and orient constraints, Passive and Active Rigid
  Bodies with fields, motion path control, etc., all affecting the
  motion of these objects and all being evaluated simultaneously.

  You will usually have to play the scene through twice before the
  solver evaluates properly for this example. The first playback
  often displays the following error from the rigid solver:

  ```
  // Error: basellist::take: cannot locate item //
  ```

This cryptic error is displayed when the rigid solver is unable to account for some piece of geometry in the evaluation. In this example, this error and the problems that result from it normally disappear on the second playback.

It is normal for the constraints to behave in a unpredictable manner when you rewind. However, they should realign normally once the animation plays back for a few frames.

7 Offset control arms group

- Rewind to frame **1**.

- Select *mainControl, controlArmsGroup;* and the *controlArms* object.

- Set **translate X** for controlArms to about **-4** in the Channel Box. This provides some spacing between the engines. The engine will settle in to its new position during the thirty frame runup prior to the beginning of the motion path animation.

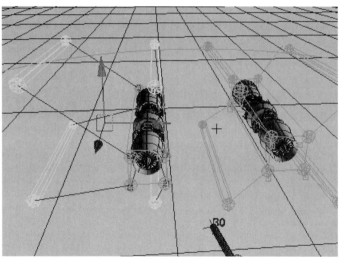

Offsetting controlArms in -X shown prior to playback

8 Display particle layers

Two particle emitters are point and orient constrained to geometry on the back of the engines. Both emit into the same sprite particle object to simulate smoke trails.

- Locate the *smokeEmitters* display layer and make it visible.

- Playback at least **30** frames. The emission rate is keyframed to begin after frame 30 and continue throughout playback.

Hardware graphics display of sprite smoke layer

Note: This smoke only renders using the hardware render buffer and would need to be composited into a final rendered image. Hardware rendering is covered in greater detail later in the book.

- The file *pods_pathDone.mb* is a completed version of this file.

TIPS AND TRAPS

Some of the following issues may arise as you go through the previous examples in this chapter:

- Sometimes the arm on the catapult will not fully recoil unless the rewind button is pressed several times. Also, the arm may offset. This is likely to happen if caching is turned on for the *rigidBody* solver. Check this first! This can also be caused if you are scrubbing in the timeline or using undo a lot in this example. This is partially caused by the fact that there are dynamic and non-dynamic constraints working together here. The undo queue may not be able to record all complex interdependent functions. In some cases, simply zeroing out the transforms on the offset geometry can serve as a temporary fix. You may have to start from scratch and do the setup again, just try to keep scrubbing and undoing to a minimum. For the catapult example, take it step-by-step.

- Be careful not to confuse dynamic (hinge, pin, sprint, etc.) and non-dynamic (orient, point, etc.) constraints. Dynamic constraints only exist between rigid body objects.

- A good solution for limiting the range of the catapult arm is to place a hidden Passive Rigid Body object just behind the *boomWheel* so the *lever* collides with it, thus stopping it before the *boom* hits the *overhead*. If the *rigidBody* is placed up higher (near the *overhead*), interpenetrations are more likely to occur since the tip of the arm is travelling faster than the base of the arm. The solver is not checking frequently enough to be able to catch interpenetrations that occur at the end of the arm.

- Notice that you cannot make the boom of the catapult a Passive Rigid Body. This is because there is already a rigid body in that hierarchy (on the launcher pad). You can only have one rigid body controlling a given hierarchy. The optimization chapter will discuss some alternatives to this limitation.

- Changing the shape of the motion path in the pod engine example is not recommended unless you have rewound to frame 1.

- Take advantage of the fact that you can keyframe a constraint on and off in the Channel Box. For example, perhaps you have a leaf dangling from a tree using a pin constraint. Keying the constraint off would allow the leaf to fall to the ground at a specific time.

SUMMARY

Rigid body constraints in Maya are an important part of working with dynamically animated geometry. Understanding the various advantages of using a specific constraint for a specific application can greatly affect how you approach a shot. Alternative methods for building and controlling hierarchies of objects through parenting and constraints using the methods outlined here is another important process to consider as you build more complicated scenes or scenes that require more control.

3 Rigid Body Optimizing

This chapter covers some fundamental tools and techniques related to making sure your rigid body simulations are as efficient as possible.

In this chapter you will learn about the following:

- The importance of stand-in geometry;
- Rigid Body and solver optimization settings;
- Collision and interpenetration troubleshooting;
- Baking simulations.

Battling tops

CHAPTER 3

WHAT IS AN OPTIMIZED SCENE?

Question: When do you need to optimize a scene?

Answer: When it runs excessively slow.

Answer: When it fails due to interpenetration errors.

Answer: When it behaves erratically and unpredictably.

You generally expect performance problems when running simulations in dense environments and expect lighter scenes to present less of a challenge to the interaction and playback.

The first objective is to ensure that a scene progresses through the simulation, only stopping or slowing down during an intensive calculation.

The second objective is to achieve playback as close to real-time as possible without having to render or playblast the scene. This is a good goal but in many cases cannot be attained due to hardware and software performance limitations.

To achieve these objectives, you will look at some typical problem areas and the necessary steps to ensure that the solver is not driven into an unsolvable situation.

The rigid solver

The rigid solver calculates the transformation attributes for rigid bodies using the attributes on the *rigidBody* nodes and the global attributes set on the rigid solver node as input. The attributes on the rigid solver node control the accuracy of the solution. The following material will help you find the right balance of accuracy versus speed.

Unpredictable or wild results

This is typically caused by values being fed into the solver that are wildly changing or exceeding the proper expected range. The proper expected range are values that make sense for the solver on a given attribute or dynamic state. If the solver encounters a value that is much larger or smaller than it was expecting, it may tell an object to travel much faster or farther than the other objects around it are prepared to do.

The solver must make assumptions to increase its performance. When you intentionally or unintentionally stress the simulation, you may exploit an assumption that the solver is making. This can result in errors. Remember, the simulation is only an approximation.

The goal is to set the approximation to an appropriate trade-off between accuracy and interaction.

Solver grinding or failing

When a scene is grinding or no longer making forward progress, it is time to take a look at what is going on more closely. The Script Editor is the first place to look for errors and information that may be produced by the solver. Even seemingly unimportant warnings can provide a clue as to why a solver is failing farther on. Your first step should be to investigate all warnings and errors.

You should learn to associate warnings and errors with symptoms and conditions that lead to solver problems.

Slow playback

In order to speed up playback, the load on the solver must be reduced. The solver attempts to determine the solution as to where every rigid body vertex is at any given frame.

The first step is usually reducing the amount of vertices that the solver must keep track of. Using Stand Ins will accomplish this as will tuning rigid body tessellation to more coarse values. A Stand In is a less complex shape that is used to represent a more complex shape, essentially an object with less data for the solver to keep track of.

Reducing the overhead of other scene components and display functions can go a long way to improving playback (displaying in wireframe, hiding other unused objects etc.).

Caching the animation is necessary for optimizing rigid bodies that have an unavoidable geometry density. Caching can use a lot of memory in scenes with dense geometric objects. Caching will not make it easier for the solver to calculate a solution, but it will help speed up your work because it reduces the time you have to wait for the solver.

Interpenetration errors

An interpenetration error occurs when the solver can no longer guarantee the accuracy of the simulation due to one object's geometry having passed through another object's geometry. Typically, the solver stops or slows down the simulation if this error occurs.

Why doesn't the solver just continue and ignore this error?

This error is important. You want this type of feedback. You can use this information to your advantage to help adjust simulation properties so that the solver does not enter into a corrupt or inaccurate situation.

Imagine if a sharp piece of geometry spiked into another object creating an interpenetration. The only way for the object to continue on would be to reverse its direction and back itself out and continue in a less penetrating fashion. This would be a very laborious and computationally intensive moment and one that you want to avoid completely, if possible.

Avoid interpenetration errors by:

- Anticipating "at risk" objects;
- Using stand-in geometry;
- Adjusting tessellations.
- Adjusting *rigidSolver* attributes in the Attribute Editor:

    Step Size;

    Collision Tolerance.
- Increasing Damping to avoid wild velocities.
- Checking the surface normal orientations.
- Positioning objects so that there is a little gap between them before the simulation starts.

Battling tops

Battling tops

This exercise steps you through some common scene problems that lead to optimization and troubleshooting. This scene is a very simple scene that has been constructed to demonstrate some of the more common things you can check for when optimizing a more complex scene.

1 Load the scene file

- Open the file *battleTop_start.mb.*

2 Playback the scene

The scene is setup to a point where it is in need of some optimization. It also has some "errors" creating problems. Ask yourself the following questions:

- What do you notice about performance?
- What do you notice about the base object?
- What do you notice about the tops?

3 Create normals display on/off shelf buttons

- Select **Display → NURBS Components → Custom - ❐**.
- Enable **Normal (shaded mode)**.
- Press **Apply and Close** to save the options.
- Press and hold **Ctrl+Alt+Shift** simultaneously, then select **Display → NURBS Components → Custom**.

  The menu item is now loaded on to the current shelf as a shelf button.

- Repeat the above process to create the off button with the **Custom - ❐** settings to **Normals** toggled **Off**.

4 Select and display the object normals

- Select the base and the tops.
- Use your normals display shelf buttons to display the normals for the base and tops.

  The bases' normals are pointing inward. This is a common occurrence for objects that were created using surface modeling tools like revolve and sweep since the U direction of the creation curve will determine the normal direction of the resulting surface. It may be difficult to see that the normals are facing inward. It helps to dolly your camera inside one of the tops' geometry to clearly see the surface normal direction.

5 Reverse the base surface

- Select the base object.
- Select **Edit NURBS → Reverse Surface Direction - ❐** and **Reset** options.
- Press **Reverse**.

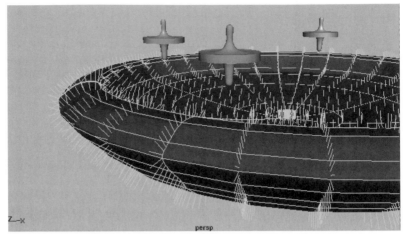

Normals displayed with correct orientation

6 Reverse the surfaces of the tops

Although this may improve performance and alleviate interpenetration problems in some scenes, for this particular scene, it hasn't solved our slow performance problem yet. Sometimes, it is just one or two things that affect the entire situation. Nonetheless, having the normals facing outward is important, so repeat the process for the remaining tops.

- Make sure the normals are facing outward for the remaining tops.

7 Rebuild the tops' geometry

Another reason for hampered playback can be geometry that is needlessly overbuilt, therefore, you will rebuild the tops' geometry to see if that will fix the slow playback.

- Select one of the tops.

- Select **Edit NURBS** → **Rebuild Surfaces -** ❏. Set the following:

    Rebuild Type to **Reduce**;

    Parameter Range to **0 to 1**;

    Direction to **U and V**;

    Use Tolerance to **Local**;

    Positional Tolerance to **1**;

    Output Geometry to **NURBS**;

    Keep Originals to **Off**;

    Click **Rebuild**.

- Repeat this rebuilding process for all the tops and playback.

- Playback to check for improvements.

- Once again, you likely will not notice a huge performance increase, but this step is still recommended to help prevent other problems that could be introduced.

Tessellation Factor for NURBS rigid bodies

As you may know, when you render a NURBS object, Maya tessellates the geometry of that NURBS object into polygons prior to rendering. A similar process occurs when the dynamics engine encounters a NURBS rigid body object. The solver assigns a Tessellation Factor to the NURBS object that determines the polygonal approximation of the shape. You can adjust the accuracy of this approximation by adjusting the **Tessellation Factor** attribute under **Performance Attributes** for each rigid body object. This attribute has no effect on polygonal rigid body objects.

By default the Tessellation Factor is 200.

If you have a highly detailed NURBS object, 200 polygons may not be enough for the solver to accurately represent that shape when calculating collisions. Although lower Tessellation Factors will mean less computation work for the solver, you will also have less accurate representation of your NURBS geometry. Being aware of this attribute can help you tune your simulations to add more or less accuracy where necessary.

By rebuilding the tops objects, you have reduced the geometric load on the solver. Another way is to adjust this Tessellation Factor attribute. The main drawback is that you do not have control over where the tessellation is most needed. In this example, you want more tessellation at the tips to avoid a sharp interpenetrating point and also at the sides to avoid interpenetration when tops collide.

Another strategy might be to convert your rigid bodies to polygons during the rebuilding process, thus creating a Stand In object for collisions and simulation.

Stand Ins

One of the best ways to clean up the performance of a rigid body is to use a Stand In object. This is very useful when you have dense or irregular objects that you want to perform rigid body dynamics to. The *rigidBody* node provides a choice of cube and sphere Stand Ins that you can select from. Alternatively, you may wish to create your own Stand In geometry, make it a rigid body, then simply parent your higher resolution object to that Stand In and hide the Stand In.

1 Substitute the base object with the lowRezBase object

Continue on your quest to get this scene optimized. One object in the scene is needlessly complex. The base object has geometry that is not involved in collisions.

- Select *base* object.
- In the Outliner, delete the associated rigid body.
- Select *lowRezBase* and unhide it if necessary.

  This object was created by duplicating the base object, then detaching the surface at the appropriate place and deleting the unnecessary geometry.

- Select **Soft/Rigid Bodies** → **Create Passive Rigid Body**.

  Now the collisions will be computed only for the area of the base that is important for this particular simulation. You can hide the *lowRezBase* again.

2 Playback the scene

Still no major improvements?

Optimizing a dynamics scene is often like optimizing for rendering. You will can try several different options until you find what works. During this process, you have cleaned up a lot of things and will continue to do so.

3 Set Tessellation for the tops' rigid bodies

The rigid body dynamics are determined from an approximation of the rigid body object's shape. This approximation is controlled by the tessellation of the rigid body unless a Stand In object is specified.

- Select *top1*.
- Open the Attribute Editor and locate the **Performance Attributes** section.

Performance Attributes section, rigid body

Stand In - selects Stand In Object Sphere or Cube.

Apply Force At - Dynamic forces applied at Center of Mass, Bounding Box or VerticesOrCVs. VerticiesOrCVs is the most accurate but the slowest.

Tessellation Factor - adjusts geometric approximation of rigid body object.

Collision Layer - selects Collision Layer participation. Objects on the same collision layer number will collide with each other. Objects on different collision layer numbers will not collide with each other. An object on collision layer -1 will collide with an object on any collision layer.

- Experiment with values on the **Tessellation Factor** attribute with **Stand In** set to **none**.

Below are the equivalent tessellations for the *top1* object set to 100, 150, 200, and 500.

Tessellation of 100   **Tessellation of 150**

   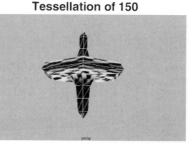

Tessellation of 200   **Tessellation of 500**

Tessellation values from 100 to 500

Note that at low tessellation values the point of the top is much sharper. This affects how the top spins and also increases the likelihood of an interpenetration. At low tessellation values the interaction of the edge of the top with other tops is less predictable.

4 Use the Attribute Spread Sheet

You've tried all of these things but nothing has solved the problem yet. When this happens, it is a good idea to have a look at the *rigidBody* nodes themselves and compare them against each other. You want to look for differences between the rigid bodies or values that stand out as excessively large or small.

- Select all the *rigidBody* nodes for the tops.
- Open **Window** → **General Editors** → **Attribute Spread Sheet...**
- Click on the **Shape Keyable** tab.
- Compare the attribute values. Do you notice any strange values?
- The InitialSpin settings are very high, with some at 15000 units per frame. This is potentially the root of the problem for this scene.
- Try lowering the values and playing the simulation again. You should notice much faster performance in the playback.

With practice, you will learn valid ranges for the different attributes and also learn how many attributes rely on each other. In other words, if you change mass, you may have to change frictions to compensate for the new motion.

Working through this process usually isn't too much fun but knowing what to check and being methodical about checking things will help you track down and solve problems. It will also help you to design things correctly when starting from scratch to help avoid potential problems.

Obviously, this scene file is very simple by design. Chances are your production shots will not be this simple. Design your work smartly from the ground up and also know what you can reasonably expect as good performance from the solver. Always look for ways to keep the number of rigid body calculations to a minimum.

A windy city

Maya is much faster at evaluating animation curve information than it is at evaluating dynamic motion in a scene. The primary reason an evaluation of existing animation curve data is faster is because the software "knows" where the object(s) is going to be at any given point in time. This is not true for a rigid body simulation. The position and orientation of all rigid bodies are calculated using rules inside each frame to produce the final result.

In this example, you will learn some additional optimization techniques. You will learn how to produce animation curve data from objects that are dynamically controlled. This process is called "baking". You will also learn how to create and work with multiple rigid body solver nodes and the advantages to this approach.

The example scene is a basic trash can object that will bounce down a stairway and into an alleyway. You will place trash objects inside the trash can and have the trash bounce around inside.

When you consider what you will need to accomplish this motion, you will hopefully realize that you'll need the trash can to be active so it can bounce down the stairs but you also want it passive so that the trash inside it will bounce around without affecting the motion of the can. This seems like an unattainable situation. How can something be Active and Passive simultaneously? Well, it cannot, but by using a simple baking technique you can achieve these results.

Another challenge here will be getting these interdependent objects reacting to each other without stalling the solution due to interpenetration. Hopefully, you can use what you learned in the previous section of this chapter to overcome any such interpenetration problems encountered.

1 Open scene file

This scene consists of an alleyway with typical urban obstructions and an average dose of garbage.

- Open the file *alley.mb*.

Animate the trash can

The trash can presents some problems that can be alleviated by using a Stand In object. You will use a cylinder as the Stand In object. This cylinder will be used to make the trash can bounce down the stairs. Later you will use a second rigid body to make trash bounce around inside the can. Your initial goal here is to have trash inside the trash can.

1 Create Passive Rigid Bodies out of the lowSteps, stairway, and floor objects

- Select the *lowStepsGroup*, *stairwayGroup*, and *floor*.

- Select **Soft/Rigid Bodies → Create Passive Rigid Body**.

    These objects are now rigid bodies under the *rigidSolver* solver.

2 Use a Stand In object for the trash can

- Make sure you have **Display → Shapes** turned **On** in the Outliner window.

- Select and unhide the *trashcanStandInShape* object.

3 Turn the trashcanStandIn into an Active Rigid Body

- Make sure *trashcanStandInShape* is still selected.

- Select **Soft/Rigid Bodies** → **Create Active Rigid Body**.

4 Connect this rigidBody to the airFields and gravityField1

- With *trashcanStandInShape* selected, **Ctrl-select** the *airField1*, *airField2* and *gravityField1*.

- Select **Fields** → **Affect Selected Object(s)**.

5 Adjust rigid body Attributes to satisfy the simulation

The ideal situation would be to have the trash can fall down the steps and also follow the curve so that it ends up at the bottom of the stairs and continues down the alley. Use the following settings as a guide. All other un-noted attributes are assumed to be default.

trashCan rigid body settings:

> **Mass** to **15**;
>
> **Bounciness** to **0.4**;
>
> **Damping** to **0.1**;
>
> **Static Friction** to **0.2**;
>
> **Dynamic Friction** to **0.2**;
>
> **Collision Layer** to **0**;
>
> **Stand-In** to **none**;
>
> **Apply Force At** to **verticiesOrCvs**.

stairwayGroup rigid body settings:

> **Mass** to **1**;
>
> **Bounciness** to **0.6**;
>
> **Damping** to **0**;
>
> **Static Friction** to **0.2**;
>
> **Dynamic Friction** to **0.2**;
>
> **Collision Layer** to **0**;
>
> **Stand-In** to **none**;
>
> **Apply Force At** to **verticiesOrCvs**.

airFields:

> The *airField* values are already set to give you a good start. You can leave them as they are or experiment with the *airFields* settings. However, some attributes can have a profound impact on the trash can's movement.

Bake Simulation

Once you have a decent simulation of the trash can bouncing down the stairs, you can simplify things by baking the simulation. Baking converts the dynamics induced animation to animation curves. These curves can then be tweaked and manipulated like all other animation curves in Maya.

The baking process also provides other performance benefits and functionality. You will bake the dynamic motion of the *trashCanStandIn*, delete the *rigidBody* node, then make the *trashCan* object into a Passive Rigid Body. This allows for another "layer" of rigid body dynamics to exist. Remember, Passive Rigid Bodies can be parented under surface geometry that is controlled by keyframed animation.

Currently, if you try to make the *trashCan* a Passive Rigid Body, you would get the following error:

```
Error line 1: Attempting to create a rigid body from
the shape or hierarchy "trashCan" which already
contains a rigid body.
```

You cannot have more than one object in the same hierarchy be controlled by different rigid bodies. By baking the motion of the Active Rigid Body trashcan, you can delete the rigid body and add a new Passive Rigid Body on the *trashCan* object.

1 Bake the trash can falling down the stairway

- Select the *trashcanStandIn* Transform node.

- Select **Edit → Keys → Bake Simulation - ❑**. First **Reset** the options in the dialog box (**Edit → Reset Settings**) and then set the options as follows:

> **Hierarchy** to **Selected** - You only want to bake the selected object, not the entire hierarchy.
>
> **Channels** to **From Channel Box** - You will highlight the appropriate transform attributes in the Channel Box.
>
> **Time Range** to **Start/End** - You should only need to bake about **300** frames, that should be enough. Set this value to the length of your desired simulation.
>
> **Sample by** to **1.0** - You will sample by **1** frame increments.

Bake Simulation Options window with correct preferences

- In the Channel Box select the **Translate** and **Rotate** channels.

Tip: **LMB-drag** down the Channel Box and across these attributes so that they are highlighted in black.

- Press **Bake.**

  Maya will create keyframes for each frame of the simulation and create animation curves.

2 Delete the trashcanStandIn rigid body

Shortly, you will add a rigid body to the *trashCan*. Since the *trashCan* and *trashCanStandIn* are in the same hierarchy, you need to remove the existing rigid body before you can create another one for a different object in the same hierarchy.

- Select the *trashcanStandIn* node.
- Press the **Backspace** or the **Delete** key on the keyboard.

3 Playback

Confirm that the bake is accurate. Problems with baking can arise when either you are sampling by too coarse of a sample rate and/or you are trying to bake too many channels from control points or Shape node animation. Treat these other nodes and channels as separate passes.

Also, notice that if you select the *trashcanStandIn* object, the timeline shows a series of red tick marks. These are the keyframes that now control the motion of the *trashCanStandIn*. You can also view and edit these keys using the Graph Editor.

Baking is strongly recommended as the last step before rendering any rigid body scene. It is a good idea to keep an unbaked dynamic version of your scene and a baked version that is used for rendering. Time-based rendering options, such as motion blur, work much more reliably with baked animation data than with dynamically driven animation.

Baking with the control points option turned on is a good method for baking out soft body animations prior to rendering them with motion blur. Soft bodies are covered in detail in a later chapter of this book.

Putting trash in the can

1 Make the trash can a Passive Rigid Body

- Select the *trashCan* Transform node.

- Select **Soft/Rigid Bodies** → **Create Passive Rigid Body**.

2 Add Active Rigid Body contents to the trash can

In the *alley.mb* scene file is a group named *garbage*. This group contains various pieces of refuse. You will use them to test with.

- Select one of the *paperStandIn* objects and position it inside of the *trashcan*. If you need to scale the object, do so before making it a rigid body.

- Make the paper object you selected an Active Rigid Body by selecting **Soft/Rigid Bodies** → **Create Active Rigid Body**.

- Set the **Stand In** attribute on that rigid body to **Sphere**.

- Connect this rigid body to *gravity2*, *airField1*, *airField2*.

3 Playback and tune for interpenetration

Damping, Bounciness, and **Friction** will play a big part in preventing the Active Rigid Body trash objects and trash can from reaching accelerations that can cause interpenetrations. The solver attributes of **Step Size** and **Collision Tolerance** may need to be slightly lowered. This may take some time, also, you may want to experiment with different trash pieces and their starting position/orientation within the can if interpenetration errors persist.

Trash object rigid body settings:

> **Mass** to **100**;
>
> **Bounciness** to **0**;
>
> **Damping** to **0.8**;
>
> **Static Friction** to **0.1**;
>
> **Dynamic Friction** to **0.1**;
>
> **Collision Layer** to **(separate values for each trash object)**;
>
> **Stand In** to **Sphere**.

trashCan object Passive Rigid Body settings:

> **Mass** to **1**;
>
> **Bounciness** to **0.01**;
>
> **Damping** to **1**;
>
> **Static Friction** to **0.01**;
>
> **Dynamic Friction** to **0.01**;
>
> **Collision Layer** to **-1**;
>
> **Stand In** to **none**.

rigidSolver settings:

> **Step Size** to **0.020**;
>
> **Collision Tolerance** to **0.03**;
>
> **Start Time** to **1**;
>
> **Rigid Solver Method** to **Runge Kutta Adaptive**.

The solver settings are very important and are a good place to look at early in the process of reaching a good solution. If your settings of **Damping** and **Friction** do not alleviate persistent interpenetration problems, then the solver settings of **Step Size** and **Collision Tolerance** should be lowered slightly.

The solver method also influences performance. The **Runge Kutta Adaptive** method is Maya's default method and is generally the most accurate setting. Experiment with these methods so that you are comfortable with their respective strengths and weaknesses.

It is difficult for us to give you numbers and tell you that these will work for your simulation. Getting this simulation to run is tricky. The numbers provided here are one possible solution that may or may not work for you. As you will learn, one small change in your scene changes all the interdependent and subsequent elements of the simulation. Having patience and being methodical are important. Also, making slight adjustment in the initial starting position of your simulation can have profound effects.

Moving objects to another rigidSolver

Using multiple rigid solvers gives you the ability to adjust solver settings independently. If you have groups of colliding objects but these groups will not collide with each other (perhaps they are not in close proximity), then putting them on different solvers helps optimize things.

To select the current solver:

- Select **Solvers** → **Current Rigid Solver** → **rigidSolver**.

To create a new solver:

- Select **Solvers** → **Create Rigid Body Solver**.

1 Duplicate floor object

- Duplicate the rigid body *floor* object and rename the new rigid body object *newFloor*.

  If you want to create a new separate simulation of trash blowing down the alley, it may be more efficient to create a new solver and run the objects on the new solver. Remember that objects cannot collide or be influenced by objects on separate solvers. You can, however, duplicate objects and put them on another solver or create them under a new solver.

2 Create a new rigid body solver

- Select **Solvers** → **Create Rigid Body Solver**.

  The newly created solver (*rigidSolver1*) is now the active solver. Any Active or Passive Rigid Bodies created will be assigned to this solver unless you select another solver as the current solver.

3 Move rigid body to rigidSolver1

Move the *newFloor* rigid body object to *rigidSolver1*.

- First select *newFloor's rigidBody* node then in the Command Line or the Script Editor enter:

  ```
  rigidBody -edit -solver rigidSolver1;
  ```

  You can select multiple rigid bodies and execute this command to move all over at once. There are ready-made shelf buttons in the *rigidBody* shelf that make this process quicker so you don't have to type the MEL command each time.

This new solver and floor are now ready to work with newly created rigid bodies. The new solver can have separate settings while maintaining the settings already in place for the existing trashcan simulation. If you look in the **Outputs** section of the Channel Box for the *newFloor* rigid body object, you will now see that it is connected to *rigidSolver1*. Any new rigid bodies you create in the scene will be on *rigidSolver1* and will only collide with other rigid bodies on *rigidSolver1*. In a way, this is like using collision layers. The difference is that you can control each solvers' accuracy level independently. Note that there is also a shelf button included to delete a rigidSolver node from your scene. First, you have to move all objects off of the solver you want to delete and then press the **delSol** shelf button included with the shelves in the support files.

SUMMARY

Tuning and troubleshooting rigid bodies can usually be approached by keeping the following in mind:

Know your tessellations - Surfaces or polygons, what is the solver seeing in terms of geometry?

Which way are the normals facing? This is the number one reason for problems.

Will **Stand Ins** help the solver work with this geometry?

Bake Simulation to add control to complex scenes.

Collision Layers are a good method of separating out objects that you do not want the solver to calculate collision between.

Using **Multiple Solvers** can help localize control over a specific simulation or collision/interaction.

The *rigidBody* and *rigidSolver* MEL commands can be used for creation and modification of *rigidBodies* and *rigidSolver* nodes in MEL scripts. Refer to the online MEL command reference for a list of all available flags for these commands.

A word about solver accuracy

It is also important to remember that the solver is an approximation of real world physics. The solver doesn't evaluate detailed information about subtle surface properties. Doing this detailed level of calculation (such as some systems specifically designed for engineering purposes), would be slower than existing methods. The solver is not intended to give you accuracy down to the millionth decimal point. However, there is a decent level of accuracy control there if you need it. Use rigid bodies to get some dynamic motion happening, bake and modify where necessary, and be glad you don't have to keyframe it all by hand! Also, use caching when possible to speed things up.

What units are you using?

Finally, you should always keep in mind your scene scale and units when working with dynamics and fields. In physics, gravity is measured in meters per second squared. In Maya, the same is true, however, usually people work in centimeters, not meters. Therefore, the effect of gravity seems to be off by a factor of 100. You'll often see rigid body objects floating through the scene seemingly in slow motion because of this. Things may appear okay in your hardware playback but when you view it in real time, you notice this floating motion. For example, if you are trying to match live action motion, you will most likely need to crank your gravity much higher than a magnitude of **9.8**. Start at 980 and bring it downwards. In practice, it is best to keep the scene units at centimeters; you'll find that you'll have fewer problems. Using reference footage is very important. The movie *dropBall.mpg* included with the data is reference footage that was shot to compare real world gravity with Maya's gravity in centimeters. Importing this movie footage into Maya via an image plane and mimicking the motion with rigid bodies is a good way to get an idea of how Maya's dynamics relate to real world physics.

Time to render? Time to Bake!

Baking is highly recommend before you render rigid bodies or soft bodies, especially if you are rendering with motion blur.

Intro to Particles

4

This chapter focuses on the basic concepts required to understand and work efficiently with particles in Maya. This chapter should be considered an essential framework to build upon for more advanced concepts which are discussed later.

In this chapter you will learn about the following:

- The particle Shape node;
- Basic particle attributes;
- Emitters.

Water fountain

CHAPTER 4

PARTICLE STRUCTURE IN MAYA

Particles in Maya differ from geometry in the following ways:

- Particles are points in space. They require special handling at render time because they do not contain surface information.

- Particles can be rendered using hardware or software rendering methods. The particle Render Type attribute controls which of these two methods are used.

- Individual particles belong to a common collection referred to as the *particleShape* object. Just as CV's of a geometric object belong to their Shape node, individual particles can be thought of as components to the *particleShape* node.

- Particle attributes are commonly categorized into two types: Per Particle(array) and Per Object.

Applications of particles

Particles are commonly used to simulate complex natural phenomena. Common examples include smoke, rain, sparks, gases, dust, snow, fire, and other motion that consists of complex or random motion of many individual components.

Particles can be keyframed or controlled dynamically.

Creating a particle galaxy

There are several methods for creating particle objects in Maya. In this first example, the focus will be on using the **Particle Tool**.

The Particle Tool is a quick and easy way of creating individual particles, particle grids, and random collections of particles. This can be useful for just getting some particles to start working with. This also provides you with the ability to interactively place particles exactly where you want them.

1 Sketch some particles

- Select **Particles** → **Particle Tool -** ❏ and set the following:

    Particle Name to **galaxy**;

    Number of Particles to **20**;

    Sketch Particles to **On**;

    Maximum Radius to **3**;

    Sketch Interval to **5**.

- Sketch a cross-like shape in the top view and press **Enter**.

A sketched cross of particles

Tip:	If you drag while the mouse button is depressed, you can interactively change the placement of where the particles will be dropped. The particles will be placed at the location where the mouse button is released.

- Open the Outliner to see the newly created particle object called *galaxy*.

  You will need to show shapes in the Outliner to see the *galaxyShape* node.

- Enable Outliner option **Display → Shapes**.

2 Apply a vortex field to the galaxy particles

To make the particles spin like a galaxy, you will apply a vortex field.

- Select the *galaxy* particle object.
- Select **Fields → Vortex**.
- Playback to watch the particles spin.

3 Adjust conserve on the particles

To prevent the particles from immediately spinning out of control, you can lower the conserve attribute on the particle object.

- Select the particle object.
- Set **Conserve** to **0.8** in the Channel Box then playback.

Conserve is a very important particle attribute. Conserve is short for conservation of momentum. By default it is set to 1 which means the particles will never lose any of their motion as they move through space. This is a very "sensitive" attribute so lowering it in very small increments is usually best. Normally, lowering conserve just a little below 1 will give your particle motion a more realistic looking appearance.

4 Set Initial State

Every time you rewind, the galaxy returns to the cross shape. To prevent this, you can set the Initial State of the particles.

- Playback until the particles are in a galaxy like shape.

- Select **Solvers → Initial State → Set For Selected**.

  Now when you rewind, the galaxy is in the shape it was when you set the Initial State.

5 Keyframe the particles

Traditionally, particles have been animated exclusively through fields and dynamic expressions. In Maya, you also have the option to animate the particle objects transform like any non-dynamic object. Translate, scale, and rotation can be keyframed to provide many common effects.

- Select the Transform node of the galaxy particle object.

- Set **Rotate Z** to about **-25** degrees so the galaxy is tilted at an angle.

- Playback.

- Things look fine at the first frame of the simulation but as you playback, you may notice that the particles are not orbiting around relative to the new rotation you introduced. Instead, they are revolving around the world axis defined by the vortex field's axis attributes (0 1 0).

- To make the particles orbit with respect to the -25 degree angle you've introduced, parent the *vortexField* into the galaxy particle object. Then, set **forcesInWorld** to **Off** in the Channel Box for the particle object.

- Now, the vortex 0 1 0 axis is being calculated in local space to the particle object instead of the world space. Also, the field is conveniently parented into this effect so you can keyframe the entire galaxy's translation, rotation, and scale as you wish.

- The file *galaxy.mb* shows a completed version of this setup.

Note: It is also possible to create an *empty particle object* by setting the number of particles to **0** in the Particle Tool options or by typing "particle" in the Script Editor or Command Line. Empty particle objects are commonly needed when working with particle emitters which are discussed in the next section.

EMITTERS

An emitter is like a cannon that projects particles into space. Below is a list of the different kinds of emitters available in Maya:

- Directional;

- Omni directional;

- Curve;

- Volume;

- Surface;

- Texture;

- Per-Point.

Open the file *emitterTypes.mb* to see an example of each of these.

Display in shaded mode is recommended to see the colored particles. You may also want to use the display layers provided in the scene to keep the viewport from getting overly cluttered.

Create a simple fountain using a directional emitter

1 Load the scene file

A fountain is a very simple effect that you will create to learn how to get around with the particle system in Maya.

- Open the file *fountainGeo.mb*.

  This file contains geometry of a simple fountain with no dynamics. You'll add a directional emitter and modify some of its attributes.

2 Create a directional emitter

A directional emitter allows you to specify exactly what direction in world space to emit the particles.

- Select **Particles** → **Create Emitter** - □. Set the following:

  Emitter Type to **Directional**.

- Press **Create**.

  This creates two new objects. *Emitter1* is the directional emitter that emits particles into the particle object *particle1*.

3 Position and name the emitter

- Select *emitter1* in the Outliner or Perspective window and position it slightly below the tip of the fountain's *spout*.

- Rename *emitter1* to *spray*.

- Rename *particle1* to *droplets*.

4 Playback the animation

- Set the playback range to start at frame **1** and end at frame **500** and playback the animation.

  By default, the particle emitter direction occurs along the X-axis.

5 Modify the emitter's attributes using manipulators

- With the emitter selected, press the **t** key to switch to the **Show Manipulator Tool**.

  The small circular icon below the emitter is a toggle switch that cycles the manipulator through different attributes on the emitter, so that each attribute can be quickly edited graphically. This manipulator functions similarly to manipulators on spot lights which you may already be familiar with. The *value* manip will change based on the attribute manip selection. It can be click dragged to change the attribute value.

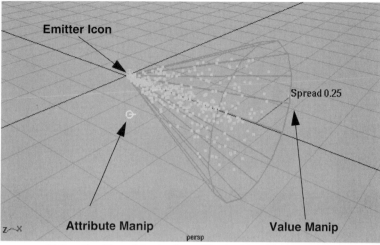

Using the Show Manipulator Tool with an emitter

- Use the manipulators or Channel Box to adjust the **Direction**, **Speed**, **Rate**, and **Spread** of the emitter until the result resembles a fountain as shown below:

The spray directional emitter with its manipulator displayed

- The following values work well for the *spray* emitter:

  Direction to **0, 1, 0**;

  Rate to **1000**;

  Spread to **0.17**.

Note: A **Spread** value of 1 corresponds to a 180 degree emission cone. **Rate** is a measurement of the number of particles per time unit that are emitted. The default time unit is seconds. **Speed** determines how fast the particles leave the emitter.

---

6 Change the particle render type to MultiPoint

- **Click-drag** select *droplets* in the Perspective window.

- Open the **dropletsShape** tab Attribute Editor, and set the following:

    Particle Render Type to **MultiPoint**;

    Depth Sort to **On**.

- Press the **Current Render Type** button and set the following:

    Color Accum to **On**;

    Use Lighting to **On**.

These options determine the draw, shading, and lighting properties of this particle object. These settings make the particles appear somewhat more like water droplets in motion. The specific details of these options will be discussed more in the rendering chapter.

7 Add gravity and turbulence to the droplets

Adding fields will help better define the particles' motion.

- With *droplets* still selected, select **Fields** → **Gravity**.

- Select *droplets* again, select **Fields** → **Turbulence**.

- Playback the scene to test the gravity and turbulence fields.

8 Increase spray's Speed attribute

Using a higher speed value causes the particles to leave the emitter faster which, in turn, allows them to travel higher before being overcome by gravity.

- Select *spray*.

- Set **Speed** to **10** in the Channel Box.

Add a secondary particle object

To give the impression of streaks in the water, you'll now add a second particle object for the emitter to emit into. The attributes of this particle object can be controlled independently from the *droplets* particles.

Fields

When a field is chosen from the Fields menu, all selected objects will be connected to that field automatically. If nothing is selected, then the field is created in the scene and objects can be connected to it using the **Dynamic Relationships Editor** or by selecting the object(s), then the field, then **Fields** → **Affect Selected Object(s)**. If you want the field to automatically be parented to the select object, use **Fields** → **Use Selected as Source of Field**.

1 Use the Particle Tool to create an empty particle object

An "empty particle object" is created when the **Number of Particles** setting in the Particle Tool's options is set to **0**. This creates an empty storage place for the emitter to later emit into. The particles will be created by the emitter, using the attributes set on the *particleShape* node.

- Select **Particles** → **Particle Tool -** ❑ and set the following:

    Particle Name to *mist*;

    Number of Particles to **0**.

- Click anywhere in the Perspective window.

- Press **Enter**.

    You may receive a warning that no particles were created. `Error: No particles can be created if Number of Particles is 0.` This is normal.

- Check the Outliner to make sure the *mist* particle object was created.

2 Establish emission for mist

Currently, there is no relationship between *mist* and *spray*. You'll now establish a connection between the two.

- Select *mist* in the Outliner.

- **Ctrl-click** to select *spray*.

- Select **Particles** → **Use Selected Emitter**.

    Rewind and playback. The *spray* emitter now emits into both *mist* and *droplets*.

3 Set display attributes for mist

Just as you defined descriptive attributes for *droplets*, you can do the same for *mist*. Use the Attribute Editor to set the following attribute values for *mist*:

Particle Render Type to **Multi-Streak**;

Depth Sort to **On**;

Color Accum to **Off**;

Use Lighting to **On**.

Turning **Color Accum** off for *mist* creates contrast against the *droplets* particles whose **Color Accum** setting, you'll recall, was turned on. Depth Sorting simply draws the particles on the screen from back to front.

Tip: When **Color Accum** is on, overlapping particles within the same particle object get their RGB values added together. This creates a more "washed-out" or additive appearance. You will only notice the Color Accum effect later, once the particles have an opacity attribute.

---

4 Connect mist to the existing gravity

- Select *mist* in the Outliner.

- **Ctrl-select** *gravity1* located inside the *fountain* group.

- Select **Fields → Affect Selected Object(s)**.

  When played back, the *mist* particles should fall with *droplets*.

The spray directional emitter emitting into particle objects droplets and mist

Understanding particle attributes

The next step is to add more specific controls to *droplets* and *mist*. This requires a clear understanding of some important concepts that will be discussed here briefly before continuing with the fountain:

- The most commonly used particle attributes exist on the *particleShape* node. The Transform node contains the traditional transform attributes (translate, scale, rotate, etc.).

- All particle objects use position, velocity, acceleration, and mass attributes. Therefore, these attributes are part of the *particleShape* node by default and cannot be deleted.

- There are many other attributes (lifespan, radius, color, incandescence, etc.) which can be added to particles. This allows you to customize each particle shape to your specific needs and also keeps things more efficient.

- Some attributes are intended to be used for only specific particle render types. For example, *spriteNum* is only intended to be used with sprite particles.

Per Particle vs. Per Object Attributes

It is important to understand the difference between the *per particle* and *per object* attributes.

- **Per particle** attributes allow each particle to store its own value for a given attribute.

- **Per object Attribute** assigns one attribute value to the entire particle object.

  It has become a common convention to name per particle attributes with a PP at the end (RadiusPP, rgbPP, etc). However, it is not an absolute requirement.

Tip: For more information regarding various particle attributes, visit Maya's online documentation.

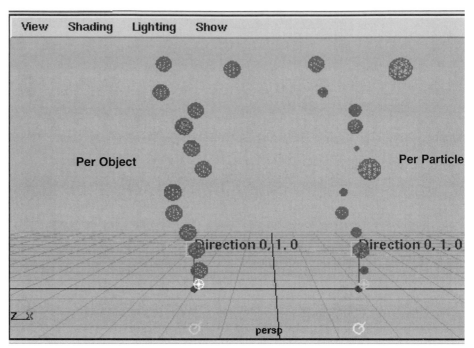

Per Object vs. Per Particle Radius

In the picture above, the particles emitted from the left emitter were given a per object radius attribute (radiusPP). The particles emitted from the emitter on the right are in the same relative position as those emitted from the emitter on the left. However, each particle has its own radius value.

Color and Lifespan attributes

You will continue working with the fountain you have just created.

1 Set per object lifespan and add color attribute to the particles

The lifespan attribute gives you control over how long the particles stay in the scene before they disappear. For now, you'll assign the same lifespan value to all the particles to keep things simple.

- Select *droplets* and open the Attribute Editor.
- In the **Lifespan Attributes** section, in **Lifespan Mode,** select **Constant**.
- Set **Lifespan** to **2.6** (this is the number of seconds).
- In the **Add Dynamic Attributes** section, press **Color** and select **Add Per Object Attribute**.
- Press **Add Attribute**.

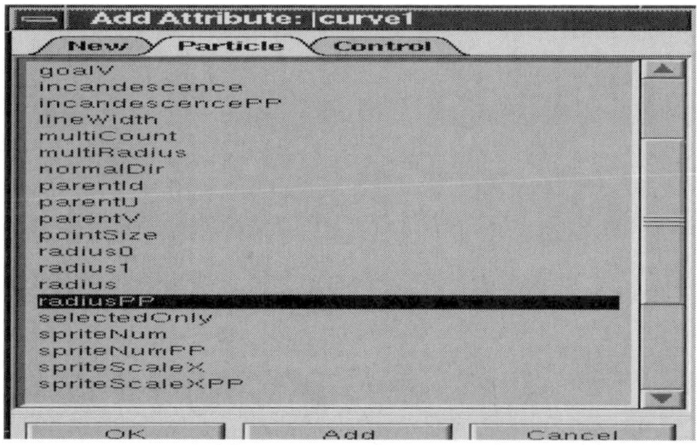

Adding a per object attribute

Fields for editing **RGB** are added in the **Render Attributes** section (and in the Channel Box) for this particle object as shown below.

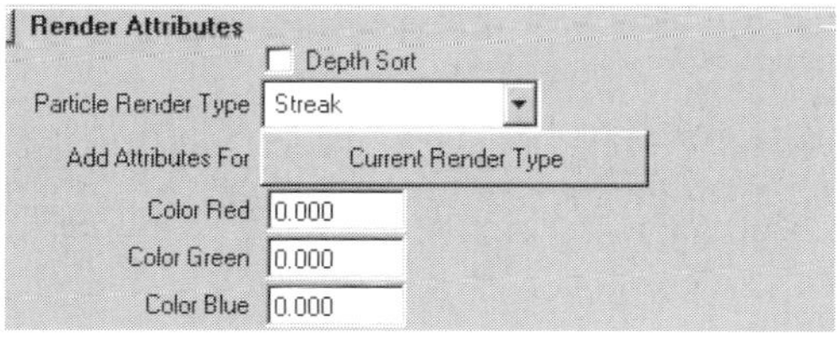

Changing the Per Object RGB values in the Attribute Editor

- Set the following attributes for **Color**:

    Color Red to **0.5**;

    Color Green to **0.5**;

    Color Blue to **1.0**.

2 Repeat the process for mist particles

- Create a Per Object Color attribute for *mist*. Use the same Lifespan value but modify the RGB values very slightly to add some variation.

3 Test the animation

- Rewind and playback the animation.

- If necessary, adjust the lifespan so the particles die near the time they are at the same **Y** coordinate as the bottom pool of the fountain.

- Select the particles and press **5** then **7** on the keyboard.

Now when you playback the animation, the particles are displayed with color and lighting.

For better results when rendering this fountain, increase the *spray's* **Rate** to **2000** and also add **Opacity** attributes to the mist and droplets.

You may notice that the particles do not collide with the fountain in this example. Particle collisions will be discussed in a later chapter.

Note: The unit for lifespan is seconds so it is important to be aware of your frames per second settings and the different results that can occur if the same file is used on two different machines with different time settings. This can happen when you use import in stead of open. When you use **File → Open Scene**, the time setting will be read from the scene file. To check the time setting, open **WIndow → Settings/Preferences → Settings...**

Omni directional emitters

Omni directional emitters can be added to NURBS, polygons, and curves. An omni directional emitter causes particle emission to occur from the CV's (or vertices) of the object it is added to. The emission from that point emanates equally in all directions, as opposed to only one specific direction which is the case with the previously discussed directional emitter.

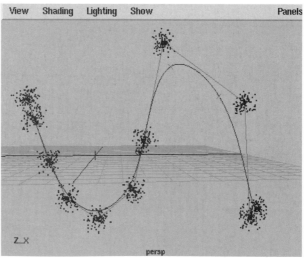

An omni directional emitter emitting from a curve's CV's

Curve emitters

Although it is possible to add a directional or omni-directional emitter to a curve, doing so will cause emission to occur only from the CV's of that curve, not from the portions of the curve between the CV's points and not from points on the curve.

A curve emitter is designed to allow omni-directional emission to occur along the entire curve, instead of only from the CV's.

1 Create a simple curve emitter

- Create a NURBS circle or create your own edit point curve using the EP Curve Tool.

- Select the curve and add a curve emitter by selecting **Particles** → **Emit from Object -** ❏ and set the following:

  Emitter Type to **Curve**.

2 Test the animation

- Playback the animation to view the curve emission.

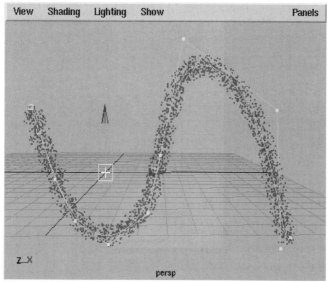

The same curve with curve emission instead of omni directional

---

Tip: It is possible to change the emitter type after the emitter has been created by editing the **emitterType** attribute in the Channel Box or Attribute Editor for the selected emitter.

Whitecaps

Curve emission with per particle attributes

In some cases, it is useful to duplicate isoparms on surface geometry and use the resulting curve as an emitter. The steps below illustrate a quick example of this workflow, and introduce you to using per particle attributes.

1 Open the scene file

- Select **File** → **Open Scene**.

- Select *basicWave.mb*.

2 Add a curve emitter to the edge of the wave

- Playback the animation to see the slight ripple motion that has been added to the object using a non-linear deformer.

- Rewind to frame **1**.

- Use the **RMB** menu to select the isoparm at the breaking edge of the ocean wave, as shown below.

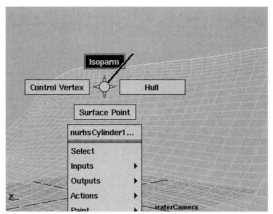

Selecting the edge isoparm of the ocean wave

- Select **Edit Curves** → **Duplicate Surface Curves**.

  A NURBS curve matching the shape of the selected isoparm is created.

- Select the NURBS curve.

- Add a curve emitter to it by selecting **Particles** → **Emit from Object** - ❐.

- Name the resulting particle object *foam* and the resulting emitter *foamEmitter*.

Tip: You can also add curve emitters to a curve on surface (COS) object. You can create a COS using tools like Intersection or Project Curve or by making the surface *live* (**Modify → Make Live**), then drawing a curve with the EP or CV Curve tools.

---

3 Adjust lifespan attribute

- Select the *foamShape* particles and change the **Particle Render Type** to **Cloud (s/w)** in the Channel Box or Attribute Editor.

- In **Lifespan Attributes,** change **Lifespan Mode** to **Constant**.

The default setting of **1.0** is fine for now.

4 Add a radiusPP attribute

Adding a **radiusPP** attribute will provide control over the radius of each cloud particle emitted.

- Open the **Per Particle (Array) Attributes** section of the Attribute Editor.

- Press the **General** button in the **Add Dynamic Attributes** section of the Attribute Editor.

- Click on the **Particle** tab and select **radiusPP** from the list of particle attributes.

- Press **OK**.

A **radiusPP** attribute field is added to the **Per Particle (Array) Attributes** section of the Attribute Editor.

Adding a radiusPP from the Add Attributes window

5 Add a ramp to control each particle's radius

- **RMB-click** on the **radiusPP** field.
- Select **Create Ramp** from the pop-up menu.
- **RMB-click** on the same **radiusPP** field and select **arrayMapper1.outValue1PP** → **Edit Ramp**.

The Ramp Editor is displayed in the Attribute Editor.

6 Edit the ramp color

- Edit the ramp so there are only two color entries - white at the bottom of the ramp and black at the top as shown below:

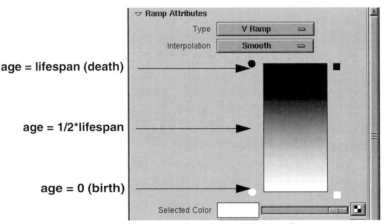

A ramp added to radiusPP to control each particle's radius over age

The vertical "axis" of the ramp represents the particle's *normalized age*. The bottom of the ramp corresponds to the particle's birth and the top of the ramp corresponds to its death.

Black corresponds to a radius value of **0**, white to a value of **1**. Therefore, with the current ramp configuration, the radius will be **1** when the particle is born and **0** when the particle dies.

Tip: In order to assign values greater than 1 for float attributes such as **radiusPP** with a ramp, it is necessary to switch to **RGB** mode in the Color Chooser, then enter the desired value in the **R** field. The numbers for **B** and **G** are ignored unless you are controlling a vector attribute.

- Set **Interpolation** to **Smooth** to provide a soft transition from black to white.

7 Test the animation

- Rewind and playback the animation.

  The radius decreases smoothly over the particle's age.

- Using these techniques, try to make the particles emit with a radius of **1.2**, stay at **1.2** until halfway through their life, then linearly decrease to a radius of **0.1** when they die.

- You may want to decrease the emission rate while you adjust the effect and boost it back up when you've got the values to your satisfaction.

- Save the file as a Maya Ascii file called *wave1.ma*.

Tip: Adjusting **Noise** and **Noise Frequency** in the ramp is an interesting way to achieve randomness. This works better with some attributes than others.

8 Adjust the Inherit Factor of the particles

Inherit Factor controls how much of the emitting object's velocity is transferred to the particles during emission.

- Select the emitted particles and set **Inherit Factor** in the Channel Box to **1.0**.

- Rewind and playback the animation.

  When **Inherit Factor** is **0**, the particle velocity is not affected by the wave's deforming motion. A setting of **1** causes the particles to emit with the same velocity the moving curve has at the time of emission. This is closer to how foam would really emit from an actual wave.

  If **Inherit Factor** was set to **0**, the particles would immediately fall down (due to gravity), even if the curve emitting them was moving up.

  Curve emission is also useful for simulating effects like shockwaves or energy pulses by adding the curve emitter to a curve and scaling the curve over time. This could be a stand alone effect or a greyscale rendering used as a displacement effect in compositing.

Normalized age

Normalized age is the relationship between a **particle's age** and its **lifespan** (age/lifespan). When a particle's age is equal to its lifespan, the particle dies.

Surface emitters

Surface emitters can be applied to NURBS and polygonal surfaces and cause emission directly from the surface rather than just from the CV's.

1 Load the file and switch to wireframe mode

- Load the file *glassEmit.mb.*

- Press **4** to ensure you are in wireframe display mode.

2 Add a surface emitter

- Use the Outliner to select *glassBase.*

- Choose **Particles** → **Emit from Object-** ❑ and set the following:

    Emitter Type to **Surface**.

- Press **Create**.

- Name the emitter *baseEmitter* and the particles *baseParticles.*

3 Switch the render type to Sphere

- Select *baseParticles* and open the Attribute Editor.

- In the Render Attributes section of the Attribute Editor, set the following:

    Particle Render Type to **Spheres**;

    Press **Current Render Type** and set **Radius** to **0.06**.

4 Test the animation

- Playback the animation.

    The particles emit from the base towards the top of the glass but remain in the scene indefinitely.

5 Add and adjust turbulence for baseParticles

Turbulence will add some fluctuation to the movement of the particles to add realism.

- Select *baseParticles.*

- Select **Fields** → **Turbulence**.

- Select the *turbulence* field and position it near *glassBase.*

- In the Channel Box set **Attenuation** to **2** for the **Turbulence** field.

- Increase **Magnitude** to **8** and **Frequency** to **2**.

6 Set the Per Object Lifespan attribute

- Use the techniques learned in the fountain example to **Set a Constant lifespan** attribute for the *baseParticles.*

    Choose a lifespan value that causes the particles to die before they reach the top of the glass.

7 Add color to the baseParticles

- Use the Attribute Editor to add an **rgbPP** attribute to *baseParticles*.

Note: If an **rgbPP** attribute is added without a lifespan present, Maya will automatically add one.

- Add a *ramp* to the **rgbPP** attribute.

  Don't edit the colors or position of the color entries yet.

- Select the *drinkingGlass* object from the Outliner and template it using **Display** → **Object Display** → **Template**.

- Press **5** to switch to shaded mode.

8 Test the animation

- Rewind and play the animation.

  As a particle's age approaches its lifespan, its color corresponds to a color higher along the vertical axis of the Ramp Editor.

- Edit the ramp so the color smoothly interpolates from white to a slightly light blue tint.

Tangent Speed and Normal Speed

Two attributes that are noteworthy when working with surface emission are Tangent Speed and Normal Speed.

These are closely related to the speed attribute that was previously discussed. Normal Speed controls the particle's speed along the vector that is normal to the point of emission. Tangent Speed controls the particle's speed along a randomly selected vector that is tangent to the surface of emission.

A good way to see what Normal and Tangent Speed do is to create a NURBS sphere and add a surface emitter to it. Increase the rate to around 300 and playback. If you view the sphere from the top view, you'll see a radial emission pattern.

Attenuation

Attenuation controls an exponential relationship between the strength of the field and the distance between the affected object and that field. Imagine a curtain being blown by the air from a fan. In reality, as the distance between the fan and the curtain increases, the effect of the air from the fan on the curtain diminishes. It is this relationship between distance and field strength that attenuation controls. An attenuation of 0 causes a constant force regardless of the distance between the field and the affected object.

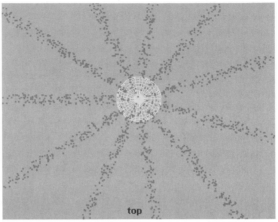

radial emission pattern

The pattern emerges because the particles are emitted from tessellated geometry. The default Tangent Speed is 0, causing the particles to move perpendicular to the faces of the tessellated geometry from which they were emitted. Adding a bit of Tangent Speed eliminates this problem. Select the emitter and increase the Tangent Speed a little and the particles will now be given some velocity along the surface tangent from which they originate. This causes them to shoot off the surface at angles and gets rid of the emission pattern seen before.

Tip: Setting both the **Normal Speed** and **Tangent Speed** to **0** is an easy way to get the emitted particles to stick to the emitting surface.

---

1 Add water droplets to the glass surface and make them stick

- Select *drinkingGlass* and untemplate it using **Display → Object Display → Untemplate**.
- Add a surface emitter to *drinkingGlass*.
- Rename the new emitter *glassEmitter*.
- Rename the corresponding particle object *glassParticles*.
- Set the following attributes for the *glassEmitter*:

    Tangent Speed to **0**;

    Normal Speed to **0**.

2 Test the animation

- Rewind and play the animation.

The emitted particles "stick" to the glass since there is no Normal or Tangent Speed. However, there are too many particles stuck to the glass. Adjusting the emitter Rate and particle Lifespan to get the precise number of particles can be difficult. Fortunately, the number of particles can be controlled directly.

3 Adjust the Max Count attribute

To limit the emission, adjust the **Max Count** attribute.

- Open the Attribute Editor for the *glassParticles*.

- Set **Max Count** to **50** near the top of the Attribute Editor.

4 Test the animation

- Rewind and play the animation.

  The **Max Count** attribute limits the total number of particles the selected particle object is allowed to hold.

Note: When a particle object is created, **Max Count** is set to **-1** by default. This means Maya sets no limits on the number of particles it can hold.

---

5 Use a ramp to control acceleration

Currently, the *glassParticles* remain stationary during playback. It is possible to control their acceleration using a ramp. This is an alternative to attaching a gravity field.

- Open the Attribute Editor for *glassParticles*.

- In the **Per Particle (Array) Attribute** section, **RMB** in the **rampAcceleration** field and select **Create Ramp** from the pop-up menu.

- Adjust the ramp so there is only one color entry (circular handle).

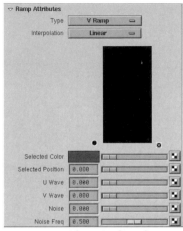

Acceleration ramp with a single color entry marker

- Move the color entry to the bottom of the ramp.

- Set the **RGB** values for the color entry to **0**, **-0.5**, **0**, respectively.

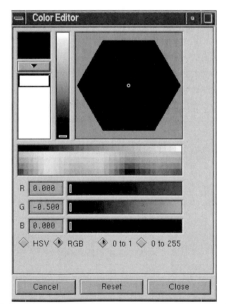

Setting a vector quantity (acceleration) using RGB

Note: When using the Ramp Editor to control **vector** quantities such as position, acceleration, and velocity, RGB corresponds to the particle's X,Y,Z respectively.

---

6 Test the animation

- Rewind and play the animation.

- Experiment with different **RGB** values to see how the acceleration of the particles is affected.

  Controlling particle motion with ramps is not really all that common. This example is very simple as it's intended to show you the purpose of this feature and also help give you some ideas of other ways to move particles around. You could potentially use textures that are mapped to the ramp handles to push particles around your scene. This would require some additional setup, but is a technique that some studios are currently using to help modify existing motion of particles without changing too much in the simulation.

TEXTURE EMISSION

With surface emitters, it is possible to control emission rate and location based on characteristics of a texture file or any 2D procedural texture. Texture emission works with textures only, not materials (Blinn, Phong, etc., or layered shaders).

Coloring particles using textures or procedurals

1 Load the file

- Load the file *paperBurn.mb*.

2 Add a surface emitter

- Select *emitPlane* then choose **Particles → Emit from Object - ❑**. Set the following:

  Emitter Type to **Surface**;

  Emitter Name to **textureEmitter**.

- Name the associated particle object *textureParticles*.

3 Set Tangent and Normal Speed

- Select *textureEmitter*.

- Set the **Tangent Speed** to **0.5** and **Normal Speed** to **1.0**.

This prevents the particles from emitting directly normal to the surface providing for a more randomized emission appearance.

4   Add a rgbPP attribute to textureParticles

An **rgbPP** attribute is required for the **Inherit Color** option of texture emission to work. This is a common oversight when setting up texture emission.

- In the Attribute Editor for *textureParticles*, add a **rgbPP** attribute.

5   Set the rate of textureEmitter

- Select *textureEmitter*.
- Set the **Rate** to **200** particles per second in the Channel Box.
- Turn **scaleRateByObject** to **On**.

If this attribute is turned on, the size of the object emitting the particles affects the rate of the particles emitted per frame. The larger the object, the greater the rate of emission.

6   Specify a texture for coloring the particles

Now you will connect a pre-made ramp texture to the emitter which will determine the color of the particles emitted.

- Open the Attribute Editor for *textureEmitter*.
- Select **Window → Rendering Editors → Hypershade...** and position it next to the Attribute Editor.
- In the Hypershade, Choose **Tabs** from the menu bar. Make sure **Show Top Tabs Only** is checked **On**.
- Select the **Textures** tab.

  This displays all of the textures currently in the scene file. An animated *fireRamp* texture has already been prepared for this example and should be visible in the Hypershade window.

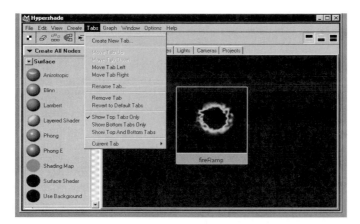

Displaying the fireRamp texture in the Hypershade window

- Locate the **Texture Emission Attributes** section of the Attribute Editor.

- **MMB-drag+drop** the *fireRamp* texture icon from the Hypershade window onto the **Particle Color** slider in the Attribute Editor for *textureEmitter*.

- Close the Hypershade window.

- Turn **Inherit Color** to **On** in the Attribute Editor or Channel Box for the emitter.

- Press **6** to switch to hardware texture mode.

7 Test the animation

- Rewind and play the animation.

  Notice the emitted particles have inherited the RGB values from the texture at the location where they were emitted. Notice that black particles are emitting from the outer edge of the texture where the color is not present. You will be fixing this shortly.

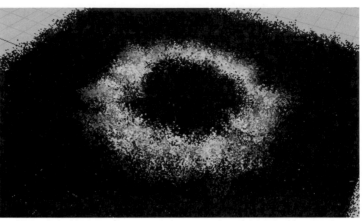

Using an animated ramp texture to color the emitted particles

---

Note: To use a 3D texture for texture emission, you'll first need to convert it to a 2D UV mapped image using **Convert To File Texture** in the Hypershade.

---

8 Change Lifespan attribute

- Set the **Lifespan Mode** to **Constant**. A default value of **1** is fine.

9 Add opacity so the particles fade out

Now you'll add opacity and a ramp to control it based on the age of the particles.

- Create a **Per Particle Attribute** for **Opacity**.

- Add a ramp to **opacityPP**.

- Edit the ramp so it has the following properties:

    Color entry 1: **Selected Position** to **0**; **RGB** to **0.9, 0, 0**;

    Color entry 2: **Selected Position** to **0.5**; **RGB** to **0.4, 0, 0**;

    Color entry 3: **Selected Position** to **1.0**; **RGB** to **0, 0, 0**.

Scaling Emission Rate with a texture

Similar to how you mapped a color image to control the color of emitted particles, you can also use the values of a greyscale image as multipliers on the emission rate of the emitter. This provides control over which portions of the surface will emit more than others. In this example, you want to shut off emission from the black areas of the ramp texture and leave emission on for the areas where there is color in the burning ring.

1 Connect a ramp to the rate

Since the areas of emission that you are interested in controlling correspond exactly to the color ramp that is being animated, the same ramp can be mapped to Texture Rate.

- Use the same method previously used to **drag+drop** the *fireRamp* from the Hypershade. This time, drag it onto the **Texture Rate** slider of the emitter.

- Turn **Enable Texture Rate** to **On**.

2 Test the results

- Rewind and playback.

  Although *fireRamp* is a color image, when mapped to Texture Rate, Maya extracts the luminance values of the color ramp and uses those values as multipliers against the emission rate at the corresponding location of the surface.

  Areas of the color map with a luminance of 0 (black), use a 0 emission rate. Areas of the color map with luminance of 1 use 100% of the emitter's rate.

  Once rendered, this fire ring could be rendered with a matte channel and combined with other textured surfaces using compositing software. These techniques will be discussed later in the book.

Texture emission with fireRamp mapped to Texture Rate

Per-Point Emission

Sometimes when working with particles, you may want to have some points on a curve or a surface emit at a different rate than other points.

This can be achieved to some extent using texture emission controls. Another option that offers some additional control is **Per-Point Emission**.

1 Open the file

- Select **File** → **Open Scene**.
- Load *basicWave.mb*.

2 Add omni emission to the edge's edit points

- Use the technique learned earlier to duplicate the edge isoparm of *oceanWave*.
- Name the duplicated curve *waveCurve*.
- Select *oceanWave*, then choose **Display** → **Object Display** → **Template**.
- Select the *waveCurve*, then press **F8** to switch to component mode.
- Set the pick mask so only **Edit Points** are available for selection.

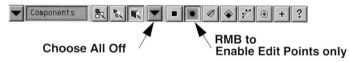

Choose All Off

RMB to
Enable Edit Points only

Setting the pick mask for edit points only

- **Drag-select** around the entire *waveCurve* in the Perspective window to select all of its edit points.
- Select **Particles** → **Emit from Object**.
- Rename the emitter *perPointEmitter*.

Notice that the **useRatePP** attribute of *perPointEmitter* in the Channel Box is currently locked and set to **Off.** This becomes important shortly.

3 Test the animation

- Rewind and playback the animation.

An even emission **Rate** of **100** PPS occurs in all directions from the edit points as illustrated:

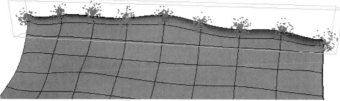

An even omni emission from the edge curve's edit points

4 Setup Per-Point Emission control

You can easily vary the emission rate for each edit point using per-point emission:

- Select the *perPointEmitter.*

- Select **Particles** → **Per-Point Emission Rates**.

  The **useRatePP** attribute of *perPointEmitter* gets automatically unlocked and set to **On** in the Channel Box.

- Select *waveCurveShape* and change the emitter **Rate** for each edit point in the Channel Box.

Channels	Object
waveCurveShape	
t Emitter Rate PP[0]	20
t Emitter Rate PP[1]	40
t Emitter Rate PP[2]	60
t Emitter Rate PP[3]	80
t Emitter Rate PP[4]	100
t Emitter Rate PP[5]	120
t Emitter Rate PP[6]	140
t Emitter Rate PP[7]	300
t Emitter Rate PP[8]	500
INPUTS	
tweak2	
curveFromSurfaceIso1	
OUTPUTS	
geoConnector1	

Per-Point Emission rates shown in the Channel Box for waveCurveShape

5 Test the animation

- Rewind and playback the animation.

  The emission rates of each edit point correspond to the changes made in the Channel Box. This style of emission can be combined with the curve emitter to add some variation to the overall effect.

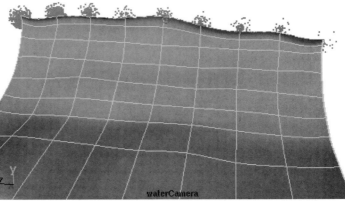

Per-Point Emission rates decreasing from left to right

There are more practical examples of when you might use Per-Point Emission but these often require the use of particle expressions which we will cover in a later chapter. For example, perhaps you have a car crashing into a wall. Points that collide with the wall at a higher velocity could be made to emit more particles at the collision point. Or, perhaps you want to emit foam from the peaks of waves. You can use Per-Point Emission setup to emit a lot of foam for certain peaks and very little or no foam for other peaks. Techniques such as these will be explored in greater detail later in this book.

TIPS AND TRAPS

The following tips and traps will give you some additional information relating to these lessons, some extra tips, and also some possible explanations for things you may run into while working with the provided examples.

- People often ask about the **currentTime** attribute found on particles. By default, Maya's particle system is plugged into the default Maya scene time. As you advance the timeline, the particles evaluate. It is possible to break the connection from the main Maya scene time and create your own custom time curve for the particles to evaluate from.

  The file *reverseTime.mb* in the demo directory demonstrates a simple example of this. For example, perhaps you want to have particles shoot out into a scene and freeze in space while other animation continues.

- To setup *reverseTime.mb* yourself, do the following:

    Create a directional emitter with **Rate** = **10**, **Speed** = **20**.

    Set timeline to end at frame **100** and advance to frame **100**.

    Select the associated particle object and cache it (**Solvers** → **Memory Caching** → **Enable**), then rewind and playback.

    Select the particle object and **RMB** → **Break Connection** on the *current Time* attribute in the Channel Box

    Rewind to frame **1**. Set *currentTime* to **1** and set a key.

    Advance to frame **50**. Set *currentTime* to **25** and set a key.

    Advance to frame **100**. Set *currentTime* to **50** and set a key.

    Playback and it plays at half speed in comparison to the original emitter/particle in the scene.

    Now select the particle object and edit its time curve in the Graph Editor. Since the data is cached, you can actually make the time curve cause the particles to get sucked back into the emitter by pulling the time curve back down to near a value of **1** at frame **100**. You can also add keyframes in the Graph Editor and adjust the curve however you want.

- To connect the particle object back to the default time in Maya, break its connection from time again, then select **Particles** → **Connect to Time.**

- The shadows in the fountain movie were made by switching the render type to blobby, making the radius very small, then rendering a software pass of the geometry using the useBackground shader on the fountain geometry. The blobbies were rendered in the same pass with primary visibility set to **Off**. This was then layered over a color pass of the fountain in compositing software. More on this type of technique is included in the rendering and compositing sections of the book.

- People often ask if particle emission can occur from Edit Points (instead of CV's). Currently, this type of emission is not available without using expressions (the emit command will be discussed later in the book).

- The *geoConnector* node on the surface associated with the emitter has a **Tessellation Factor** control. This is very similar to the Tessellation Factor used with rigid bodies. However, this controls the level of detail of the surface that the emitter uses to emit particles from. Increasing this attribute will slow things down but provide more even/accurate emission from the surface. If you have a highly detailed surface that you need very accurate emission from, increasing this number will likely be necessary.

- Patchy or sputtering emission can also be caused by a playback setting of "RealTime 30fps" in your general preferences. Set the playback to **Play Every Frame** in the animation preferences to correct the problem.

Exercises

- Load *fountainGeo.mb* and add curve emitters to the bowls so they drip water.

- Add opacity to the bubbles in the glass example. Make the bubbles fade out just before reaching the top of the glass. Also, try adding radiusPP so each particle grows slightly as it approaches the top of the glass.

- Try adding a second particle object to the bubbles emitted from the base of the glass. Use the same techniques you used with the second particle object in the fountain example.

- Combine a curve emitter and Per-Point Emission to make a wave that has more emission on one end than on the other.

- Add a second particle object to the texture emission example so the texture emits MultiPoint and Multi-Streak.

SUMMARY

Now you have seen an introduction of some different ways of creating and working with particles in Maya. At this stage, you've learned your way around with the basics of particles. Learning where everything is and the basic terminology is a very important step on the road to creating your own effects. In this lesson, you have looked at the following:

- Particle Tool, *particleShape* node, forcesInWorld, basic fields.

- Emitters:

    Directional;

    Omni directional;

    Volume;

    Surface;

    Texture Emission;

    Per-Point Emission.

- Per particle and per object attributes;
- Controlling particle motion using ramps (ramp acceleration);
- Emitting into multiple particle objects.

Later in the book you will learn how to emit particles using MEL.

In this chapter you also worked on controlling simple motion and characteristics of particles using **particle object** and **per particle attributes** such as:

- lifespan and lifespanPP;
- rgb and rgbPP;
- radius and radiusPP;
- acceleration;
- rate and ratePP.

There are many more attributes that are special to particles. These will be discussed in greater detail later, however, they all are accessed and manipulated in the same way.

5 Rigid Bodies & Particles

Now that you have been introduced to particles and rigid bodies, we will combine the two into one exercise to show you some ways they can work together. It is common for a rigid body event, such as collisions, to result in a particle-involved dynamic event. Getting the two to work together can help create realistic movement that otherwise would require intensive keyframing.

In this chapter you will learn about the following:

- Particle and rigid body collisions;
- Additional rigid body optimization using collision layers;
- Rigid body surface emission.

Shattering window

Breaking a window

In this example, you are going to create a shattering window. You will be incorporating some of the tools that you have been working with up to this point, as well as some more advanced techniques.

1 Open the scene

- Open the scene called *breakingGlass.mb*.

    This scene consists of a window and a floor. The window glass is made up of three elements whose visibility is keyframed at different times so the window first appears unbroken and then broken.

    glass - Unbroken pane of glass (initially visible, then keyed invisible).

    outsideGlass - Full pane after break (initially invisible, then keyed visible).

    glassShards - Broken pieces that you will animate (initially invisible, then keyed visible).

2 Make the glass shards into Active Rigid Bodies

In order for the window to dynamically shatter and be influenced by fields, the shard pieces need to be made into Active Rigid Bodies.

- Open the *glassShards* group and select all the individual *shards*.

- Select **Soft/Rigid Bodies → Create Active Rigid Body**.

- Edit the attributes in the Channel Box on the *rigidBody* nodes as follows. Make sure you see "..." near the top of the Channel Box indicating that these edits will occur for all selected items.

    InitialVelocity Z to **1.5**;

    InitialSpin Y to **5**;

    Mass to **0.5**;

    Bounciness to **0**;

    Damping to **1**;

    Dynamic to **Static Friction** to **0**;

    Stand In to **None**;

    ApplyForcesAt to **verticesOrCvs**.

3 Assign alternate shards to separate collision layers

Collision layers are used to organize collections of rigid bodies into layers that the rigid body solver can handle independently.

The idea here is to put adjacent shards on separate collision layers. This will prevent excessive collision and interpenetration of neighboring objects that are initially in contact. This will also increase the performance of the solver since there are fewer potential objects that each shard can collide with (shards can only collide with objects in the same collision layer or an any object on collision layer -1).

- Select all the shard *rigidBody* nodes.

- Open **Window** → **General Editors** → **Attribute Spread Sheet...**

- In the Attribute Spread Sheet, switch to the **Shape Keyable** tab and enter alternating values of **1** or **2** for the **Collision Layer** attribute as you go down the list of selected rigid body objects.

Tip: You can also key the **Collisions** attribute on or off for adjacent rigid bodies. This puts each object on its own collision layer so that they do not collide with one another.

Selection for collision layer assignment

4 Make the floor a Passive Rigid Body

Now you will make the shards collide with the floor.

- Select *floor*.
- Select **Soft/Rigid Bodies** → **Create Passive Rigid Body**.
- Set **Collision Layer** to **-1** in the Channel Box.

  Setting Collision Layer to **-1** causes the object to collide with all other rigid body objects, regardless of their collision layer setting.

5 Create Air fields to blow the shards

- Select all the *shard* rigid bodies.
- Select **Fields** → **Air** – ❐ and set the following:

  Magnitude to **25**;

  Attenuation to **1**;

  Max Distance to **30**;

  Direction to **0, 0, 1**;

  Speed to **0.5**;

  Component Only to **Off**;

  Spread to **0.3**.

- Press **Create**.
- Position the air field slightly behind the window facing out through the window in the Z direction.

6 Create Gravity fields for the shards

- Select all the shards again, then select **Fields** → **Gravity**.
- Set **Magnitude** to **12** in the Channel Box.

7 Test the animation

The glass shards should fly out of the window and collide with the floor. Notice that only shards on the same collision layer collide with each other.

One interesting way to tune this type of animation is to get a reasonable simulation, then go back to individual objects and change things like their **Mass**. By creating individual mass values for each object, you can improve the natural motion and interaction.

If you find, for instance, that two pieces are interpenetrating noticeably, you can select one and change its mass or even its collision layer to fix the problem.

Make some pieces of glass surface emitters

1 Create surface emitters to throw out some glass

Since rigid bodies can also be surface emitters, you will select four or five shards to act as surface emitters for a couple of frames.

- Select four evenly spaced shards.

- Select **Particles → Emit from Object -** ❐ and set the following:

    Emitter type to **Surface**.

    This creates one emitter for each selected shard and parents the emitter to the shard.

2 Set keyframes for the rate

- Go to frame **1** and keyframe the **Rate** to a value of **1000**.

- Go to frame **10** and keyframe the **Rate** to a value of **0**.

3 Connect the particles to the Air and Gravity fields

- **Shift-select** *particle1* then *gravityField1*.

- Select **Fields → Affect Selected Object(s)**.

- **Ctrl-select** *particle1* then *airField1* in the Outliner.

- Select **Fields → Affect Selected Object(s)**.

4 Set particles to collide with the floor

- **Ctrl-select** *particle1* and *floor* in the Outliner.

- Select **Particles → Make Collide**.

5 Increase particle Inherit Factor

Increasing the Inherit Factor will cause the motion of the particles to inherit the speed and direction of the shards they are emitted from.

- Select *particle1*.

- In the Channel Box, increase the **Inherit Factor** to about **2**.

6 Adjust particle bouncing

The particles are now colliding with the floor but they are not sliding when they hit, instead they abruptly bounce. To adjust how the particles react to the colliding surface, do the following:

- Select the particles.

- Locate the *geoConnector* node in **INPUTS** section of the Channel Box.

- Adjust **Resilience** and **Friction** values until the particles slide more naturally upon collision. As a start, try values of 0.2 for both attributes. You'll see how dramatically different the particles now respond when they collide.

7 Playback and tune

Spend some time adjusting the various rigid body and/or field attributes to change the motion to your liking. You can also try incorporating some of what you learned in previous lessons to add more interesting characteristics to the particles, such as color or opacity.

TIPS AND TRAPS

- If the glass shards appear partially shattered when the scene file is opened, select all the shards and use **Modify → Reset Transformations** to correct this.

- Make sure the placement of the Air field is positioned behind the glass shards to get the proper effect.

- If the collisions are not occurring between the particles and floor, make sure you did not **Shift-select** in the Outliner when you selected the objects prior to issuing the **Make Collide** command. You should be **Ctrl-selecting** in the Outliner.

- Resilience controls how much rebound occurs in the particle collision. You can even use negative numbers with Resilience, however it is rare that you would need this. The online Dynamics documentation fully describes the differences between resilience and friction. Refer there for more details.

- You can also use the **Set Rigid Body Interpenetration** and **Set Rigid Body Collision** menu options under the **Solvers** menu to produce the same basic result of setting different objects on different collision layers. Set Rigid Body Interpenetration has the same effect as putting all selected objects on different collision layers. Set Rigid Body Collision has the effect of all selected objects being on the same collision layer. This is just another way of doing the same thing but makes it faster since you don't have to manually change all the numbers. However, it can be tricky to keep track of what things are set to collide and what things are not. The advantage of collision layers is that you can very clearly see which objects will be colliding just by looking in the Attribute Spread Sheet.

SUMMARY

You should now have a good idea how to setup and work with collision layers, basic particle collisions, and methods for integrating particles with rigid bodies. One of the big challenges with rigid bodies is handling objects that are stacked together. You have seen that collision layers are useful for handling this situation and also provide a method for speeding up the solver evaluation.

In upcoming lessons, you will take this a step further to work with particle collision events which cause a user defined action to occur when a particle collision occurs.

6 Particle Collisions

In this chapter you will learn how to create and tune Particle Collisions by:

- Creating particle to surface collisions;
- Creating and editing particle collision events;
- Setting particle collision event procedures;
- Applications.

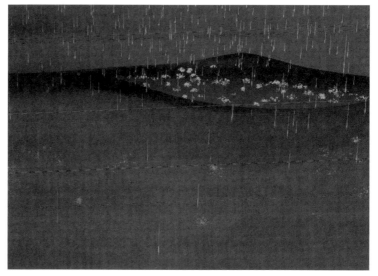

Rain drops

Creating Particle to Surface Collisions

To enable a particle to collide and interact with a geometric object (including soft bodies, trimmed objects, and deforming geometry), you will use the **Particles** → **Make Collide** menu command.

Particles can collide with geometry but cannot collide with each other.

Particle Collision Events

With the Particle Collision Event, you can trigger the following events when a particle collides with a collision object:

- Emit new particles;
- Execute a MEL procedure;
- Kill particles.

The collision can be caused by either moving particles or by moving or deforming geometry.

Collision events obey trimmed surfaces.

Rain drops

This exercise will introduce you to the Collision Event Editor.

1 Open rainDrops.mb

- Open *rainDrops.mb.*

    This scene file contains three pieces of geometry:

    rainCloud - polygonal plane;

    rainSurface - NURBS surface obtained from trim;

    mounds - NURBS surface.

2 Add a surface emitter to the rainCloud object

- Select the *rainCloud* plane.
- Select **Particles** → **Emit from Object - ❑** and set the following:

    Emitter Type to **Surface.**
- Press **Create.**
- Set the emitter's **Rate** to **1** and **Speed** to **10.**

3 Set attributes for particleShape1

- Set the following attributes for *particleShape1*:

  Particle Render Type to **Multi-Streak**;

  Line Width to **1**;

  MultiCount to **3**;

  Multi Radius to **0.01**;

  Normal Dir to **2**;

  Tail Fade to **0.5**;

  Tail Size to **0.5**.

4 Make rainSurface a collidable object

- Select *rainSurface*.

- Select **Particles** → **Make Collide**.

  This will create and connect a *geoConnector* node to the *rainSurface* object. This node contains the collision attributes of **Tessellation Factor**, **Resilience**, and **Friction**.

  The *rainSurface* geometry will now show up as an option for connecting the particle object as a collision in the Dynamics Relationship Editor.

5 Connect rainSurface to particle1

- Open the Dynamic Relationships Editor in **Window** → **Relationship Editors** → **Dynamic Relationships...**

- Select the *particle1* object.

- Select **Collisions** under **Selection Modes.**

- Select *rainSurfaceShape1*.

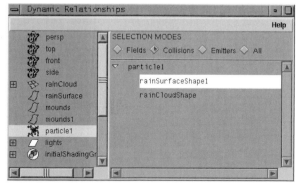

Connecting collisions to rainSurfaceShape1

The connection is made between the *rainSurfaceShape1* and the *particleShape1* nodes via the *geoConnector* node. Now, the particles will collide with that surface.

6 Test the scene

Test the scene for proper playback. You should see the particles now colliding with *rainSurface*.

Adjust the **Resilience** and **Friction** as desired.

Tip: You can also do this collision and connection in one step by first selecting the *particle*, then the *surface* it is to collide with, then press **Particles →
Make Collide**.

---

7 Use the Particle Tool to create an empty particle object

You will soon make the colliding particles split into new particles. Creating an empty particle object now will give those new particles somewhere to be stored.

- Use the Particle Tool to create an empty particle object.

    When created, the empty particle object is called *particle2*.

8 Connect Particle2 to collide with rainSurface

You can setup collision and connection in one step without using the Dynamic Relationship Editor.

- **Shift- select** *particle2*, then *rainSurface* object.
- Select **Particles → Make Collide**.

Using the Particle Collision Event Editor

1 Open Collision Event Editor

- Select **Particles → Particle Collision Events...**

    This editor is the graphical interface to the event MEL command.

Selection and Events Section

The top two list panes provide selection of valid objects to create events for and for selecting events to edit.

The next section provides fields that give information about the selected event and allow for editing the event name.

You can create multiple events for each particle selected in the left-hand list. You can also update the list of particle objects by pressing the **Update Object List** button.

Below that section is a section which displays whether you are in edit or creation mode and a button to add a New Event to the particle you are working with.

The next section lets you choose which collision the event occurs on or all collisions.

From this editor, you can choose actions to occur when a particle collides with its collision objects.

2 Set event options

- Select *particle1* in the **Objects** section.
- Set the following options as directed:

  All Collisions to **On**;

  Type to **Split**;

  Num particles to **20**;

  Spread to **1**;

  Target Particle to **particleShape2**.

  (Type in *particleshape2* next to Target Particle. This is the empty particle object that was created using the Particle Tool)

  Inherit Velocity to **0.8**.

Emit vs. Split

"**Emit**" is when the particle emits new particles and lives while "**Split**" is when the particle emits new particles and dies. If a new target particle is not specified for Split, then it uses the same particle object as the colliding particle. Also, when emit is used, the age of the new particles starts at 0. When split is used, the age of the new particle is inherited from the colliding particle.

Random # Particles

Checking this attribute will create a random amount of emitted particles with a min range of 0 and a max range of the following attribute Num Particles.

Num Particles

Sets the amount of particles emitted at collision or the max range of particles if Random # Particles is selected.

Spread

Controls the spread of emitted particles. Valid values are from 0 to 1.

(Cont'd on next page)

Event Type Section

(Cont'd)

Target Particle

The Target Particle field is where you can choose the particleShape that you want to emit upon the collision event. If you do not select a particle, one is created for you.

Inherit Velocity

This value controls what percentage of the parent particles velocity will be assumed by the new Split or Emitted particles.

The Event Actions Section

The Event Actions section is where you can call a MEL procedure at the time of collision. Later in this lesson we will look at this section more closely.

3 **Create Event**

- Press **Create Event**.

4 **Test the animation and add gravity**

Playback the simulation add apply gravity to *particle2*.

Select *particle2*, then **Fields** → **Gravity**.

5 **Add two events to the particle2**

- Open **Particles** → **Particle Collision Events...**
- Select *particle2* in the object list pane.
- Press **Create Event**.
- Rename this first event from *event0* to *firstEvent* in the **Set Event Name** field.
- Press **New Event**.

  You are now in create mode.

- Press **Create Event** at the bottom of the window.
- You have now created another new event for *particle2* called *event1*.
- Rename this event *secondEvent*.

6 **Set Event Options for firstEvent**

Set the following options as directed:

All Collisions to **Off**;

Collision Number to **1**;

Type to **Split**;

Num Particles to **2**;

Spread to **0.5**;

Target Particle to **particleShape2**;

Inherit Velocity to **0.5**.

7 Set Event Options for secondEvent

Set the following options as directed:

All Collisions to **Off**;

Collision Number to **2**;

Type to **Split**;

Num Particles to **1**;

Spread to **0.5**;

Target Particle to **particleShape2**;

Inherit Velocity to **0.5**.

8 Run the scene and tune

- Adjusting lifespan and render attributes for *particle1* and *particle2* will help refine the simulation.

Trampled underfoot

The scene file *footDust_start.mb* contains a character and floor of particles. You will make the character kick up a cloud of particles as he walks through the scene.

Character walking through dust

1 Open the scene

- Open the file *footDust_start.mb*.

  Note the scale of the grid. This scene is built on a larger world scale. Some attributes on the dynamic objects may need to be set in relation to this larger scale. It is good practice to keep this in mind.

2 **Test the animation**

You will see the character walk through the particles.

3 **Create a radial field on particle1**

- Select *particle1*.

- Select **Fields** → **Radial** - ❑ and set the following:

  Make sure this is *not* a volume field. **Volume shape** should be set to **none** for this radial field. The other settings should be something like:

    Magnitude to **1**;

    Attenuation to **1**;

    Max Distance to **5**;

    Use Max Distance to **On**.

4 **Point Constrain the field to the left foot**

- Select the left foot *Ball* joint.

- In the Outliner, select **Display** → **Selected** to see the object nested in the hierarchy.

- In the Outliner, **Ctrl-select** *Ball* and the radial field. *Ball* is one joint back from the toe joint of the character.

- Select **Constrain** → **Point**.

- Create another radial field and constrain it to the other foot.

5 **Test the animation**

Playback the scene to ensure that the fields and particles are interacting.

6 **Set the floor particles to collide with the floor object**

- Select the *particle1* object, then **Shift-select** (Hypergraph) **Ctrl-select** (Outliner) the *stageBase* object.

- Select **Particles** → **Make Collide**.

7 **Create a collision event for the floor particles**

- Select **Particles** → **Particle Collision Event...**

- Select *particle1* in the **Objects** section.

- Press **Create Event**.

- Select *event1* in the Events Selection pane.

- Enter the following Event Type options:

    All Collisions to **On**;

    Type to **Emit**;

    Random # Particles to **On**;

    Num Particles to **10**;

    Spread to **1**;

    Target Particle to **particleShape2**;

    Inherit Velocity to **1**.

8 Playback and Tune

There are various places to fine-tune this example. Particle **Lifespan** and **Max Count** on *particleShape2* control how many particles are in the scene.

Resilience on the *stageBase* object's *geoConnector* will control how the particles react with the floor. Adjusting the field attributes (especially magnitude and max distance), will also make a big difference.

Particle Collision Event procedure

You have learned how to create and edit collision events. Now, let's take things a little farther and explore the options for triggering a more complex animation at the time of collision.

The Particle Collision Event also has a section called **Event Actions**. From this section you can enter an Event Procedure. An Event Procedure is typically a MEL script that is called when a collision occurs and the event is triggered. There are a multitude of applications that can utilize this functionality. For example, perhaps you want to move an object to the location of a particle collision or perhaps you want to query the UV coordinates and find out or modify the shading information at a collision point. In many production environments, there may be other proprietary rendering systems or software applications that require you to pass information to. Having access to this level of information and being able to modify that information for use inside of Maya (and outside of Maya for other applications), is what makes this a powerful feature.

There is one requirement for the script that is called by the Particle Collision Event. It must have the following format and argument list:

```
global proc myEventProc(string $particleName, int
$particleId, string $objectName)
```

Where `myEventProc` is the name of the MEL procedure and also the name of the script (*myEventProc.mel*), `$particleName` is the name of the particle object that owns the event, `$particleId` is the particle number of the particle that has collided, and $objectName is the name of the object that the particle has collided with.

These arguments, which are also variables, are the place holders for holding the information that is passed to the script from the Particle Collision Event.

1 Open the scene and enter MEL commands

This scene will be setup to accept a specific Particle Collision Event procedure. It contains the rain objects you used before.

- Open the scene *collision_script.mb.*

Enter the following commands in the Script Editor to create a special node and establish the connection to the *ground* surface:

```
createNode closestPointOnSurface;

connectAttr -f ground.worldSpace[0]
    closestPointOnSurface1.inputSurface;
```

The *closestPointOnSurface* node is a very useful node for querying the world and UV position of a point on a surface.

2 Set particle1 to collide with ground

- **Shift-select** *particle1* and then *ground* in the viewport (persp).
- Select **Particles → Make Collide**.

3 Add the script procedure to a Particle Collision Event Action Event

- Select **Particles → Particle Collision Event...**
- Press **Create Event**.
- Set **Original Particle Dies** to **On**.

Note: Do not select **Emit** or **Split** as the **Event Type**.

- Enter *partCollisionPrnt* into the Event Procedure field under the **Event Actions** section. This is the name of a script that is included as part of the dynamics support files. This script needs to be in your current Maya script path to be found by the software.

4 Create a point light in the scene

- The script that will be executed at collision time will print out information but will also take a point light in your scene and move it to the X,Y, Z location of collision.
- **Create → Lights → Point Light** (the name should be *pointLight1*).
- Press **5** then **7** to switch to hardware lighting mode.

5 Open the Script Editor and playback the scene

The *partCollisionPrnt* script is executed each time a particle collides with the surface. The *partCollisionPrnt* script then prints the position on the surface where the collision occurred. The script also moves the point light you created to these world coordinates.

Sample output from the Script Editor:

```
partCollisionPrnt("particleShape1", 0, " ground");

CPOS XYZ          10.51686562 2.943025257e-15 -10.38921561

CPOS UV           0.9370036721 0.9316994754

POS Position      10.51686562 2.943025257e-15 -10.38921561

POS UV Position 0.9370036721 0.9316994754
```

6 Open the partCollisionPrnt.mel script

If you want, you can use a text editor or the Script Editor to read through the *partCollisionPrnt*. Unless you know MEL, this script may not make a lot of sense to you. But, you will be able to see the basic framework of the collision event procedure and get an idea of how this type of effect is set up.

The procedure *partCollisionPrnt* does a few things. First, it takes the arguments given to it from the Particle Collision Event and puts these values into global variables:

```
$particlePositions

$particleVelocitys

$hitTimes

$particleHitCount

$currentHitTime
```

These variables can then be accessed from other procedures or expressions in Maya. Use this upper portion of the script as a template for your own Particle Collision Event scripts.

The second portion uses two types of point-on-surface nodes to get and maintain collision information as it pertains to the surface.

closestPointOnSurface returns information about a point on the surface in relation to the worldspace position information that the $particlePositions variable is getting from the Particle Collision Event each time a particle collides with the surface.

pointOnSurface is an operation that can create a *pointOnSurfaceInfo* node. This node will maintain information about a point on a surface even if the surface is animating and deforming.

TIPS AND TRAPS

- People often ask about the difference between Emit vs. Split. They determine what happens to the particle that originally collided. Emit keeps it in the scene, Split will kill the particle. This also affects what happens to the age of the new particle. Emit resets the age of the new particle to 0 and Split starts the age of the new particle at whatever value the old particle's age was when the collision occurred. The file *emitVsSplit.mb* in the demo directory is a very basic demonstration of this.

- As the character walks through the grid of particles, everything may appear to work fine for the first part of the walk cycle but not later in the cycle. This is because there is a **Max Count** set for *particleShape2*. This is just to keep the number of particles in the scene to a reasonable level. If you want, you can set the value to -1 and use the level of detail attribute on *particleShape2*, instead of Max Count.

- When entering the name of a script to be executed by the collision event procedure, don't type the ".mel" portion of the script name into the Collision Event Editor.

- If errors occur, check to make sure the script is in your scripts directory or try sourcing the script by typing "source partCollisionPrnt" in the Script Editor. Always check the output to the Script Editor to help track down problems.

- A great way to find out where Maya is looking for your scripts is to type: `internalVar -userScriptDir;` into your Script Editor.

- If you make any changes to the *partCollisionPrnt.mel* script yourself, you will need to type: `source partCollisionPrnt;` in the Script Editor before Maya will be aware of those changes you made to the script.

- If using IRIX, a fun example is to have Maya play a sound when a collision occurs. To do this, use a system command and the sfplay unix command along with any *.aiff or sound file. Store the following commands as soundPlay.mel in ~/maya/version/scripts:

```
global proc soundPlay (string $particleName, int
$particleId, string $objectName)

{

system ("sfplay mySound.aiff");

}
```

There is a completed version of this script in the scripts directory. There are also some example sound files included with the Dynamics data. sfplay is an IRIX command, so this will not work on Windows systems.

- The file *dieOnFrustumExit.mb* shows how to make particles die when they leave the camera frustum. This is a very simple file where a polygon has been fit to the camera frustum and a collision event is used to kill the particles. This can be useful when dealing with very large numbers of particles for memory management.

- The event MEL command can be used in MEL scripts and expressions to customize the behavior of particle collisions events beyond what is in the Collision Event Editor. Additionally, particles have an "event" attribute that keeps track of how many collisions each particle has had. For much more information on this and many other particle attributes, refer to the **particle** entry in the *Node and Attribute Reference* section of Maya's online documentation.

SUMMARY

The Particle Collision Event is a very powerful method of controlling particles and their behavior. It provides a logical method of emission and/or death, based on collision. The ability to execute a procedure at collision also opens up a large range of possibilities for creating geometry or manipulating virtually any other part of Maya or even your system at times of collision.

7 Particle Expressions

This chapter focuses on different techniques for controlling particle motion with special attention placed on particle expressions.

In this chapter you will learn about the following:

- Fundamental physics concepts;
- Maya's particle evaluation process;
- Initial State;
- Creation vs. Runtime Expressions;
- Linstep and smoothstep functions;
- The particleId attribute;
- Absolute Value;
- Sin and cosine.

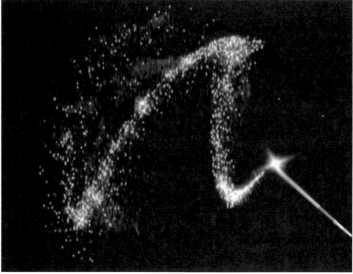

Magic wand

Fundamental physics concepts

There are some basic rules that govern the motion of objects in the universe that are directly applicable to a discussion of particles in Maya. Newton's first law states the following:

```
Force = Mass x Acceleration
```

This is more commonly written as `F = ma`.

Force and **Mass** are known quantities in Maya. Acceleration is calculated by the dynamics system based on these values. The resulting values are used to control the particle's motion.

> **Force** - a generated quantity that can come from things like *fields*, *springs*, and *expressions*.
>
> **Mass** - an attribute that exists by default on particle objects. Therefore, since two items in the equation are known, the third (acceleration) can be determined through simple division:
>
> ```
> a= F/m
> ```

This rule forms the basis of the underlying architecture Maya uses to calculate particle attributes such as position, velocity, and acceleration. Understanding this relationship is not always necessary, but can be useful when deciding how to set something up, or when troubleshooting.

Some useful definitions

There are some common terms and definitions that come up frequently regarding particle attributes and quantities related to particles.

> **Scalar** - a numerical quantity with only one specific component. *Time* and *mass* are examples of scalar values represented by values like 20 or -3.5.
>
> **Vector** - a quantity with magnitude and direction. In Maya, this is represented as three distinct numerical components grouped together in brackets, i.e. <<1,2,3>> or <<5,-2,1>>.
>
> **Float** - a decimal numerical value, i.e. 2.3, 0.001, 3.14, etc.
>
> **Integer** - a non-decimal whole number, i.e. -1, 0, 57, etc.
>
> **String** - a collection of alphanumeric characters, i.e."hello"
>
> **Boolean** - a value that is either *true* or *false, on* or *off, 1* or 0.
>
> **Variable** - a location in memory used to store information that is one of the above data types, i.e. `float $hello` defines $hello as a storage space for decimal numerical information that can be accessed in expressions and scripts.
>
> **Position** (vector) - a particle's *location in the world* is its **position**.

Velocity (vector) - a particle's *change in position over time*. This is a measurement of both **Rate** and **Direction**. To visualize velocity, imagine an arrow pointing in the direction of the object's motion with the arrow's length proportional to the speed of the object.

Speed (scalar) - a particle's measurement of *rate only* (without respect to direction).

Acceleration (vector) - a particle's measurement of the *change in velocity* over time.

Propagation: the evaluation process

Propagation is the method Maya uses to determine a particle's attribute values by basing the calculations for the current frame on the result that was determined from the previous frame.

Propagation is like a "piggy-back" effect. For example, frame 2 gets information from frame 1, it does some calculations, then positions the particles. Next, frame 3 gets the result from frame 2, does its calculations, positions the particles, and moves to frame 4. The cycle continues throughout the playback of the animation.

So what happens at frame 1?

Frame 1 in the above example is the **Initial State** of the system. Initial State refers to the values that exist in any dynamic object's attributes at the initial frame of a dynamic simulation. It is from this Initial State that propagation occurs.

Note: The **Initial State** of a simulation is not necessarily the first frame in the playback frame range but, instead, is determined by the **start frame** attribute on each particle object.

Creation vs. Runtime Expressions

It is important to understand the difference between creation and Runtime Expressions.

Creation Expression - evaluated only once for each particle in the particle object when the particle is born.

Runtime Expression - evaluated at least once per particle per frame but not at particle birth.

In Maya, two types of Runtime Expressions are available, Runtime before Dynamics and Runtime after Dynamics. Runtime before dynamics is the same as the Runtime in prior versions of Maya, Runtime after Dynamics is new.

Note: Particle expressions are also commonly referred to as *rules*. The term *rule* comes from *Dynamation* which uses *creation* and *runtime rules*.

- Each particle object stores all of its expressions in one of two places: the **Creation Expression** or the **Runtime Expression**.

- All **Creation Expressions** are stored in the creation portion of the Expression Editor for that particle object.

- Likewise, all **Runtime Expressions** on a given particle object reside in the runtime segment of that particle object.

**Toggle between
Runtime before Dynamics,
Runtime After Dynamics
and Creation**

The Expression Editor can toggle between displaying the Runtime and Creation Expressions for the selected *particleShape* node. The expressions are evaluated in the order they appear in the Expression Editor.

Tip: Runtime and Creation will be greyed out unless the *particleShape* node is the selected item. If you select the particle object in the modeling view, you can press the down arrow on the keyboard to navigate to the *particleShape* node.

---

1 Create a simple Creation Expression

Now you will write a simple particle expression. Remember that all of the expressions used in this chapter are available on your shelf if you have installed the preferences that come with the support files for this book.

Typing them out is good practice, though, and is recommended if this is new territory for you.

- Open the file *runtimeCreation.mb.*
- Switch to shaded mode and playback.

  This scene contains two pre-made directional emitters with an **rgbPP** attribute already added to both *particleShape* nodes. Right now, the rgbPP value is <<0,0,0>> so the particles emit as black.

- Open the Attribute Editor for *particleShape1.*
- **RMB** on **rgbPP** and select **Creation Expression**.
- Enter the following expression in the Expression Editor:

  ```
  rgbPP = <<rand(1),0,0>>;
  ```

  In the above syntax, the double brackets indicate a vector quantity. There are three entries in a vector quantity, called X, Y, and Z components. The components get separated by commas. In this case the first (X component) corresponds to a red color, the second (Y component) to a green color, and the third (Z component) corresponds to blue.

Note: It is common to see many different attributes assigned values on the *same line* in the Expression Editor. Each should be separated by semi-colons. i.e. `rgbPP = <<1,0,1>>; lifespanPP = rand (4,6);`

---

2 Create a simple Runtime Expression

- Select *particleShape2.*
- **RMB** on **rgbPP** and select **Runtime Expression Before Dynamics**.
- Enter the following expression in the Expression Editor:

  ```
  rgbPP = <<0,0,rand(1)>>;
  ```

3 Test the results

- Make sure you are in shaded mode.
- Rewind and then playback.

  The particle shape with the Creation Expression gets a random red color assigned to it only once during the animation. The particle shape with the Runtime Expression reassigns a new random blue value on each frame of the animation.

Note:	The syntax **rand(1)** picks a random value between 0 and 1. The result is always greater than 0 but less than 1. You can also define a more specific range by using two numbers with rand. For example **rand (20, 30)** picks a random value greater than 20 and less than 30. This example uses a range from 0 to 1, since RGB values range from 0 to 1.

Use the same techniques to create additional creation and Runtime Expressions to control other attributes such as radiusPP, lifespanPP, or opacityPP.

APPLIED PARTICLE EXPRESSIONS

You should now have a better understanding of the difference between Runtime and Creation. The next step is to use these concepts in conjunction with normalized age to establish a relationship between time and the attribute values.

The following "template" can be used when writing a particle expression to animate from **quantity A** to **quantity B** over the particles **age**:

```
A+((B-A)*(age/lifespan))
```

1 Mimic a ramp behavior with a particle expression

In a previous lesson, you learned to change the color of a particle over its age based on a ramp. This section teaches you how to do the same thing using an expression. This is handy if you need some specific control that you can't get from a ramp.

- Open the file *fountainExpression.mb*.
- Open the Attribute Editor for *mist*.
- Set **Lifespan Mode** to **Constant** to **2.6**.
- Add an **rgbPP** attribute to *mist*.
- **RMB-click** in the **rgbPP** field and choose **Runtime Expression Before Dynamics...**
- Following the template from above, substitute values for white (A), light blue(B), and normalized age into the Expression Editor as shown below:

```
$normAge = age/lifespan;

vector $start = <<1,1,1>>;

vector $end = <<0,0,0.8>>;

rgbPP = $start+(($end-$start)*$normAge);
```

- Drag the contents of this expression to the shelf. You'll use it again later.

- Press **Create** and close the Expression Editor.

- Press **5** to switch to shaded mode.

- Rewind and play the animation.

  The expression causes the particles to slowly transition from white to blue over the particles' age in the same fashion ramps controlled their color in a previous lesson. You can adjust the start and end colors in the expression to your liking once you see the effect the expression is having.

- The particles at the very base of the stream where the particles leave the emitter are black. See if you can use what you've already learned to fix this.

Linstep and smoothstep

Linstep and smoothstep are built-in functions within Maya that return a value between 0 and 1 over a specified range for a given unit (frames, fps, lifespan, age, etc).

Linstep produces a linear curve while smoothstep produces a linear curve with an ease-in and ease-out appearance at the tangents.

The syntax template for a linstep (or smoothstep) statement is as follows:

```
linstep (start, end, unitParameter)
```

One advantage of using linstep and smoothstep is that the range of the effect can occur over any defined interval instead of being limited to the particle's age.

It is also possible to make the range of the values for linstep or smoothstep extend beyond the range of 0 to 1. For example, to make a particle's radius increase from 0 to 5 over the course of frames 8 - 20, the following Runtime Expression could be used:

```
radiusPP = 5* linstep (8, 20, frame)
```

To make a linstep curve decrease instead of increase, subtract the linstep statement from 1. Below is a common linstep function that will cause opacity to fade out linearly over the particle's age if placed in the Runtime Expression.

```
opacityPP = 1-(smoothstep(0, lifespanPP, age));
```

| Note: | Graphs for the linstep and smoothstep function are provided in Maya's online documentation. |

Taking it a step beyond ramps

So far, what you've done could be done using ramps. The idea has been to get you familiar with how to enter expressions and how their evaluation works in Maya. Now, you'll control a particle attribute such as radiusPP using a dynamic attribute like velocity. This is more difficult to accomplish with ramps and lends itself well to an expression.

1 Set mist render type to sphere

Although you may not want to render the final shot in sphere mode, for this example you will use the sphere render type, since the effects of the expression are easiest to see with that render type.

2 Double check that rgbPP expression is still present

- Look in the Runtime Expression for rgbPP to make sure the expression you used for rgbPP above is still assigned to the particle object. If you deleted it, **drag+drop** it from the shelf back into the Expression Editor.

3 Add a radiusPP attribute and enter a Runtime Expression

- Add a **radiusPP** attribute.
- Enter the following Runtime Expression for radiusPP. You may want to enter a few carriage returns below the expression that is controlling rgbPP to make things more readable.

```
float $startRadius = 0.1;

float $endRadius = 0.5;

vector $vel = velocity;

float $y = $vel.y;

radiusPP = $y/10 * ($startRadius + ($endRadius-
$startRadius) * $normAge);
```

The above expression changes the radius of the spheres based on a factor of their velocity in the **Y** direction but also based on their normalized age. Notice that the radius decreases when the particle drops slow down and increases as they speed back up.

What happened to the RGB values?

You may have noticed that now the spheres begin white but turn black at some point instead of being colored. Any ideas why this happened?

4 Use the numeric render type to track down the problem

The numeric render type is useful for determining what values a specific particle attribute holds.

- Playback so you have some emitted particles.

- Select the *mist* particles.

- Set **Particle Render Type** to **Numeric**.

- Press **Current Render Type** and enter **radiusPP** in the Attribute Name field.

  This displays the numeric radius value held for each particle. As you playback, the values start positive, then become negative. Since the expression used is returning negative radius values, the spheres get turned "inside out." This is why you see black instead of color.

5 Correct the expression so only positive radius values are used

- Open the **Runtime Expression** for **radiusPP**.

- Edit the last line of the expression so it appears as follows:

  ```
  radiusPP = abs($y/10 * ($startRadius +
  ($endRadius-
  $startRadius) * $normAge));
  ```

  The only difference is that you enclosed what you previously had within **abs()**. Abs is a function that takes the **absolute value** of the value within parentheses. This tells the expression to check the value in parentheses, and make it positive if it is negative.

- Press **Edit** and **Close**.

6 Test the results

- Playback in numeric mode again to verify that the numbers stay positive throughout.

- Switch **Render Type** back to **Sphere** and playback to see that the RGB values now display correctly.

Particle motion examples

The file *expressionExamples.mb* contains several particle objects in different display layers. Each particle object has its own Creation and/or Runtime

Expression illustrating a common or interesting technique used with particle expressions.

A magic wand

This is an application for controlling particle color over time to create the common pixie dust effect.

Magic wand

1 Load the file

This scene consists of a cylinder object called *wand* and some standard lighting.

- Open the file *magicWand.mb*.

2 Create an emitter and parent it to the wand geometry

- Create a directional emitter with default values.
- Rename emitter *dustEmitter*.
- In the Outliner, **MMB-drag** *dustEmitter* onto *wand*.
- Select *dustEmitter* and translate it to the end of the *wand* geometry.

3 Add a Directional emitter to the dust particle object

- Rename *particle1* to *dust*.
- Select *dust*.
- Select **Particles → Emit from Object**.

    This creates an emitter that will emit particles from the dust particles. It also creates another particle object.

- Rename the added emitter *trailEmitter*.
- Rename the new particle object *dustTrail*.

4 Adjust Emitter attributes

- For the *dustEmitter* set the following:

    Emitter Type to **Directional**;

    Rate to **800**;

    Directional Y to **1**;

    Spread to **0.5**;

    Speed to **2**.

- For the *trailEmitter* set the following:

    Emitter Type to **Directional**;

    Rate to **1**;

    Directional Y to **1**;

    Spread to **0.2**;

    Speed to **0**.

5 Create fields for the pixie dust

- Add **Gravity** to *dust* and decrease **Magnitude** to **1**.
- Add a separate **Gravity** field to *dustTrail* with **Magnitude** to **1** and **Attenuation** to **0**.
- Add **Turbulence** to *dust.* Set the **Magnitude** to **2**.

6 Adjust dust particle shape attributes

   Particle Render Type to **Points**;

   Normal Dir to **2**;

   Point Size to **2**.

7 Adjust dustTrail particle shape attributes

   Particle Render Type to **Streak**;

   Line Width to **1**;

   Normal Dir to **2**;

   Tail Fade to **1**;

   Tail Size to **0.05**.

8 Add Per Particle (Array) Attributes to the dust particle shape

- Select *dust*.

- Add a **rgbPP** attribute.

9 Add Per Particle (Array) Attributes to the dustTrail particle shape

- Add a **rgbPP** attribute.
- Add a **opacityPP** attribute.

10 Create a Creation Expression for the lifespanPP of the dust particle shape

- Set **Lifespan Mode** to **LifespanPP** only.
- Use the following creation expression to control the dust particle lifespan on a per particle basis:

```
lifespanPP = rand(1,3);
```

This expression assigns a random lifespan value greater than 1 and less than 3 seconds to each particle.

11 Create a Runtime Expression for the rgbPP of the dust particle shape

- Use the following classic twinkle expression to control the color of the particles on a per particle basis:

```
rgbPP = <<1,1,1>> * (sin(0.5*id + time * 20));
```

Here is a breakdown of what is going on:

<<1,1,1>> : this is the rgb vector value of white. The expression multiplies a number against this value to change its overall value by <<0,0,0>> (black) and <<1,1,1>> (white).

sin(.5 * id + time * 20) : sin is a function that can create an oscillating value between 1 and -1.

By multiplying sin by variables like `particleId` and `time`, we can get values that are unique and changing rhythmically. This is a very important function of expressions, especially particle expressions.

0.5 * id : when working with per particle expressions, it is useful to work with the `particleShape.particleId` attribute. This attribute, as you have seen, gives us a unique value for each particle that this expression is applied to.

0.5 * id + time * 20 : again time is a great incrementer. Multiplying by 20 in this case dictates the frequency or how fast this sin functions repetition.

Why does this expression work?

What is strange about this expression?

Alternate expression #1:

Here is an alternate expression that does not use negative values against the rgb vector:

```
rgbPP = <<1,1,1>> * ((sin(0.5 * id + time * 20)
*0.5)+0.5);
```

This example offsets the sin function to provide values that fall between 0 and 1. To do this, the sin is multiplied by 0.5 to cut the amplitude in half. An offset has also been added to keep its values above 0.

Will this be better or worse?

Alternate expression #2:

How about even a simpler method? Just like tossing a coin, we can make some of the particles dark gray and some white to cause a blinking effect:

```
if (rand(1) > 0.5)
rgbPP = <<1,1,1>>;
else
rgbPP = <<0.3,0.3,0.3>>;
```

The point is, there are always many different ways to do similar things. Be careful about making things overly complicated when you don't really need to. But, at the same time, you should allow enough control in your expressions to be able to achieve the effects you want.

12 Make a Creation Expression for the lifespanPP

- Select *dustTrail* particle shape.
- Add the following Creation Expression:

```
lifespanPP = rand(2,5);
```

For the *dustTrail*, we want these particles to live a little longer.

13 Create Runtime Expressions for the rgbPP and opacityPP of the dustTrail particle shape

You will create the same type of **rgbPP** expression and also an **opacityPP** expression to control, not only the **Color**, but also the **Transparency** of the particles.

```
rgbPP = <<1,1,1>> * ((sin(.5 * id + time * 20)
*.5)+.5);
opacityPP=(1-((linstep(0,lifespanPP, age))) *.0005);
```

1-linstep(0,lifespanPP,age) : the linstep function is used here to provide a linear change of value between 0 and 1 over time. 1- linstep gives us the reverse, returning values from 1 to 0 over the particle's age. This value is different for each particle based on the lifespanPP Creation Expression you already made.

14 Playback and tune

Experiment with field attributes, render types, or multiplier values in the expressions to tune the results.

Exercises

- Simulate the effect of gravity using a particle expression instead of a field.

- Create a particle expression that assigns a random radius value between 1 and 4 to a particle as it is emitted.

- Create a particle expression that changes each particle's color from yellow to blue over its age.

- Create a particle expression using a dynamic attribute such as velocity, acceleration, position, or mass and rand, sphrand, noise or dnoise.

TIPS AND TRAPS

- **Appendix A** of this book provides a more in-depth explanation of each expression in the *expressionsExample.mb* file. To learn more about the specific expression syntax, refer to this appendix.

- **mag** is a function in Maya that finds the magnitude of a vector (also known as the length). This is useful for representing a 3 component vector with a single value. mag does the following math automatically for the user:

  ```
  distance^2 = (x2-x1)^2 + (y2-y1)^2 + (z2-z1)^2
  ```

  mag is often useful to help determine the distance one point in space is from another point in space. For an example of this, look at the *waveBodyCamDist.mb* file included in the demo directory. The mag function is used to determine the distance from each wave particle to the camera.

- In the fountain exercise of this chapter, the fountain may emit black particles on the first frame. To fix this, add a Creation Expression that sets the color to white. The Runtime Expression doesn't evaluate at age=0.

- Expressions are evaluated in the order they are typed in the Expression Editor from top to bottom. For more specific information about the order of evaluation of Maya's dynamics, refer to Appendix A of this book.

- People often look through some of the expression examples and see things like `position0` and `velocity0` and wonder what they are.

  When you save Intial State on a particle object, that information needs to be stored somewhere. Most static particle attributes (i.e., position, velocity, acceleration, mass, etc.), have an **Initial State** attribute which is designated by the 0 as in `position0`. Also, when you add a new array attribute to a particle object via **Modify** → **Add Attribute...**, there is an option for **add inital state attribute**. When you check that **On**, it adds a "0" attribute for the custom attribute.

- Specifically, with the wave example in *expressionExamples.mb* file, people often ask why `position0` is even in that expression at all.

  `position0` is the location of where the particle is located in space at Initial State. Let's say it is <<1,1,1>>. Next, Maya evaluates a noise function like dnoise(stuff) for each frame. That noise function produces a vector value, for example, say it's <<2,3,4>>. We can do one of two things in each frame. We can take the current position of where the particle is (position) and add <<2,3,4>> to it, or we can take the original location of the particle at its Initial State (`position0`) and add <<2,3,4>> to it. We choose to do the latter because we will always be offsetting the particle from a constant/known location in space (`position0`). This gets done in rapid succession on each frame. This produces a smoother motion and more predictable motion than if you added the noise function to position. It also lets us work with the particles in world space instead of having to move the particle relative to where it was the last evaluated frame. The best way to test this is to just try changing position0 to position in your expression. You'll see the results aren't as good when you playback.

SUMMARY

You now have a foundation for creating some of your own particle expressions. An entire book could be dedicated to applications of particle expressions. In this chapter, we have chosen to show you how to get started and give you some examples to get you going. Particle expressions should be considered another tool within Maya's dynamics. Not all situations lend themselves well to using expressions. However, they give you access to a lower level of information that, in some cases, is not accessible through graphical methods such as ramps or the Attribute Editor. Expressions can also provide a solution for getting results that would be difficult or impossible to keyframe and can give your simulations the ability to have decision-making built into them.

8 Flow

Flow is a Maya clip effect that allows you to quickly and easily make particles follow the shape of a specified curve.

In this chapter you will learn about the following:

- How to make particles flow along a NURBS curve;

- How to combine deformers and animation with dynamics;

- How to combine fields with flow controlled particles;

- How to adjust important flow parameters.

A tornado

Use flow to create a basic tornado effect

There are many ways to create a tornado effect in Maya. In this example, we'll give your brain a rest from particle expressions to demonstrate the simple and easy to use flow effect.

1 Open the file

- Select **File → Open Scene**.

- Open *tornadoCurve.mb*.

2 Apply a lattice deformer

- Select *tornadoCurve*

- Select **Deform → Create Lattice - ❑**. Set the following:

    Divisions to **5, 9, 2**;

    Autoparent to Selection to **On**.

- Press **Create**.

3 Add relative clusters

- Select the *ffdLattice* node, then press **F8** to switch to component mode.

- Select the top three rows of lattice points.

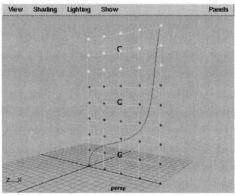

Adding clusters to the lattice points

- Choose **Deform -→ Create Cluster - ❑** and make sure **Relative Mode** is **On**.

- Press **Create**.

- Create two additional clusters for the three middle and bottom rows.

Note: Making a cluster **Relative** forces the cluster to receive its transform information from the Transform node directly above it in the hierarchy. This prevents the *double transformations* that normally occur when clusters are parented to geometry. It is possible to toggle the relative mode **On** and **Off** in the Attribute Editor on a cluster that has already been created.

---

4 Group the clusters under the tornadoCurve

- **MMB** in the Outliner and parent the three cluster handles to *tornadoCurve*.

5 Keyframe the lattice/curve

- Select *tornadoCurve*.
- Rewind to frame **1**.
- Move *tornadoCurve* to **-12**, **0**, **12**.
- Press **Shift+W** to keyframe the translation channels.
- Advance to frame **110** and set another keyframe using **Shift+W**.
- Advance to frame **160**.
- Move *tornadoCurve* to **0**, **0**, **0** and set another keyframe.
- Advance to frame **300**.
- Position the *tornadoCurve* at **-12**, **0**, **-12** and set another keyframe.

  You can also add keyframes to the cluster handles if you wish to animate the shape of the funnel, instead of only the position.

  It is best to get the motion of the curve the way you want it before animating the clusters.

6 Add flow to the curve

- Select *tornadoCurveShape*. (Make sure to pick the Shape node.)
- Select **Effects** → **Create Curve Flow -** ❑ and set the following:

  Flow Group Name to **tornadoFlow**;

  Num Control Segments to **6**;

  Particle Lifespan to **3**;

  Goal Weight to **0.62**.

- Press **Create**.

A new node called *tornadoFlow* is created. This hierarchy contains all the flow components and attributes Maya needs to control the flow of particles along the curve.

The Transform node was likely selected if you receive an error similar to the following:

```
includeEffectsGlobals.mel line 557: Command failed to
execute: duplicateCurve
```

You must select the *Shape node tornadoCurveShape* node before creating the flow.

Note: Deformers can be added to a flow path curve after flow has already been applied. Flow does not interrupt the curve history.

---

7 Test the results

- Rewind and playback the animation.

    The particles follow the shape of the curve as they are emitted. They reach the end of the curve in three seconds (90 frames) since **Lifespan** is set to **3**.

    The particles don't flow exactly along the curve's path. This is due to a low **Goal Weight** setting. Goal Weight values closer to **1** cause the particles to adhere more closely to the curve's shape.

    If you want to adjust these values, select the *tornadoCurveFlow* group in the Outliner.

8 Adjust flow parameters

- Select the circle (control segment) at the upper end of *tornadoCurve* and scale it up.

- Scale the other circles along the curve in a similar fashion so they increase in scale from the bottom of the curve to the top as shown:

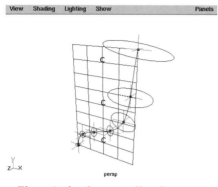

Flow circles from small to large

Tip:	To adjust the control segments (rings) along the length of the curve, pick the selection handle (or pick the *Flow* group in the Outliner), at the beginning of the curve and edit the attributes called *Locator_xx_pos* in the Channel Box. (*xx* corresponds to the number of the control segments.)

---

9 Enable Display Thickness

You can get a better sense of the volume the particles will fill by enabling the display thickness attribute for refining your circles.

- Select *tornadoFlow*.

- Set **Display Thickness** to **On** in the Channel Box.

  There are additional display attributes such as **Display Subcircles** and **Display All Sections**. These values are used for advanced refinement of the curve and to help smooth out sharp bends in the flow path, if necessary.

- Once satisfied with the shape, set all display attributes back to **Off.**

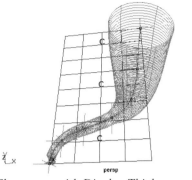

Flow curve eith Display Thickness enabled

10 Add and adjust a vortex field

- Select the particles, then choose **Fields** → **Vortex - □**. Set the following:

  Magnitude to **20**;

  Attenuation to **0**.

- Select the vortex field and position at the base of *tornadoCurve*.

- Use the Outliner to parent the vortex field to *tornadoCurve*.

11 Add a ramp to control radius over age

- Switch the **Particle Render Type** to **Cloud (s/w)**.

- Add a **radiusPP** attribute.

- **RMB** to create a ramp on **radiusPP**.

- Adjust the **R** value of the ramp so the **Radius** starts at **0.1** and dies at **0.9**.

Tip: The radius could also be increased over age using the Runtime Expression:
```
radiusPP = 0.1 + ((0.9-0.1) *
smoothstep(0,lifespan,age));
```

Since the Goal Weight is fairly low, the vortex field adds to the acceleration of the particles and allows them to spin as they flow. As the Goal Weight value is increased, the effect from the vortex is less, but the particles adhere more closely to the curve.

When combining fields with flow effects, the curve usually acts up acting as a general guide for the particles, not an absolute pathway for them. This allows the field to influence the particle.

Surface Flow

You can also guide particles along a NURBS *surface* using a different but closely related clip effect called Surface Flow. To see how this works, do the following:

- Create a simple NURBS plane and scale it up.

- Deform it using **Edit Surfaces** → **Sculpt Surfaces** from the Modeling menus so it looks somewhat like terrain.

- Select the plane and choose **Effects** → **Create Surface Flow** and adjust the resulting attributes for the Surface Flow in the Channel Box.

TIPS AND TRAPS

- If double transformations occur when moving the lattice, turn **On** relative mode on the cluster.

- You can move control rings along the length of the curve by selecting the flow group, then **MMB-dragging** on the Locator_xx_pos entries in the Channel Box. The proximity of the rings to each other controls the amount of time it takes the particles to jump between each ring.

- By default, there is not an easy way to make each particle travel along the path with an individual lifespan, (i.e. some particles take five seconds to reach the end whereas others take three seconds). This could be done with expressions but is not part of the built-in functionality of the flow effect.

- Sometimes one particle shoots out at the beginning and gets away from the flow curve. This can be fixed by setting the opacity on that one particle to 0 or by killing it using a Creation Expression based on its id. Lifespan mode will need to be lifespanPP only.

```
if (id==0)

lifespanPP = 0;
```

If that doesn't fix the problem, check your timeline to see if the start frame is set to 1 or 0. If it is at 0, try it at 1 and if it is at 1, try it at 0. This seems to fix the problem sometimes, and is likely to be some strange refreshing problem in the Dependency graph.

If that still doesn't fix it, select the offending particle in component mode and set its opacity or lifespanPP to 0 in the Component Editor.

- Both the flow and Surface Flow clip effects are MEL scripts that simply setup a variety of settings for the user. If you would like to view the contents of the flow MEL script, you can type `whatIs flowAlongCurves` in your Command Line and then view the resulting script with a text editor. This is a great way to learn MEL.

- The flow clip effect adds a lot of expressions into your scene. This is good reference information for you to learn more about expressions and expression syntax. Run the flow clip effect on a curve and look at the expressions in the Expression Editor; you may be able to pick up some tips. These expressions primarily focus on goalU, goalV, and goalOffset. These are covered in greater detail later in the Goals chapter of this book.

- People often ask if you can change the shape of the circular control rings. The answer is yes, you can change the shape, but it doesn't change the motion of the particles.

SUMMARY

The flow clip effect is a handy method for getting particles to go where you want them to go. In some cases, it can provide as much control as complicated expressions, without having to write them yourself.

Use flow for things like:

- Water flowing;
- Energy streams;
- Flocking;
- Smoke.

Other cases where you need to guide particles and fields alone do not provide enough control.

9 Goals

This chapter focuses on working with Maya's particle goal functionality.

In this chapter you will learn the following:

- Creating goal objects;
- Goal parameters;
- Fun with goals;
- Per Particle Goal attributes and functionality.

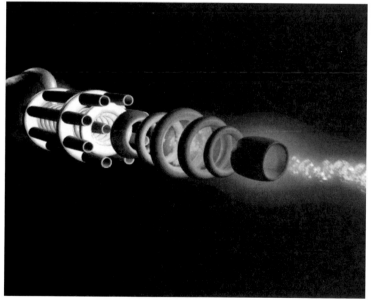

Ray gun

CHAPTER 9

PARTICLE GOALS

One of the more powerful methods that you have for controlling particle position and motion is through the use of goals. A goal is a location in space that a particle will move towards. You can create goals out of curves, lattices, polygons, NURBS surfaces, particles or Transform nodes. A particle can also have multiple goal objects.

When a goal is created, new attributes are added to the *particleShape*. In the Attribute Editor, under Goal Weights and Objects you will see an attribute with the name of the goal. This is the Goal Weight. In the Per Particle (Array) Attributes you will see a **goalPP** attribute. Together with the **Goal Smoothness** attribute, these attributes control how each particle moves towards the goal.

Particle goals are a big part of soft body dynamics. You will be looking at goals for soft bodies in the soft body section as well. The concepts covered in this lesson will be directly employed in the soft body lessons.

Creating particle and non-particle goals

Creating a particle goal object involves selecting the particle, then the object or objects that will be used as the goal objects and then selecting the menu Item **Particles → Goal**. You have the option of using particles or geometry objects as the goal objects. In the Goal Options window, you can specify if you want to use the transform of the object as the goal. By default, this option is off, and the components of the goal object will be used as the goal. When more than one object is an active goal for a particle, the resulting goal will be a combination of the goal objects' positions and the Goal Weights that have been set for each goal on the *particleShape*.

Goal Weights and goalPP

Goal Weights can be set for all particles at the same time or on a per particle basis. The per particle Goal Weight is controlled by the **goalPP** attribute. This is a dynamically added attribute. It is automatically added when a goal is created for a particle object. The goalPP weight is then multiplied by the Goal Weight of the particle object for a total particle Goal Weight. A Goal Weight of 1 means the particle will stick to its goal immediately. A Goal Weight of 0 means it will not move towards the goal at all.

Goal Smoothness

Goal Smoothness controls how particles accelerate toward a goal object. A low Goal Smoothness value will make the particle take large steps towards the goals, a higher vale will cause the particle to take smaller steps. The ratio between goalSmoothness and goalWeight controls how far the particle will travel towards the goal in each step.

A ray gun

In this example, you will control particle movement with goal objects only. You will notice that using goals instead of expressions and fields has many advantages.

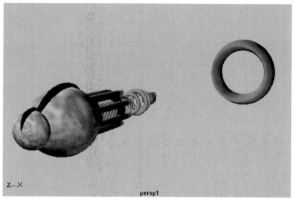

Ray gun and target wall

1 Open the scene file

- Open the file *rayGunStart.mb*.

   This scene file consists of a *rayGun_group* and a target wall. The *rayGun_group* has several objects underneath as children:

   Gun - This is the group that holds the *rayGun* geometry.

   targetFocus - This is the goal for the particles.

   circleEmitter - This is the particle emitter.

   pointLight - This is the gun's light source.

   coneControl - This is another object that is used for particle control.

2 Add a curve emitter to the curveEmitter object

This emitter will serve as the particle source.

- Select the *circleEmitter* object.

- Select **Particles → Emit from Object -** ❑ and set the following:

   Emitter type to **Curve**.

- Press **Create**.

3 **Add the targetFocus object as a goal to the emitted particles**

This object will be the main destination for the emitted particles. Notice that it has a **Post Infinity Linear Rotation** applied.

- In the Outliner, select the particle object then **Ctrl-select** the *targetFocus* object.

- Select **Particles → Goal**.

4 **Playback to see the results**

- View *particleShape1* Goal attributes in the Attribute Editor.

- Note attributes for **Goal Weights and Objects**:

  Goal Smoothness;

  targetFocusShape;

  Goal Active.

- Experiment with these values.

  Attributes that affect particle motion in general and their affect on particles being moved by goals are listed below:

  Dynamics Weight;

  Conserve;

  Level Of Detail;

  Inherit Factor.

  Play with these values and combinations of these values in concert with **Goal Smoothness** and the *targetFocusShape* **weight**.

  Conserve is a very important attribute for controlling the acceleration of particles towards their goals. If you find that particles are overshooting their goal object, you may be able to dampen their movement with this attribute.

  Dynamics Weight may not have much of an effect, but notice that if it is 0, the simulation will not compute. This is a global control for the particle object, scaling how much the various dynamic contributors such as fields affect this particle object. If you want to scale the effect of all fields by a little, it is much easier to lower this value than to try and adjust all field magnitudes, especially if they are all keyframed.

  Inherit Factor controls the amount of velocity inherited from the emitting object. This only comes into play here if the position of the gun is keyframed.

- Tear off a copy of the Emitter's Attribute Editor by clicking on the **Copy Tab** button and adjust emission attributes for the curve emitter while you are adjusting the *particleShape* attributes.

The main attributes at work are **Conserve, Goal Weight,** and **Goal Smoothness**. Experiment with these attributes to get a feel for how the particles are being driven.

▷ **Time Attributes**	
▷ **Collision Attributes**	
▷ **Soft Body Attributes**	
▽ **Goal Weights and Objects**	
Goal Smoothness	9.612
targetFocusShape	0.573
Goal Active	☑
coneControlShape	0.592
Goal Active	☑
▷ **Particle Instancer**	

Goal attributes on the ParticleShape

5 Add coneControl as another particle goal object

- Add the *coneControl* object as another goal object for the rayGun particles.

Experiment with adding in this object's Goal Weight to the particle object.

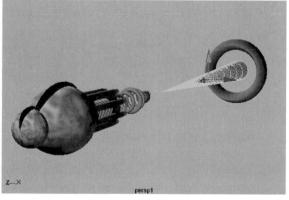

ray gun

Tip: To remove a goal object's influence, toggle off Goal Active.

---

6 Experiment with different Animation, Scale, and Position settings on the Goal objects

- Note if you set the goalWeight to 1 for the *coneControl* object and 0 for the *targetFocus* object, the particles line up on the CV's of the cone. Conversely, if you set the goalWeight to 1 for *targetFocus* and 0 for *coneControl*, the particles gather on the CV's of the targetFocus object.

- You can animate the goal objects around the scene if you want. Notice in this case the targetShape object is already animated...it is rotating.

- Mixing the Goal Weights between the two objects produces some very interesting results. Don't forget to also lower conserve and adjust goalSmoothness values.

7 Note a goalPP attribute was added to the particleShape

Maya adds the **goalPP** attribute to the *particleShape* when a goal is created for the particle. This attribute allows you to set Goal Weights on a per particle basis. The total Goal Weight per particle is the object Goal Weight multiplied by the goalPP value. The default value of goalPP is 1.

8 Animate the rayGun_group

- Animate the *rayGun_group* as if the gun is tracking an object or trying to disintegrate a moving target.

- Set keyframes at frames **1** and **100**. You may want to use Gimbal rotate manip to move the *rayGun_group* as if it were on a turret.

9 Parent the particle object into the rayGun group

When you animate the *rayGun_group* transform, all of the child objects, including the goal objects, will translate and rotate together. The particles will move towards their respective goals but will react in world space.

- **Drag+drop** the particle object into the *rayGun_group* in the Outliner.

- If you get strange offsetting of the particles after you parent them into the hierarchy, toggle the *emissionInWorld* attribute for the particle object. This may fix that problem.

The file *rayGunFinal.mb* is a finished version of this example.

Drips on a surface

In this example, you will make particles travel along a NURBS surface as though they are water droplets. You will keep track of where the particle was emitted on the surface and move it along the surface by incrementing the goal value for each particle on each frame of the animation. In the last example, the particles travelled directly to the CV's of the goal objects and now you will learn how to move them along the surface.

Water droplets traveling along a surface

1 Open Scene file

- Open *faucetUV_start.mb*.

2 Add surface emitter

- Select *faucetSpout* in the Outliner.
- Add a surface emitter to *faucetSpout* with a **Rate** of **10**.

3 Enable need parentUV flag and set particle lifespan mode

- Select the emitter and enable **Need Parent UV**.
- Select the particles and set **Lifespan Mode** to use **lifespanPP only**.

4 Make faucetSpout a goal for the particles

- Select the particles, then *faucetSpout*, then **Particles → Goal**.
- Set the **Goal Weight** to about **0.9** and playback to watch the particles build up on the surface of the faucet.

5 Add goalU, goalV, parentU, parentV particle attributes

- Select the particle object and press the **General** button in the **Add Dynamics Attributes** section of the Attribute Editor.
- Select the **Particles** tab and add **goalU** and **goalV** attributes.

<table>
<tr><td>Note:</td><td>ParentU and ParentV attributes are automatically added when Need Parent UV is enabled.</td></tr>
</table>

The parentUV attributes establish the UV coordinates where a particle was emitted from the surface. At birth, the goal and the parent should be the same so the particle has a goal *on* the surface instead of at the CV of the surface. Enter the following **Creation Expression**:

```
goalU = parentU;

goalV = parentV;
```

6 Add a Runtime Expression

To get the particles to move along the U direction of the surface, you will change the **goalU** attribute on each frame with the following **Runtime Expression**:

```
goalU = goalU - 0.1;
```

7 Refine region of emission and make particles drip off

The expressions below have some new lines added to them, allowing particles to exist only on a specific part of the faucet. The Runtime Expression has been modified to have the Goal Weight for each particle shut off when the particle reaches a certain U location on the surface.

Creation:

```
goalU = parentU;

goalV = parentV;

if ((parentU > 10) || (parentU <2))

lifespanPP =0;
```

<table>
<tr><td>Note:</td><td>The double pipe "| |" is the OR operator. In this case, if the particle was emitted between U values of 10 and 2 (the lower part of the faucet), it will stay alive, otherwise it will be killed.</td></tr>
</table>

Runtime:

```
goalU = goalU - 0.1;

if (goalU <=2)

goalPP = 0;

else

goalPP = 1;
```

8 Add gravity to the particles

Adding gravity gives the particles downward motion after the Goal Weight has been set to 0.

The file *faucetUV_Finish.mb* has a completed version of this file. Some additional expressions and particle instancing were added to make the drop objects and to make them grow/orient correctly.

Exercise

- Use what you've learned about goals to write "M a y a" in particles.

TIPS AND TRAPS

- **Dynamics weight**: An error occurs if Dynamic weight is set to 0, so set it above 0 when using goals.

  Dynamics weight allows you to scale the effects of dynamics (fields, collisions, springs, goals).

  A value of 0 causes fields, collisions, springs, and goals connected to the particle object to have no effect. A value of 1 provides the full effect. A value less than 1 sets a proportional effect. For example, 0.6 scales the effect to 60% of full strength.

  Expressions are unaffected by Dynamics weight.

- The shelf buttons **fauC** and **fauR** are for the Creation and Runtime Expressions, respectively. The Creation Expression finds out where the particle left the surface and sets the goal to that UV location. It also kills any particles that are not within a defined UV region of the surface.

- The **MinMax RangeU** and **MinMax RangeV** attributes in the Shape node of the Attribute Editor make it easy for you to determine the UV range of a surface. This is useful when working with goalUV expressions. Also, the feedback line will show you this info if you are in Isoparm pick mode.

- In the faucet example, the Runtime Expression is what moves each particle along the surface. Incrementing the goal on each frame of the simulation is what moves it along the U (and/or V) direction. This expression also determines when the goalPP value will be set to 0. This is what causes the particle to drip off the end of the faucet. You may want to add gravity to the particles and add a collision object beneath the faucet that makes the particles die on contact.

- In the finished file *faucetUV_Finish.mb*, geometry has been instanced to the particles and their **aim direction** has been set to **velocity** so the drip orients itself. Also, there is a custom attribute called **growth** that affects the **scale** of the drop based on its position along the surface (using a linstep expression).

- parentUV and goalUV used to work only with NURBS. Support for polygons was added in Maya Version 6.

- If setting a value using goalPP, it is good practice to set the Goal Weight slider to 1 when creating the goal. This is important because the goalPP attribute always get multiplied by that number. Therefore, if the goal is created with a value of 0 and goalPP is set to 0.5, the resulting goalPP value will be 0, not 0.5 as would normally be expected.

- Is possible to change the "goal mapping" that Maya uses? By default, the first particle will go to the first CV or vertex of a goal object. This mapping cannot be changed currently. In other words, you can't make the first particle go to the fifth CV and the 2nd to the 1st CV.

- People commonly ask if there is an *easy* way to apply a black and white ramp to the surface and have the greyscale of the ramp control the particle Goal Weight. Currently, this involves quite a convoluted work around to accomplish, so the short answer is no. Applying a ramp to goalPP will change the goalPP weight of all particles in that particle object with respect to the particle's lifespan, not the surface UV coordinates. This doesn't mean that it isn't doable, it just isn't a quick and simple solution.

- The file *mGoalNormalized.mb* is a somewhat more advanced file that demonstrates two things. Firstly, it is an example of how to write a letter in particles. Secondly, it shows how to use an expression to check to see if a given particle has reached its goal. The particles are colored using the values of a ramp. The particle's color is at the bottom of the RGB ramp at birth and at the top of the ramp once it reaches the goal.

Additional demonstration: goalAtoB.mb

A file called *goalAtoB.mb* in the demo directory shows an interesting application of goalPP, particle expressions, and blobby surface rendering.

- This file was set up by creating two polygonal letters with the text tool.

  A surface emitter was added to each letter.

The scene was played until the A filled up with particles. The **Max Count** of the B particles was set to the **count** of the A particles.

B particles were made to be a goal for A particles (set goalWeight to 1 when the goal is created).

A locator was animated in the scene to check the distance between the B particles and the moving locator. This distance check was done using a Runtime Expression. As the locator moves further from the B particles, the goalPP value of the A particles gets set to 1. The goalPP value gets multiplied by the number that the original goal was created at. The goalPP is set to 0 until the locator gets closer to the A particles, then they transition over to a setting of 1, which makes the particles jump to stick to B particles. The particles were rendered as blobby surfaces. An expression was added to control the radius size.

SUMMARY

Goals are an intuitive, fun, and powerful method of particle manipulation. They can be used to solve particle movement problems that only complex expressions can mimic. Mixing goals with fields and other animation is often the best way to achieve the most control of your particles. In this chapter, you have learned about the following:

- Creating goal objects;
- Setting Goal Weight and Smoothness;
- Recognizing and understanding goals and particle hierarchy;
- Working with Per Particle Goal attributes;
- goalU and goalV attributes, parentU, parentV, and parentId attributes.

10 Soft Bodies & Springs

Controlling surfaces with dynamic motion is accomplished using Soft bodies.

In this chapter you will learn about the following:

- Creating soft bodies;
- Changing soft body parameters;
- Using particle springs;
- Using and creating soft body applications;
- Applying Goal Weighting.

Water dripping out of a water facet

CHAPTER 10

SOFT BODIES

When you make geometry or a lattice a soft body, Maya creates a corresponding particle object. The particle object is placed in relation to the surface, based on options that you select when you create the soft body. A duplicate surface can be created and used as a goal object to help control the soft body and maintain its shape.

NURBS and polygonal surfaces can be made into soft bodies. The particles are created and placed at the corresponding CV's or vertices. If the particles move, the corresponding CV's/vertices follow, thus changing the shape of the geometry. Soft bodies are great for achieving flowing-like motion of a geometry object, such as a flag in the wind or a candle flame.

Dynamic springs can also be applied to the particles to control the tension that exists between the particles and thus, the CV's or vertices.

Creating soft bodies

Creating a soft body object involves selecting the geometry to be made a soft body and then selecting from the Dynamics menu, **Soft/Rigid Bodies** → **Create Soft Body -** ❑.

The soft body creation options allow you to make the selected object a soft body in the following manner:

> **Make Soft**: - This option directly makes the selected object a soft body.
>
> **Duplicate, Make Copy Soft** - This option duplicates the object and makes this duplicate the soft body. This is useful for making the original object a goal for the soft body.
>
> **Duplicate, Make Original Soft -** This option duplicates the object in question but makes the original selected object the soft body. This option enables the creation of a duplicate for use as a goal object.

If you are duplicating, you can choose to **Duplicate Input Graph** of the selected object as well as automatically **Hiding** or making a **Goal** of the **Non-Soft Objects**. It is often necessary to duplicate input graph if the object you are making soft contains deformers or animation.

A dripping faucet

In this example, you create a soft body water droplet that uses goals to drip out of a water faucet. You will also see how to emit a soft body object from an emitter.

1 Open the scene file

- Open the file *faucetDrips.mb.*

  This scene file consists of a faucet and some spheres for use as dripping water goal targets.

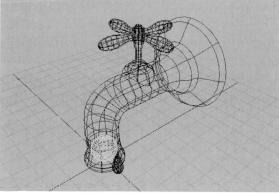

The faucetDrips.mb file

2 Make drip into a soft body

- Select the drip object.

- Select **Soft/Rigid Bodies** → **Create Soft Body - ❑**. Set the following:

  Creation Option to **Make Soft**.

- Press **Create**.

  This will turn the drip object into a soft body. Note the *dripParticle* object that is created under the *drip* object.

3 Add drip and drop targets as goals

- In the Perspective window, **Shift-select** the *dripParticle* object and the *dripTarget* object.

- Select **Particles** → **Goal - ❑** to create a goal object for *dripParticle.*

- Set the **Goal Weight** to **0.5** for now.

- Repeat this for the *dropTarget.*

4 Playback the scene

Note that the *drip* object assumes a location between the goal objects.

5 Create an emitter for the drip soft body

Maya enables you to emit soft body particles from an emitter. To do this, you will create an emitter and connect the soft body particles to this emitter.

- Select **Particles** → **Create Emitter - ❑**.

  Create a Directional emitter and set its **Rate** to **300**.

  After you create the emitter, you can delete the particle object that was created with the emitter. You may want to come back and lower this emission rate later. This rate will determine how quickly the water droplet is emitted.

- Rename this emitter *dripEmitter.*

6 Connect dripParticle to dripEmitter

- **Shift** or **Ctrl-select** the *dripParticle* object and the *dripEmitter* object.

- Select **Particles** → **Use Selected Emitter**.

  This will connect the *dripParticles* to be emitted from the *dripEmitter.*

7 Turn off "Enforce Count From History"

On the *dripParticleShape*, there is an attributes section called **Soft Body Attributes**. These are the attributes that control soft body specific behavior of the particles.

- Turn **Off** the **Enforce Count From History** attribute.

  This will allow the soft body to exist without all its particles while it is being emitted. In other words, before all its particles have been born.

8 Set Max particle count to the number of soft body particles

You don't need more particles in the *dripParticle* object then the number of particles needed to satisfy the soft body.

- Set **Max Count** equal to **Count,** which in this case is **56**.

9 Set Lifespan and Initial State

Initially, the particles should not be in the scene because you want them to spit out of the emitter. Therefore, you can set the lifespan to 0, set Initial State, then set the Lifespan to a high number.

- Set the **Lifespan Mode** to **Constant** to **0**, rewind.

  The particles will disappear.

- Select particles then **Solvers** → **Initial State** → **Set for Selected**.

- Set the **Lifespan** to **1000**.

- Rewind.

10 Create an expression for target Goal Weights

By setting your playback range to 30 frames and playing back, you can get a feel for what the Goal Weights should be set to for the drip to progress from the drip to the drop.

- While playing back from the timeline, adjust the Goal Weights of the *dripTarget* and *dropTarget* to simulate the drip falling under the influence of each in succession.

- Under the **goalPP** attribute for *dripParticleShape*, enter the following as a creation rule:

```
dripParticleShape.goalPP = 1;
```

This expression sets the particle goalPP value to 1 at particle birth.

- Under the **goalPP** attribute for *dripParticleShape*, enter the following as a runtime rule:

```
dripParticleShape.goalWeight[0] =
1-(linstep(5,40,frame));

dripParticleShape.goalWeight[1] =
linstep(0,40,frame);
```

These two expressions control the Goal Weight attributes and apply linstep functions to each. Goal Weight attribute values are stored in an array called `goalWeight[]`. The Goal Weights are then accessed in order of how they were created. You could, alternatively, animate the Goal Weights using keyframes for more precise control of the motion and timing. It is recommended that you try both methods to learn how they both work. In practice, you'll find that the keyframing method is likely to give you more artistic control.

11 Playback the scene

You should see the particle progress from the drip to the drop targets. Work with the goalWeight expressions to fine-tune this motion.

Goal Smoothness will also play a part in the motion of the drip. A value of **6** will suffice.

12 Add gravity to the dripParticle

The *dripParticle* is behaving linearly towards its goal targets but has no life, bounce, or globbiness. You can add fields to the particles to get them to act a little less orderly.

- Select the *dripParticle* object and select **Fields → Gravity**.

A large **Magnitude** may be necessary to influence the particles above the Goal Weight dominance. Try a value of **50**.

13 Playback the scene and tune as necessary

SPRINGS

Springs and soft bodies often work hand and hand. You will often find that a goal object is not always appropriate for controlling a soft body that is deforming or colliding with another object.

- Springs are useful for controlling particles that will respond to forces with cohesion.

- Springs can be established between particles.

- Springs can be established between particles and surface CV's or polygonal vertices.

- Springs can be established between surface CV's and/or polygonal vertices.

Springs often require **Stiffness** settings above **100**. Springs may gain little benefit from higher **Damping** values, though. Experimentation is required for each application, but if you find that a higher **Damping** value results in poorer spring response, your object may require more springs, or you may need to increase the **Oversampling** of the simulation.

Overlapping springs and springs connected in multiple directions will have profound results on the simulation. Generally, you want to build a framework of springs on your object. Experimentation is required.

Adding and removing springs from a spring object

The scene file *softBodySpringCompare.mb* contains three examples of soft body spring approaches. They are all under a gravity field and will collide with the floor. When you play this back, you will notice some strange behavior.

- The first sphere is a soft body with no springs.

- The second example is a sphere with a wrap deformer which is a soft body with springs.

- The third example is a sphere with a lattice deformer which has been made into a soft body with springs applied.

When you playback this scene file, you will notice that only the lattice sphere is resisting the force of the floor when it collides. This is because only the lattice example has springs in place positioned to oppose this force. The other two spheres either explode or simply collapse. These objects need to have springs added in specific places and also need to have their spring attributes adjusted.

There are several methods to create or add springs to a spring object. You will learn each of these three methods on a very basic example so you can clearly see how the process works.

> **WireFrame Walk Length** - Adds springs along the wireframe segment as determined by the Walk Length.
>
> **All** - Adds springs between all the components that are selected.
>
> **Min/Max** - Adds springs between the selected components that fall between the Min/Max criteria.
>
> **Set Exclusive** - Used to make the spring creation take place between objects and not between the components on the object.

1 Open the scene file

- Open the file *softBodySpringCompare.mb*.

2 Add springs to the WrapSphere's Spring object using Wire Walk Length

- Select the *simpleSphereParticle* particles from the viewport in component mode.

- **Ctrl-select** the *wrapSphere's* spring object in the Outliner or **Shift-select** in the Hypergraph.

- Select **Soft/Rigid Bodies** → **Create Springs -** ❑ and set the following:

    > **Add to Existing Spring** to **On**;
    >
    > **Don't Duplicate Springs** to **On**;
    >
    > **Creation Method** to **WireFrame**;
    >
    > **Wire Walk Length** to **2**.

- Press **Create**.

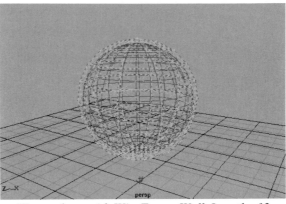

Wrap sphere with WireFrame Walk Length of 2

3 Play back the animation

Note the sphere still collapses. There are still no springs directly opposing the particles journey to the floor.

4 Add springs to the WrapSphere's spring object using selected particles

- **Shift-select** the *simpleSphereParticle's* particle components that lie on the bottom of the sphere and the top of the sphere from the viewport in component mode.

- **Ctrl-select** the *wrapSphere's* spring object in the Outliner or **Shift - select** in the Hypergraph.

- Select **Soft/Rigid Bodies** → **Create Springs -** ❐. Set the following:

   Add to Existing Spring to **On**;

   Don't Duplicate Springs to **On**;

   Creation Method to **All**.

- Press **Create**.

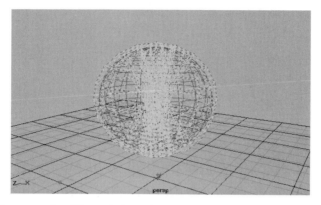

5 Add springs to the WrapSphere's spring object using Min/Max

When you find that selecting all the components and manually building springs is too tedious, you may find that you can use the Min/Max criteria to distribute the springs in the right quantity.

- Undo the last group of springs that were created in the above step or select them in the viewport and delete them by pressing **Backspace**.

- **Shift-select** all of the *wrapSphere's* particle components.

- **Ctrl-select** the *wrapSphere's* spring object in the Outliner or **Shift - select** in the Hypergraph.

- Select **Soft/Rigid Bodies → Create Springs - ❒**. Set the following:

    Add to Existing Spring to **On**;

    Don't Duplicate Springs to **On**;

    Creation Method to **Min/Max**;

    Min Distance to **4.6**;

    Max Distance to **8**.

- Press **Create**.

    You may find that trial and error is the best method for determining what min and max will work best. Another method is to use the **Modify → Measure → Distance Tool**.

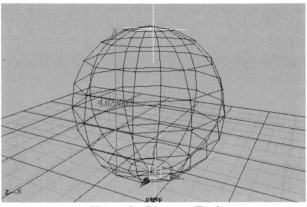

Using the Distance Tool

Working with per spring attributes

The three spring object attributes **StiffnessPS**, **DampingPS**, and **RestLengthPS** are per spring attributes. These attributes can have values set for individual springs through the Component Editor.

The scene file *springCube.mb* contains a polygonal cube that is 4 units in width, height, and length. This cube has springs applied to it by one wire Walk Length method.

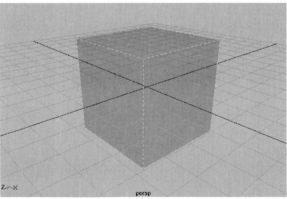

Soft body cube with springs at each corner.

1 Open the scene file

- Open the file *springCube.mb*.

  Note the spring object **restLength** size is **4**.

2 Change the restLengthPS on one of the cube's springs

- Set the **RestLengthPS** to **On** in the Attribute Editor.

- In component mode, select one of the cube's springs.

- You may need to use a pick mask to select an individual spring. It is sometimes hard to see if a spring is selected.

- Open the Component Editor and press **Load Components.** This will make it easier for you to see what is picked. Sometimes you have to **drag-select** over a spring a few times to pick it.

- Enter a value of **2** for the **restLengthPS** attribute.

- Playback.

- Enter a value of **6** for the **restLengthPS** attribute.

- Playback.

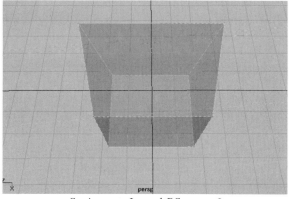

Spring restLengthPS set to 6

3 Change the value of the spring object's End1 Weight

- Select the spring object in Outliner and enter **0** for the **End1 Weight** attribute.

  This will eliminate the force acting on the start of the spring. All of the force of the added **restLength** will be applied to the end of the spring.

  End1 Weight and **End2 Weight** control at what percentage forces will act on either end of the spring.

  > 1 (default) = 100%
  >
  > 0 = 0%

- Playback.

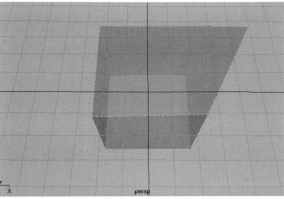

Spring End1 Weight set to 0

Shooting hoops

In this example, you will animate a basketball net using a soft body, rigid body, and a wrap deformer. You will also use Maya Artisan to paint Goal Weights and will set up collisions between the basketball and the soft body net. Some basic MEL commands will be used to automatically create the geometry for the net.

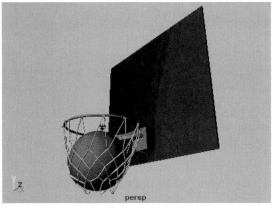

Basketball scene

1 Open File

- Open *hoops_start.mb*.

This file contains a basketball net constructed of NURBS curves, a basketball, and a polygon object that will be used as a wrap deformer.

2 Setup deformation of net curves using a wrap

- In the Outliner, select *net* then **Ctrl-select** *wrapObject*.

- Select **Deform** → **Create Wrap**.

  This creates a wrap node for each grouping of NURBS curves and one *wrapObjectBase* node.

- Pick a vertex on *wrapObject* and move it so you can see how modifying the wrap object deforms the curves of the net. Undo as necessary to get the net back to its original shape.

3 Make the wrap deformer a soft body

Making the wrap deformer a soft body lets you control the wrap's vertices using particles and goals instead of relying only on keyframes.

- Select *wrapObject*.

- Select **Soft/Rigid Bodies** → **Create Soft Body - □**.

  Set the following options:

    Creation Options to **Duplicate, Make Original Soft**;

    Duplicate Input Graph to **On**;

    Hide Non-Soft Object to **On**;

    Make Non-Soft a Goal to **On**;

    Weight to **0.5**.

  This places particles at the wrap object's vertices and makes the Non-Soft Object a goal.

4 Test the soft body motion

You can quickly get an idea if the soft body motion is happening simply by selecting *wrapObjectParticle* and adding a turbulence field. When you playback, the net should move around from the turbulence. If it does, then set the particle's Goal Weight to 1.0, delete the Turbulence field, and move ahead. You will adjust Goal Weights later using Maya Artisan.

5 Setup rigid body basketball and rim, apply gravity

- Select *basketBall* and make it an **Active Rigid Body** with the following settings:

    Mass to **40**;

    Damping to **0**;

    applyForcesAt to **verticesOrCVs**.

- Select *hoopShape* and make it a **Passive Rigid Body**.

- Add **Gravity** to *basketBall* and set **Magnitude** to **980**.

6 Setup particle collision between ball and soft body

- In the Outliner, select *wrapObjectParticle*, **Ctrl-select** *basketBall.*

- Select **Particles** → **Make Collide**.

- Set the **Particle Collision** attribute on *basketBall's* node to **On**.

- Select the particle object, locate the *geoConnector1* node in the Channel Box and set **Resilience** to **0.2** and **Friction** to **0.1**. These values control the bounciness of the particle collision. You will likely have to come back and tune these later on.

7 Paint soft body Goal Weights

Currently, the net will just break apart or cause wild motion since no Goal Weighting adjustments have been made.

- Make sure the *wrapObject* is selected.

- In the persp view, **RMB** on the *wrapObject* and select **Paint**→ **WrapObjectParticleShape** → **goalPP**.

- The *wrapObject* turns white, indicating that the weighting value for all particles is currently 1.

- To view/modify the Maya Artisan options, double click the current tool icon at the end of the mini bar or choose **Modify** → **Attribute Paint Tool -** ❑.

Option window for Attribute Paint Tool

- Set **Operation** to **Scale** and **Value** to about **0.5**. Paint around the surface of the wrap and smooth out the weighting. Be sure the weights for the particles at the top of the rim are **1**.

Paint the goalPP weights of the soft body wrap deformer

8   Add springs to the soft body

To further refine the motion of the particles after you have adjusted
Goal Weighting, you can add springs.

- Select *wrapObjectParticle.*

- Select **Soft/Rigid Bodies** → **Create Springs -** ◻.

- Set the following spring options as a guide:

   Don't Duplicate Springs to **On**;

   Creation Method to **Wireframe**;

   Wire Walk Length to **1**;

   Use RestLengthPS to **On**;

   Stiffness to **20**;

   Damping to **0.050**;

   EndWeights to **1.0**.

9   Adjust attributes to tune the simulation

There are many elements that interact to make up this simulation.
Experiment with the placement and attribute settings for the ball,
gravity settings, particle conserve, geoConnector attributes, Goal
Smoothness/Weighting, spring settings, and wrap deformer attributes
until you are satisfied with the motion.

Tip:	To prevent stretching of the net caused by particles intersecting with the rigid body, you may need to increase the oversampling slightly. However, changing the oversampling will slow things down and may require you to adjust other attributes to compensate for the new motion.

10 Review alternate methods

The file *hoops_Finish.mb* contains a working version of this example, based on the steps laid out above.

The file *hoops_With_Fields.mb* shows an alternate setup for the same type of thing. This file uses volume fields instead of particle collisions. This helps prevent some of the unexpected stretching that occur with the particle collision method.

There is also a display layer called *netGeo* that has the extruded geometry for the net in place.

Dynamic dyno

In this exercise, you will use soft bodies to create dynamic influence objects on a character. Influence objects are used with Maya's smooth skinning to create under the skin movement like muscles and fat. By making the influence objects dynamic, they will react to gravity and the forces imparted on them from the character's movement.

Dynamic Dyno

1 Open the scene file

- Open the file *dynoStompStart.mb.*

  This scene file contains an animated dinosaur with left foot, leg, and hind quarters skinned. Layers are provided for visibility and color coding. Two polygon primitives (*bellyInfluence, legInfluence*) are provided for influence objects.

  Objects have also been created to serve as mount points on the skeleton. These are polygon cubes and have been parented to the appropriate skeleton joints.

  The animation is a run loop from frames **1** to **34**. A bind pose frame is keyed at frames **0** and **40**.

2 Add influence objects to the dinosaur skin

Smooth skinned surfaces are animated through the use of influence objects. To add an influence object to a smooth skinned skeleton, you will need to first make sure the skeleton is in its bind pose.

If a skeleton has inverse kinematic controls placed on it, it may not be able to achieve it's bind pose. Disabling the IK solvers temporarily will allow the skeleton to go to it's bind pose.

- Disable IK Solvers by selecting **Modify → Evaluate Nodes → IK Solvers**.

- Place the skeleton in it's bind pose by selecting **Skin → Go To Bind Pose**.

- Position the influence objects as illustrated:

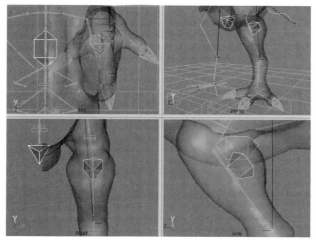

bellyInfluence and legInfluence objects positioned on stomach and leg

- **Ctrl-select** the *left_legSkin* 2(under the *dinoLeg* group) and the *bellyInfluence* object in the **Outliner**.

- Select **Skin** → **Edit Smooth Skin** → **Add Influence - ❒**.

- Set the **Add Influence Object** options as shown below:

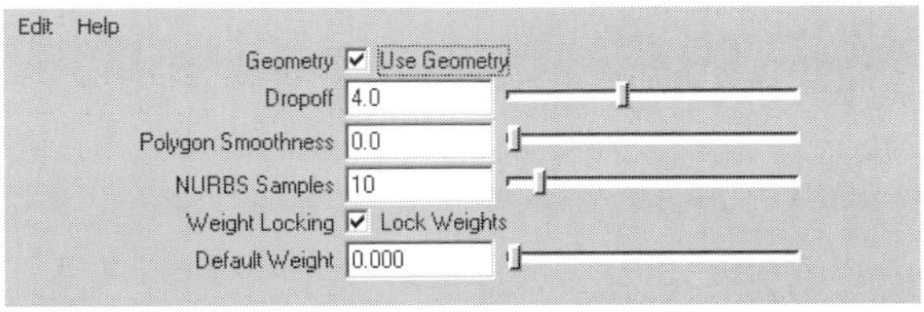

Add influence object options with Weight Locking and Default Weight of 0

Setting **Geometry** to **Use Geometry** will take the influence objects shape into consideration (including deformations that occur on the influence object).

Setting the **Weight Locking On** with a **Default Weight** of **0** will ensure that the new influence object does not disrupt the existing weighting of the smooth skinned surface.

- Press **Add** to add the influence objects to the selected skin.

- Repeat for *legInfluence*

Confirm that the influence objects were created. The Outliner will show two new objects, *BellyInfluenceBase* and *LegInfluenceBase*.

- Select the *left_legSkin2* object.

- Open the **Skin** → **Edit Smooth Skin** → **Paint Skin Weights Tool - ❒**.

Selecting the option box for the Paint Skin Weights Tool will open the Maya Artisan paint window. In the list of influence objects, you should now see *bellyInfluence* and *legInfluence*.

- Do not make any changes to the skinWeights yet. Close this window and continue by pressing **q** to exit the current tool. You will come back to this tool later.

3 Create a soft body out of bellyInfluence

The influence objects will have flexibility and react dynamically to skeleton movement and gravity. They will be soft bodies. As soft bodies, they will use particles to dynamically control the polygon influence objects shape and position.

- Select the *bellyInfluence* object.

- Select **Soft/Rigid Bodies** → **Create Soft Body - ❒**.

Set the option box settings to:

Edit	Help

Creation Options	Duplicate, Make Original Soft ▼
Duplicate Input Graph	☐
Hide Non-Soft Object	☑
Make Non-Soft a Goal	☑
Weight	.50

Soft Body options for creating a duplicate goal

4 Create a spring object for the soft body

The influence objects will work as areas of mass like muscle and fatty loose skin. To get these objects to bounce and move with a tenuous consistency, you will use springs to hold the soft body together and springs to attach the influence object to the skeleton.

- Select the *bellyInfluence* soft body.

- Select **Soft/Rigid Bodies → Create Springs - ❐**.

  Name this spring object in the option box and set as follows:

Edit	Help

Spring Name	bellyInfluenceSprings
Spring Methods	
Add to Existing Spring	☐
Don't Duplicate Springs	☐
Set Exclusive	☐
Creation Method:	Wireframe ▼
Min Distance	4.600
Max Distance	8.000
Wire Walk Length	1
Spring Attributes	
Use Per-Spring Stiffness	☐
Use Per-Spring Damping	☐
Use Per-Spring RestLength	☑
Stiffness	1.0
Damping	.20
Rest Length	0.000
End1 Weight	1.000
End2 Weight	1.000

Spring creation options, wireframe walk

5 Create a spring object to connect the soft body to the skeleton

This will be a different spring object that connects the influence object to the skeleton via the polyCube mount points on the groin joints.

- Press **F8** to enter component mode. Set your component mask settings to allow selection of **Poly Vertices** and **Particles** only.

Component Selection set to Vertices and Particles

You should hide the *left_legSkin* by turning off visibility of the **legSkin** display layer.

■ Select one of the end particles of the *bellyInfluence* soft body and two of the polyCube vertices:

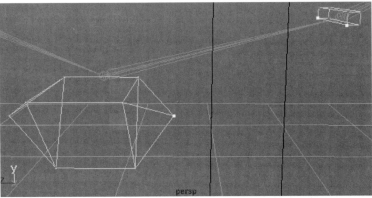

Particle and Poly Vertices selected in component mode.

■ Select **Soft/Rigid Bodies** → **Create Springs - □**.

Set the options to create a new spring named *bellyConnectSprings* using min/max settings adequate to ensure the length falls between the needed distance:

Spring creation options using min/max

Repeat this for the other side of the *bellyInfluence* soft body to attach it to the other polyCube mount point. This time add the new springs to the existing *bellyConnectSprings* object.

- Select the **Particle** on the other side of *bellyInfluence* soft body and the **Poly Vertices** on the other mount cube and the *bellyConnectSprings* spring object in the Outliner.

They *all* need to be selected to **Add to Existing Spring**.

- Select **Soft/Rigid Bodies** → **Create Springs -** ❏.

Set the options to add to the *bellyConnectSprings* using min/max settings adequate to ensure the length falls between the needed distance:

Add to spring options

6 Enable IK solvers and playback the animation

Enable the IK solvers and playback the animation. You don't need to make the dino leg visible just yet. Establish that the soft body is following the skeleton.

- Select **Modify** → **Evaluate Nodes** → **IK Solvers**.
- Playback the animation.

7 Adjust the spring and particle settings

The main attributes involved in the simulation are the particle **Goal Weight** and **Smoothness** and the **Spring Stiffness** and **Damping**.

Adjust these values until the soft body begins reacting appropriately during playback. The spring values may be quite high for the connection springs and lower for the soft body springs.

8 Save Initial State to preserve the loop

You want the soft body to begin and end its motion in sync with the loop. To do this, you can play out to the last frame of the loop (frame 35), then Set Initial State for All Dynamic. Setting the frame range back to 1 to 34 will preserve the loop and dynamics will begin and end at the same place.

- Set **Frame Range** from **1** to **35**.
- Playback the simulation and **Stop** on **Frame 35**.
- Select **Solvers** → **Initial State** → **Set For All Dynamic**.
- Set the **Frame Range** back to **1** to **34**.
- Playback the simulation.

  You may need to do this again after more tweaking or adjustment of any dynamic parameters that cause the looping motion to become asymmetrical.

9 Paint smooth skin influence weighting

Now that you have the motion of the influence object doing what you want, you can paint in how much influence this object will have and where the influence will affect the smooth skin.

- Show the *left_legSkin* object by turning on the visibility of the display layer.
- Select the *left_legSkin* object.
- Select **Skin** → **Edit Smooth Skin** → **Paint Skin Weights Tool - ❑**.

  This Maya Artisan Painting Tool is used exclusively for painting skinning influence weighting.

- In the Paint Weights window, select the *bellyInfluence* object it should have a hold on:

Paint Skin Weights window with bellyInfluence object selected

- Select **Toggle Hold Weights On Selected** to turn **Off** the hold on the *bellyInfluence* object.

Note: A hold prevents an influence object from getting its value changed by using the Paint Weights Tool on it or other adjacent influence objects. Smooth skinning works by sharing the influence weight among the influence objects that are connected to a surface. A total value of 1 is always maintained. Holding will prevent the individual influence object's participation of this total value from changing.

- Enter shaded mode by pressing **5**.

- Select the **Add** operation with an **Opacity** of around **0.5** and a **Value** of around **0.3**.

- Paint the influence of the *bellyInfluence* object into the *left_legSkin* surface.

- Work additively to build up the influence.

   The influence should appear as a lighter shade (black = 0 influence, 1 = max influence).

- Playback to see the effect of the influence as you work.

- Smooth out the painting using the Smooth Operation.

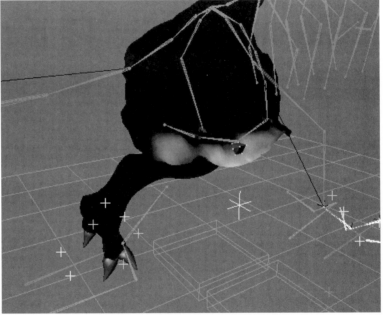

View of paint skin weighting for the bellyInfluence object

Experiment with where you are painting. The *bellyInfluence* object can also drive other areas of the dinosaur that are experiencing jiggle and shake, not just the stomach.

10 Repeat steps for the legInfluence object

The *legInfluence* object that you created can work in the same manner. Note that the mount points are on separate joints and mimic the location of muscle attachment points. See if you can create an influence object that reacts to the leg movement stretching and contracting as well as shaking like a muscle.

The issue of portability often comes up. Can you parent these influence objects, springs, and particle objects into the dinosaur skeleton?

What advantage does this hold over using rigid bodies as influence objects?

A bungee cord

In this exercise, you will create a bungee cord that will dangle from the crane cage, stretch as it is pulled down, and wrinkle as the jumper is pulled back up. You will use a soft body curve to create the cord. The jumper will be connected to the soft body cord with a dynamic constraint.

You'll work in world scale, using centimeters as units. This scene is quite large, and you will have to adjust the grid settings and possibly the camera clipping planes as well to work comfortably.

1 Open the scene file

- Open *bungeeStart.mb.*

bungeeStart.mb

2 Set the grid options

- Select **Display → Grid -** ❒.
- Set **Grid Lines** to every **500** units and set **Subdivsion Lines** to **5**.
- Set **Orthographic Grid Numbers** to **Along Edge**.

Grid Options window for bungeeStart.mb

3 Create the curve for the cord

The bungee cord needs to be about 50% of the height of the platform.

- Press **F3** to go to the Modeling menu set.
- Turn on **Grid snap**.
- Select **Create EP Curve Tool -** ❑ → **Reset Tool**.
- In the side or front view, create a curve from <<0, 4000, 0>> to <<0, 2000, 0>>.
- Turn **On** CV display. Select **Display** → **Nurbs Components** → **CVs**.

This curve is not very useful yet, because it lacks definition. There simply aren't enough CV's to allow it to deform correctly.

4 Rebuild the curve

- Select **Edit Curves** → **Rebuild Curves - ❒**. Set the following:

   Rebuild Type to **Uniform**;

   Parameter Range to **0 to 1**;

   Keep Ends to **On**;

   Number of Spans to **18**;

   Degree to **3**.

Rebuild Curve Options window

- Rename the curve to *cordCurve*.
- turn **Off** CV display.

Note: The *cordCurve* must be rebuilt to exactly 18 Spans. You'll need to think about the length of the springs, and there needs to be enough detail to allow it to deform properly, of course, but there is another reason as well. The number of CV's must be uneven. A 3 degree curve with 18 Spans has 21 CV's, in this case cordCurve.cv[0:20] (*number of CV's = Spans + Degree*). A polygonal goal object with just three vertices can be used as a goal for the first and last soft body particle. You'll see this later in the tutorial.

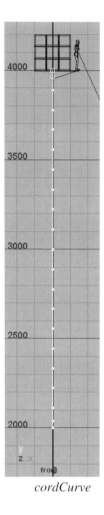

cordCurve

5 Create a soft body

- Press **F4** to go to the Dynamics menu set.
- Select *cordCurve.*
- Select **Soft/Rigid Bodies** → **Create Soft Body - ❑**.
- Set **Creation Options** to **Make Soft**.
- Click on **Create**.

6 Turn on Numeric Display for the particle

- Expand *cordCurve* in the Outliner and select *cordCurveParticle.*

- Open the **Render Attribute** section in the **Attribute Editor** and set **Particle Render Type** to **Numeric**.

Note: If you choose **Numeric**, but don't click on Add Attributes for **Current Render Type**, the particleIds will be displayed as integer values, not floats, making them easier to read.

---

7 Add Springs

- With *cordCurveParticle* still selected, select **Soft/Rigid Bodies** → **Create Springs - □**.
- Select **Edit** → **Reset Settings**.
- Set the **Spring Name** to *cordSprings*.
- Set **Creation Method** to **Wireframe**.
- Turn off **Use Per-Spring RestLength**.
- Click on **Create**.

Spring Name	cordSprings

▼ Spring Methods

Add to Existing Spring	☐
Don't Duplicate Springs	☐
Set Exclusive	☐
Creation Method:	Wireframe ▾
Min Distance	0.000
Max Distance	0.000
Wire Walk Length	1

▼ Spring Attributes

Use Per-Spring Stiffness	☐
Use Per-Spring Damping	☐
Use Per-Spring RestLength	☐
Stiffness	1.000
Damping	0.200
Rest Length	0.000
End1 Weight	1.000
End2 Weight	1.000

Spring Options window

The cord now needs to be attached to the cord anchor. A small object called *anchor* has been created under *cage*. You will use *anchor* as a goal for the particle object, but only the first and last particle will have a Goal Weight of 1. These two particles will then drag along the other particles because they are connected by springs. The curve was built with 21 CV's.

Anchor only has three vertices. When a polygonal object is used as a soft body goal, the particles will move towards each of the vertices in turn. Particle 0 will move to vertex 0, particle 1 will move towards vertex1, and so on. When the number of particles is larger than the number of vertices, the particles will behave as follows:

particleID	vertex
0	0
1	1
2	2
3	0
...	...
18	0
19	1
20	2

The polygonal object can be used to control where the start and end of the curve will go. In this example, particle 0 will go to vertex 0 and particle 20 will go to vertex 2.

8 Display vertex numbers

- In the Outliner, select *anchor*.

- Select **Display → Custom Polygon Display -** ❑.

- **Edit → Reset Settings**.

- Turn on **Show Item Numbers: Vertices**.

- Click **Apply and Close**.

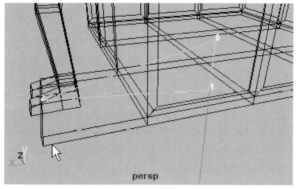

Custom Polygon Display Options window

The anchor with vertex numbers displayed

9 Set a particle goal

- Open the Outliner and select *cordCurveParticle*, **Ctrl-select** *anchor*.

- Select **Particles** → **Goal** - ❑.

- Set the **Goal Weight** to **1**, and turn off **Use Transform as Goal**.

Goal Options window

- **RMB-select** all particles in *cordCurveParticle*.
- Open the Component Editor. In the **Particles** tab, notice the **goalPP** column.
- **LMB-drag** over all rows except the rows for **pt[0]** and **pt[20]**.
- Type **0**.

	Position X	goalPP
cordCurveParti		
pt[0]	0.000	1.000
pt[1]	0.000	0.000
pt[2]	0.000	0.000
pt[3]	0.000	0.000
pt[4]	0.000	0.000
pt[5]	0.000	0.000
pt[6]	0.000	0.000
pt[7]	0.000	0.000
pt[8]	0.000	0.000
pt[9]	0.000	0.000
pt[10]	0.000	0.000
pt[11]	0.000	0.000
pt[12]	0.000	0.000
pt[13]	0.000	0.000
pt[14]	0.000	0.000
pt[15]	0.000	0.000
pt[16]	0.000	0.000
pt[17]	0.000	0.000
pt[18]	0.000	0.000
pt[19]	0.000	0.000
pt[20]	0.000	1.000

Setting the goalPP in the Component Editor

Only the first and last particle will now have a goalPP weight of **1** and move towards *anchor*.

10 Playback the animation to position the cord

- Set the playback range to **1000** frames.
- Playback.

You will need to make some adjustments to get the cord to hang correctly. Notice how particles 0 and 20 are at *anchor* immediately and how the other particles follow them, but shoot beyond the goal object.

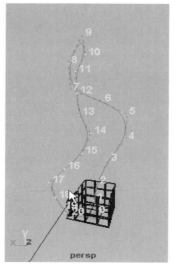

Particles moving beyond the goal

11 Add gravity to make the cord hang

- Select *cordCurveParticle*, then select **Fields** → **Gravity**. Set the **Magnitude** to **980.**

- Playback again.

Note: 980 is the correct magnitude when you're working in centimeters. It gives the correct timing when dropping things. When you drop something from a height of 40 meters as in this exercise, it would take about 2.9 seconds to hit the ground.

---

12 Adjust the springs

Notice that the cord now drops much too far.

- Select *cordSprings1Shape* and set the following:

    Stiffness to **100;**

    Damping to **5;**

    Rest Length to **40.**

- Playback to (around) frame **1000**.
- Stop the playback.

Note:	You may want to set **Playback Looping** to **Once** in the **Preferences** to make it easier to go to frame 1000. Remember that it is very important that **Playback Speed** is set to **Play every frame.** Scrolling the timeline may give incorrect results.

The cord should now be hanging from the anchor like this:

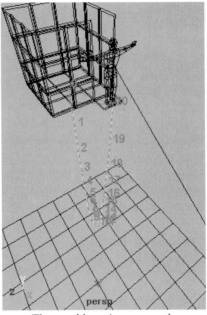

The cord hanging correctly

13 Set the Initial State

This position will be used as the starting position for the particles, the Initial State.

- Make sure you're at (or around) frame 1000 and the cord is hanging as illustrated above.
- Select *cordCurveParticle*.
- Select **Solvers** → **Initial State** → **Set for Selected**.
- Playback the scene and verify that particles now start at the intial position you just set at frame 1000.

14 Drop the cord

Once the initial position has been set, one of the ends of the rope can be released. This can be done by setting the **goalPP** of the particle to **0**.

- Select particle number20, *cordCurveParticle.pt[20]* ;
- Set the *goalWeight* for particle 20 to 0.

	Position Y	Position Z	Mass	lifespanPP	goalPP
cordCurveParti					
pt[20]	4000.000	-64.489	1.000	340282346638	0

The Component Editor for particle 20

- Playback the animation.
- You won't need to see the particles anymore. Hide the *cordCurveParticle*.

15 Adjust the springs

Notice that the springs are not stiff enough. The cord falls through the floor. Adjust the spring Stiffness and perhaps Rest Length.

- Adjust the **Spring Stiffness** until the cord no longer hits the ground. Make sure to leave some extra space for the jumper. A **Spring Stiffness** between **145** and **200** should work.

16 Place an object at the end of the cord

A simple object can be used to connect the jumper to the cord. An expression can query the world space position of the particle. The jumper should not be connected to the cord directly.

- Create a primitive cube. You may want to increase the **Width**, **Depth** and **Height** of the *polyCube* node so that you can see it more clearly in the Perspective views.
- Rename the cube to *cordEnd.*
- Select **Window → Animation Editors → Expression Editor...**
- Use the following expression to query the position of cordCurveParticle.pt[20]:

```
float $cordEndPosition[] = `getParticleAttr -at
worldPosition cordCurveParticle.pt[20]`;

cordEnd.translateX = $cordEndPosition[0];

cordEnd.translateY = $cordEndPosition[1];

cordEnd.translateZ = $cordEndPosition[2];
```

Playback the scene and notice how *cordEnd* remains attached to the end of the curve.

You couldn't have attached the jumper to the cord directly because it would have been too difficult to animate the motion of the jumper. Making it a rigid body would not have worked either, since you cannot write expressions for the position of a rigid body object. There are two objects in the scene, *l_ankle* and *r_ankle* that will be connected to *cordEnd* with spring constraints.

17 Make cordEnd a Passive Rigid Body

- Select *cordEnd*.

- Select **Soft/Rigid Bodies** → **Create Passive Rigid Body**.

- Select the *rigidBody* below *cordEnd*.

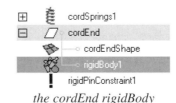

the cordEnd rigidBody

- Rename the *rigidBody* to *cordEndRigidBody*.

18 Connect l_ankle and r_ankle to cordEnd

- Go to frame **1**.

- If you made *cordEnd* very large, now is a god time to set it's size to 10x10x10 cm.

- Select *l_ankle* and **Ctrl+select** *cordEnd* in the Outliner.

- Select **Soft/Rigid Bodies** → **Create Spring Constraint**.

- Rename the constraint to *l_ankleSpringConstraint*.

- Repeat for r_ankle and rename the constraint to *r_ankleSpringConstraint*.

- Set the values for both constraints as follows:

  Spring Stiffness to **100**;

  Spring Damping to **10**;

  Spring Rest Length to **25**.

19 Connect jumper to l_ankle and r_ankle

To connect jumper to the ankle objects, use pin constraints.

- Select *l_ankle,* **Ctrl-select** jumper in the Outliner.
- Select **Soft/Rigid Body** → **Create Pin Constraint**.
- Use all views to move the pin to the center of *l_ankle.*
- Rename the constraint *l_anklePinConstraint.*
- Repeat for *r_ankle* and rename to *r_anklePinConstraint.*

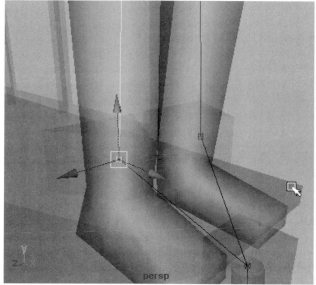

Positioning the pin constraint

- Move the center of gravity to the jumper's head.

20 Connect objects to gravity

- Select *jumper* and the *gravityField* and select **Affect Selected Object(s)**.
- Repeat for *l_ankle* and *r_ankle.*
- Playback.

21 Final adjustments

There are still a number of things you'll want to adjust to fine-tune the motion of jumper.

The following steps will prevent the jumper from falling through the platform:

- Make the *cage* a Passive Rigid Body.

- Select *cage* and select **Soft/Rigid Bodies** → **Create Passive Rigid Body** so that jumper can collide with it.

  Notice that jumper may spin wildly.

- Set the **Damping** of the *rigidBody* below jumper to a value above 0 to make the motion less nervous.

  The position of the pin constraint has a lot of influence on the motion of the jumper.

- Experiment with positions in front of and behind jumper.

- The pin constraint connects to the center of gravity.

- Adjust the position of the center of gravity. Try placing the center of gravity behind jumper to make him fall forward.

Complete the exercise by extruding a primitive circle along the curve.

Optional Exercise: Zeppelin

The file *zepStart.mb* contains a dirigible, a *simpleSphere* object, and the ground.

- Use the *simpleSphere* object as a wrap deformer for the *airShip*.
- Turn *simpleSphere* into a soft body and spring it up.
- Make the plane a Passive Rigid Body.
- Set the ground as a collision object to the soft body particles.
- Apply gravity to the soft body and watch it crash...beware, this file can get a bit slow at times.

TIPS AND TRAPS

Using MEL commands to generate net surface

In the basketball net example, you may have noticed the netGeo display layer. The net geometry was created using a series of extrusions. The MEL commands for this are listed below. This MEL code is also stored on the *softbodies* shelf.

```
select -clear;
select -hi -all;
select -tgl nurbsCircleShape1;
string $curves{} = `ls -sl -type "nurbsCurve"`;
for ($each in $curves)
{
```

```
extrude -ch true -rn false -po 0 -et 2 -ucp 1 -fpt 1
-upn 1 -rotation 0 -scale 1 -rsp 1 "nurbsCircle1"
$each;
}
select -clear;
```

A blow torch

The file *welderTorch.mb* contains a character holding and lighting a acetylene blow torch. The flame for the blow torch has been animated using soft body techniques. The flame is point and orient constrained into the character. The motion of the flame is done with soft body goals and a volume turbulence field.

SUMMARY

Soft bodies provide a direct manipulation of surface geometry with dynamic forces. They can also indirectly affect skinned surfaces through the use of dynamic influence objects.

There are several other applications for this feature including modeling, collision modeling, and fluid-like effects. The main limitation to using soft bodies is that the particles do not collide with each other or obey interpenetration checking of the surface. This is where cloth takes over for dynamically simulating fabrics and materials that must react to themselves.

11 The Emit Function

Maya provides additional control of particle placement and emission using the MEL command called emit.

In this chapter you will learn about the following:

- Common uses for the emit function;
- Common emit syntax and options;
- How to use simple conditional statements;
- How to add and work with custom attributes;
- How to construct strings of commands;
- How to use the *eval* MEL command;
- Emitting particles when rigid body collisions occur.

Fireworks

Up to this point, the examples have relied on the Particle Tool and the predefined emitters such as surface, directional, omni direction, etc. to place particles in the scene. For most applications, these provide an adequate starting place.

There are cases where some additional control may be required that is difficult or not possible using the default emitters.

ADDING PARTICLES TO AN EXISTING PARTICLE OBJECT

If you have created a cloud of particles with the Particle Tool and realize you need to add a few more particles to change the shape, one common practice is to use the *emit* command.

Using the emit function with the position flag

1 Create a particle cloud

- Use the Particle Tool to create a random cloud of particles.

- Set the **Particle Render Type** to **Sphere**.

- Set the **Radius** to **0.3**.

- Rename the particles *addParticles*.

2 Add three particles to the existing particle object using emit

- Select **Window** → **General Editors** → **Script Editor**.

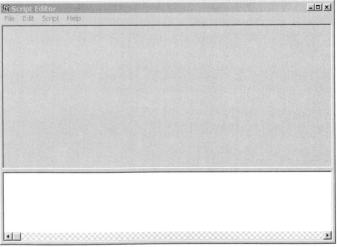

The Script Editor

- Enter the following lines in the lower window of the Script Editor:

```
emit -object addParticles -position 1 1 1;
emit -object addParticles -position 2 2 2;
emit -object addParticles -position 3 3 3;
```

- Press the **Enter** key on the numeric keypad.

  Each line above adds one particle to the existing *addParticles* particle object. The `position` flag is followed by the world space coordinate where the particle gets placed into the scene.

  You could also use the **Command Line** instead of the Script Editor to enter the emit command. The Command Line is the pink text field in the lower left corner of Maya's main window and can be toggled on and off using **Display → UI Elements → Command Line**.

Tip: Individual particles cannot be removed from a particle object. However, you can set an individual particle's **opacityPP** to 0 or its **lifespanPP** to 0 using the particleId in an expression or by setting the value in the Component Editor.

Use a locator to define particle placement

You can make this process more interactive by setting it up so the *emit* command places the particle at the coordinates of a locator.

- Select **Create → Locator**.
- Type the following in the Script Editor:

```
float $locX = `getAttr locator1.tx`;
float $locY = `getAttr locator1.ty`;
float $locZ = `getAttr locator1.tz`;
string $partObject[] = `ls -type "particle"`;
emit -object $partObject[0] -position $locX $locY
$locZ;
```

- **MMB-drag** the above text to the shelf.
- Move the locator to a location in space where you want to add a new particle
- **Select** the locator and the particle object.

- Click the new shelf button to automatically add a new particle into the selected particle object at the position of the locator.

- Repeat the process as desired.

Tip: Add the contents of the shelf button to a **hot key** to make this even more interactive.

"EMITTING" BASED ON OTHER PARTICLES

The *emit* function can set any attribute for a particle, not just its position. In the following example, *emit* is used to set position and velocity on newly spawned particles to make it appear as though the dying particles are emitting new particles.

1 Create a directional emitter

- Select **Particles → Create Emitter**:

    Change **Emitter Type** to **Directional**.

- Rename the emitter *primaryEmit.*

- Rename the particles *primaryParticles.*

- Set the following attributes for *primaryEmit:*

    Spread to **0.25**;

    Direction to **0, 1, 0**;

    Speed to **10**;

    Rate to **100**.

- Set the following attributes for *primaryParticles:*

    Particle Render Type to **Spheres**;

    Radius to **0.2**;

    Lifespan Mode to **lifespanPP only**.

2 Create an empty particle object

- In the Script Editor, type the following:

    ```
    particle -n secondaryParticles;
    ```

    This will create an empty particle object named *secondaryParticles*.

3 Set the Render Type for secondaryParticles

- Select *secondaryParticles* and set the following:

  Particle Render Type to **Multi-Streak**;

  Lifespan Mode to **lifespanPP only**.

4 Connect gravity to primaryParticles

- Select *primaryParticles*.

- Select **Fields → Gravity**.

5 Add a Runtime Expression to lifespanPP for primaryParticles

- Add the following to *primaryParticles'* Runtime Expression:

```
$pos = position;

$vel = velocity;

if ($vel.y<0)

{

lifespanPP = 0;

emit -object secondaryParticles -position ($pos.x)
($pos.y) ($pos.z) -at velocity -vectorValue ($vel.x)
($vel.y) ($vel.z);

}
```

6 Test the expression

- Rewind and playback.

  Just as *primaryParticles* begin to fall, the *emit* function is invoked and new *secondaryParticles* replace them with the same velocity and position.

Tip: A full description of the flags used by the emit function are listed in the online MEL documentation in the scene commands section.

---

7 Edit the expression to add color to secondaryParticles

- Add an **rgbPP** to *secondaryParticles*.

- Edit the Runtime Expression on *primaryParticles* as shown:

```
$pos = position;

$vel = velocity;

$col = sphrand(1);

if ($vel.y<0)
```

```
{
lifespanPP = 0;

emit -object secondaryParticles -position ($pos.x)
($pos.y) ($pos.z) -at velocity -vectorValue ($vel.x)
($vel.y) ($vel.z) -at rgbPP -vectorValue ($col.x)
($col.y) ($col.z);
}
```

8 Test the results

- Press **5** for shaded mode.

- Rewind and playback.

   A random color is assigned to each particle in *secondaryParticles*.

   In essence, you have created the framework for a fireworks effect with what you've done in this example. In the next section, you will take what you've done here a few steps further.

Fireworks

You can take the *emit* function a step further by repeatedly invoking the command in a looping structure to create a fireworks effect. Here you will create a fireworks effect and will also learn how to add custom attributes to the particle object and emitter so you can customize the launching and explosion characteristics.

1 Create the emitting cannon and the initial particle object

- Create a **Directional** emitter with the following settings:

   Rate to **5**;

   Spread to **0.25**;

   Direction X to **0**;

   Direction Y to **1**;

   Direction Z to **0**;

   Speed to **10**.

- Rename the emitter *launcher* and the particle object *fireworks1*.

2 Add custom attributes to launcher

Custom attributes are attributes that the user can tailor to his or her specific needs. Below you will add several custom attributes to the emitter that will later be used in particle expressions to modify the motion of the particles and the amount of emission that occurs.

To add custom attributes to the emitter, follow these steps:

- Select *launcher* and choose **Modify** → **Add Attribute...**

The Add Attributes window

- Add the following custom attributes to *launcher*. All the Attribute Types are *Scalar* and *Keyable*.

Attribute Name	Data Type	Default Value
antiGrav	Integer	5
showerUpper	Integer	30
showerLower	Integer	30
streamUpper	Integer	1
streamLower	Integer	1

Table of custom attributes to be added to Launcher

3 Add and adjust attributes for fireworks1

- Add a **per object Color** (rgb) attribute to *fireworks1*.

- Set the attribute values for *fireworks1* as follows:

  Max Count to **3**;

  Particle Render Type to **Streak**;

  Red to **0.8**;

  Green to **0**;

  Blue to **0**;

  Line Width to **1**;

  Tail Fade to **0.1**;

  Tail Size to **3.6**;

  Lifespan Mode to **lifespanPP only**.

4 Connect fireworks1 to gravity

- Select *fireworks1*.
- Select **Fields → Gravity**.

Make the secondary particle object

The secondary particle object represents the small projectiles that leave the initial projectile when its velocity reaches 0. These will be created using the emit function.

These secondary particles will act as leading particles for the long streaks of sparks that will be added later. Wherever the leading particles go, the streaks of sparks will follow. The secondary particles are the glowing tips of the streaks.

1 Create the "leading" particle object

- Type the following in the Script Editor:

```
particle -n fireworks2;
```

  This will create an empty particle object named *fireworks2*.

2 Add/modify attributes for fireworks2

- Change the **Particle Render Type** to **Spheres** and set a small **Radius** value (**0.05** works well).
- Set **Lifespan Mode** to **lifespanPP only**.

3 Create and connect gravity

- Select *fireworks2*.
- Select **Fields → Gravity**.

Create the final particle object and emitter

Now you will create the stream of sparks that follow behind the leading particles.

1 Add a directional emitter to fireworks2

- Select *fireworks2*.

- Add a **Directional** emitter by selecting **Particles** → **Emit from Object**.

- Rename the emitter *sparkEmit* and the new particle object *fireworks3*.

2 Adjust attributes for sparkEmit

- Select *sparkEmit* and set the following attributes:

    Rate to **40** (you can increase rate later for more detail);

    Spread to **0.25**;

    Speed to **1**;

    Direction to **0 1 0**.

3 Set the attributes for fireworks3

- Select *fireworks3* and set the following attributes:

    Particle Render Type to **MultiPoint**;

    Multi Count to **15**;

    Multi Radius to **0.2**;

    Color Accum to **On**;

    Depth Sort to **On**.

Add expressions to the particle objects

Now that the particle objects have been built and the appropriate fields connected, you can add expressions to the various particle objects.

1 Use emit to spawn the "leading" particles into fireworks2

- Add the following Runtime Expression to *fireworksShape1*:

```
vector $pos = fireworksShape1.position;
vector $vel = fireworksShape1.velocity;

float $antiGrav = launcher.antiGrav;
int $upperCount = launcher.showerUpper;
```

```
int $lowerCount = launcher.showerLower;

int $upperLife = launcher.streamUpper;

int $lowerLife = launcher.streamLower;


if ($vel.y < 0)

{

fireworksShape1.lifespanPP = 0;

  int $numPars = rand ($lowerCount, $upperCount);

 string $emitCmd = "emit -o fireworks2Shape ";

  for ($i=1; $i<=$numPars; $i++)

  {

    $emitCmd += "-pos " + $pos + " ";

    vector $vrand = sphrand(10);

    $vrand = <<$vrand.x, $vrand.y + $antiGrav,
$vrand.z>>;

    $emitCmd += "-at velocity ";

    $emitCmd += "-vv " + $vrand + " ";

    float $lsrand = rand ($lowerLife, $upperLife);

    $emitCmd += "-at lifespanPP ";

    $emitCmd += "-fv " + $lsrand + " ";

  }

  eval ($emitCmd);

}
```

Note: `//Error: An execution error occurred in the runtime`
`expression for fireworksShape1.`
`//Error: line 1: fireworksShape2: Object not found for`
`-object flag.//`

This execution error will appear for the above runtime rule if the name of *fireworksShape2* particle is not changed to *fireworks2Shape* within the expression.

What does this expression do?

- This expression creates the "flares" at the tips of the fireworks trails.

- For a detailed description of each line in the above expression, refer to the Emit Appendix at the end of this book.

2 Create a non-dynamic expression to control launcher's rate

A non-dynamic expression is an expression that is not contained within a Runtime or Creation Expression. Non-dynamic expressions are evaluated once per frame.

- Select *launcher* and add the following in the Expression Editor:

```
launcher.speed = rand (12,18);

if (frame%20==0)

launcher.speed = 22;
```

This expression varies the speed at which a particle leaves the cannon so the fireworks explode at different heights. Every 20th frame, a particle gets launched much higher.

Note: The **creation** and **runtime** radio buttons are dimmed in the Expression Editor since the expression is being added to *launcher*, which is *not* a particle shape object.

---

3 Assign a random lifespan to the spark trails

To control how long the spark trail burns, add the following to the Creation Expression of *fireworksShape3*:

```
fireworksShape3.lifespanPP = rand (0.3, 0.7);
```

This causes each particle in the spark trails of the fireworks to die before they are one second old.

4 Playback and adjust

After you have played the animation and are comfortable with how this process works, try setting different values for lifespanPP and other particle and attribute values, including the custom attributes you added to the emitter.

The files *emitFinal.mb* and *emitFinal2.mb* are finished versions of this example. Increasing the *sparkEmit* rate, adding opacity to *fireworks3*, and working over a black background will give you a better looking example.

Emission on contact

In this example, you will learn how to emit particles at the location where rigid bodies collide. The catapult will throw a rigid body object on the ground and you will make it emit particles at the contact points.

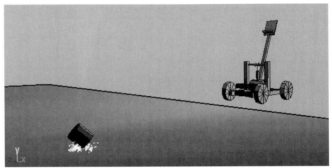

A catapult launches an object

1 Open File

- Open *rigidCollisionEmit_start.mb*.

    This file contains the catapult with an object being launched and colliding with the ground. The rigid bodies are already set up.

2 Create an empty particle object

Type "particle" in the Script Editor or Command Line to create an empty particle object. This particle object will be used later to hold the particles that are emitted when a collision occurs. Set the following attributes:

> **Particle Render Type** to **MultiPoint**;
>
> **Color Accum** to **On**;
>
> **MultiCount** to **7**;
>
> **MultiRadius** to **0.3**;
>
> **Point Size** to **2**;
>
> **Max Count** to **600**;
>
> **Conserve** to **0.9**;
>
> **Lifespan Mode** to **lifespanPP only**.

- Add an **rgbPP** attribute.
- Add an **opacityPP** attribute and add the default ramp to it.

3 Enable contact data attribute on the rigidSolver

The rigidSolver has an attribute called *contactData*. If this attribute is **On**, you can use MEL to find out information about when and where rigid body collisions occur. This attribute is **Off** by default since it requires extra work for the solver to manage this data.

- Select *DaBomb*.

- Locate the *rigidSolver* node in the Channel Box and set the **contactData** attribute to **On**.

4 Add a non-dynamic expression to DaBomb

An expression applied to *DaBomb* will be used to check the velocity of the rigid body, find out when and where a contact has occurred, and emit particles into *particle1* at that location.

- Select *DaBomb* and open the Expression Editor.

- Add the following expression or drag and drop it from the **Emit Shelf** (the shelf button is called **cont1**). The expression in the shelf button is extensively commented. It is listed below for reference but is not described in detail in this text.

```
if (frame > 60)
{
float $vel[] = `rigidBody -q -vel DaBomb`;
float $speed = mag(<<$vel[0],$vel[1],$vel[2]>>);
int $num = $speed * 5.5;
int $contact = `rigidBody -q -cc DaBomb`;
string $cPos[];
string $each;
if (($contact > 0) && ($num > 0))
{
   $cPos = `rigidBody -q -cp DaBomb`;
   for ($each in $cPos)
   {
   string $emit = ("emit -o particle1 -pos " +$each);
      for ($x=1;$x<$num;$x++)
      {
         $emit += (" -pos " + $each);
      }
      $emit += (" -attribute velocity");
```

```
            for ($x=1;$x<=$num;$x++)
            {
                vector $rand = (sphrand(1) + <<0,4,0>>);
                $emit += (" -vectorValue " + $rand.x + " " +
            $rand.y + " " + $rand.z);
            }
            eval($emit);
        }
    }
}
```

5 **Connect particles to gravity**

  - There is already gravity in the scene; connect the particles to it.

6 **Make particles collide with floor and DaBomb**

  - Select *particle1*, **Shift-select** *floor*.

  - Select **Particles** → **Make Collide**.

7 **Add Creation Expression to particles**

  Finally, you'll set the lifespanPP of the particles, color them, and set their mass which affects the quality of the collision. Add the following Creation Expression (or **drag+drop cont2** from the **Emit Shelf**):

```
mass = 500;
lifespanPP = rand (0.8,1);
rgbPP = <<0.9,0.6,0.1>>;
```

Exercises

- Add **rgb**, **Opacity**, and **Radius** attributes to the fireworks where appropriate and control them over the particle's age using ramps or expressions.

- Add per point emission so the fireworks sparks emit at different rates. Perhaps they will emit at different rates depending on their velocities.

- Can you think of a way to make each fireworks' explosion a different color? (Hint: research the parentId attribute).

- Review the *rigidBody* and MEL command in the documentation to see what other flags are available to query.

- Review the code examples for the *emit* command in the online documentation.

- See if you can design another method in Maya to create emission on collision without using expressions (Hint: use a soft body object, particle collisions, and a particle collision event).

SUMMARY

Now that you've had some exposure to the emit command, you have another tool available for you to achieve the effects you are working on.

The key concepts discussed in this lesson were:

- Using emit to add particles to a particle object.

- Using emit to place new particles based on the position of other particles.

- Constructing an emit statement using a looping structure and the *eval* command.

- Adding an emitter to particles created with *emit*.

- Emitting particles at rigid body contact points.

You'll likely come across cases where the methods discussed here are applicable to a situation you are trying to simulate. Be careful about getting side-tracked by the more technical approach of using emit if the same effect is easily accomplished using the Particle Tools available in the interface.

12 Particle Instancing

This chapter focuses on Maya's Particle Instancer, a tool for placing geometry at the location of individual particles.

In this chapter you will learn about the following:

- How to make geometry match particle movement;
- How to add animated geometry to particles;
- How to use cycles to instance a sequence of geometry;
- How the Particle Instancer uses custom attributes;
- How to add randomness to particle instanced geometry;
- Important qualities of Hardware Sprites;
- How to create software sprites using the Instancer.

Dragonflies

WHAT IS AN INSTANCE?

An instance in Maya is similar to a duplicated object. The primary difference is that an instance contains no actual surface information but is just a redrawn version of some original object. That original object acts like a master to all of its instances. The instance takes on all shading and surface characteristics of the original and will update as the original is updated. Since instances contain less information than duplicates, Maya can handle them faster.

WHAT IS PARTICLE INSTANCING?

Particle instancing (also commonly called particle replacing) is the process of using the position and behavior of particles to control the position and behavior instanced geometry. For example, you could model a honey bee, animate it flapping its wings, then use particle instancing to apply that flapping bee to a number of particles. By replacing each particle with a piece of instanced geometry, you can easily create a scene with swarming bees.

Particle instancing is not behavioral animation

Although some complex results can be obtained using particle instancing, it is important not to interpret the Particle Instancer as a full-featured behavioral animation system or flocking system. For example, you could build a fish swimming, then instance that swimming fish onto particles to simulate a school of fish. However, each fish just follows its own particle; there are no behavioral relationships established between the individual instanced elements.

The Instancer node

Maya uses the Instancer node as the "engine" to perform particle instancing. Although use of the Instancer node is not limited only to particles, the most common inputs it receives are from particles and from the geometry that will be instanced to those particles.

Inputs to the Instancer node in the Dependency graph

Creating an Instancer node

Example: Instancing animated dragonflies

1 Open the scene file

- Open the file *dragonFly_start.mb*.

2 Animate the wings flapping

- Select *leftWing* then **Shift-select** *rightWing* in the Outliner.

- Use **Shift+E** to keyframe only the rotation channels of both wings simultaneously as follows:

    Frames **1** and **5**, wings are angled down;

    Frames **2** and **4**, wings are straight;

    Frame **3** wings are angled upward.

Tip: You can **MMB-drag** in the timeline to advance frames without scrubbing through the animation. This makes it easier to setup one position at two different frame numbers for cycling. You can also use the **RMB** menu in the timeline to cut, copy, and paste keyframes.

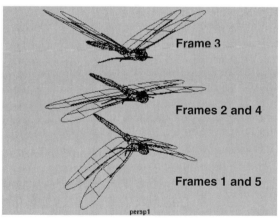

dragonFly shown with three different wing positions

3 **Create a grid of particles**

- Select **Particle → Particle Tool - □**:

  Particle Name to **flyParticles**;

  Conserve to **1**;

  Number of Particles to **1**;

  Create Particle Grid to **On**;

  Particle Spacing to **12**;

  Placement to **With Text Fields**;

  Minimum Corner to **-25, 0, -25**;

  Maximum Corner to **25, 0, 25**;

  Click in view.

- Press **Enter**.

  Setting particle spacing to **12** allows enough space inbetween each particle so that the instanced dragonflies will not intersect.

4 **Randomly offset the flyParticles**

- Add the following Creation Expression to the position attribute of **flyParticles**:

```
float $randY = rand (-3,3);
float $randXZ = rand (-1,1);
vector $offset = <<$randXZ, $randY, $randXZ>>;
position = position + $offset;
```

- Press **Create** to offset the particles from the grid. You can repeatedly offset the particles by pressing the rewind button.

- With the particles selected, set Initial State by selecting **Solvers → Initial State → Set for Selected**.

- **MMB-drag** the contents of the expression to a shelf, delete the expression, and close the Expression Editor.

5 **Instance the dragonfly to the particles**

- In the Outliner, select **dragonFly**.

- Select **Particles→Instancer (Replacement) -□** and set the following:

  Particle Instancer Name to **flyInstanced**.

- Press **Create**.

  This creates an Instancer node in the scene and creates an instanced version of the dragonfly for each particle.

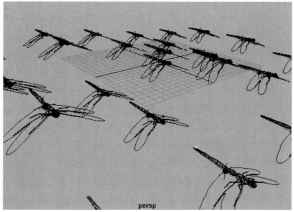

The Particle Instancer Options window

The instanced dragonflies

6 Hide the original dragonfly object

- Select *dragonFly*.
- Select **Display** → **Hide** → **Hide Selection**.

7 Add a vector attribute to the particles

Now, you will add some variation to the size of each of the instanced dragonflies.

- Open the Attribute Editor for **flyParticlesShape**.

- Press **General** in the **Add Dynamic Attribute** section and set the following:

  Attribute Name to **bugScaler**;

  Data Type to **Vector**;

  Attribute Type to **Per Particle (Array)**;

  Add Initial State Attribute to **On**.

- Press **OK**.

8 Assign values to bugScaler with a Creation Expression

- **RMB** in the *bugScaler* field and select **Creation Expression**.

- Add the following to the Expression Editor:

```
if (frame==1)
{
$rand = rand (0.4, 1.5);
bugScaler = <<$rand, $rand, $rand>>;
}
```

This expression picks a random number greater than 0.4 and less than 1.5 for each dragonfly and assigns that value to the *bugScaler* attribute.

- Press **Edit** and close the Expression Editor.

9 Set the Instancer to use bugScaler to scale each instance

- Select *flyParticlesShape*, open the **Particle Instancer** section of the Attribute Editor, and expand the **Instancer (Geometry Replacement)** tab.

- Under General Options, set **Scale** to **bugScaler**.

Any attribute added to the particle object can be fed into the various control attributes of the Instancer node. In this case, you are computing a value with an expression, storing that value in the *bugScaler* attribute, then assigning *bugScaler* to the scale option in the Instancer node. The ability to use any attribute value for any of the connections to the Instancer is what gives the Instancer its flexible control, since you are able to control the contents of those attributes with your own expressions.

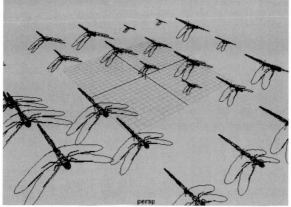

Instanced dragonflies with random positioning and scaling

10 Comment out the expression and set the Initial State

Since *bugScaler* is set at frame 1, the scale of the bugs will change every time the Rewind button is pressed. Once you are satisfied with the scale of the bugs, you can delete or comment out the expression and set the Initial State. Use two forward slashes (//) at the beginning of each line to comment out the expression.

If the *bugScaler* attribute always resets to 0 upon rewind (the bugs disappear), you probably forgot to set the Initial State.

It is a good idea to save your file before setting Initial State.

- Select the particles.
- Comment out (//) or delete the expression.
- Select **Solvers → Initial State → Set for Selected**.

11 Apply a uniform field to the particles and playblast

- Use the following settings for the uniform field:

  Direction X, **Y** and **Z** to **1, 0, 0**, respectively;

  Magnitude to **15**;

  Attenuation to **0**.

- Select **Window → Playblast - ❑** to preview the motion of the dragonflies.

Tip:	If you wanted each particle to move differently, you could apply an acceleration Runtime Expression to the particles instead of using a uniform field.

Cycling through a sequence of butterflies

1 Open the scene

- Open the file *butterfly.mb.*

  This scene contains one butterfly with no animation on it. You will create an animated cycle using the instancer and several duplicates of the butterfly.

2 Setup a cycle using duplicated snapshots of the butterfly

- Use the Outliner to select *origButterfly.*
- Make eight duplicates of the object.
- Hide *origButterfly.*
- Position the wings of each duplicate as shown in the image below.

  To rotate both wings simultaneously, select *polyRightWing*, **Shift-select** *polyLeftWing*, then use the **Rotate Tool**.

Note:	Do not **drag-select** a box around the butterfly and move it. This causes the items below the top hierarchy to be offset from the base object's coordinate system and will cause offsetting from the particles during instancing. Instead, select the top node of the duplicated object in the Outliner before moving it.

- Name the duplicated butterflies *postion1*, through *position8*.

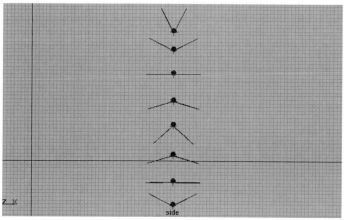

Eight butterflies producing one complete flapping cycle

3 Create particles in the scene

- Use the Particle Tool to create a cloud of about twenty particles with a maximum radius around 20.

- Rename the particles *butterflyParticles.*

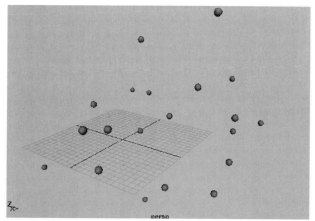

Cloud of twenty particles to be used for butterfly instancing

4 Set basic Instancer options

- Use the Outliner to select *Position1* through *Position8*. Make sure *Position1* is selected first and *Position8* is selected last, since the order they are selected will determine the cycling order used by the Instancer node.

- Select **Particles → Instancer (Replacement)** - ❏ and set the following options:

  Particle Instancer Name to **butterflyInstancer**;

  Cycle to **Sequential**;

  Cycle Step Size to **1**.

- Press **Create**.

The list of objects the Instancer will use is shown in the Instanced Objects list. The number beside the object is called the **Object Index**. The first object in the list is always index 0. The Instancer uses this index value to determine which object in the sequence of butterflies to display at a given point in time.

A cycle setting of **Sequential** causes the Instancer to cycle through the object indices in sequence rather than not using any cycling at all. A **Cycle Step Size** of **1** causes the Instancer to display each object index for 1 frame before changing to the next item in the list.

List of instanced objects and their object indices in the Instancer window

5 Make a test run

- Select and **Hide** *position1* through *position8*.

- Playback to view the instanced objects cycling.

All butterflies cycle through the eight positions in exactly the same fashion.

Instanced butterflies all with the same initial object index

6 Add a custom attribute to control cycling on a per particle basis

It was previously stated that the **Cycle Step Size** determines how long the Instancer will display each object index before switching to the next item in the list. Since the particleId is unique for each particle, it can be used to control this duration on a per particle basis. This is accomplished by multiplying the particleId by the age and storing the result in a custom attribute which, in turn, gets fed into the Age control of the Instancer's cycling options as explained below.

- Select *butterflyParticles.*
- Press the **General** Button in **Add Dynamic Attribute** section.
- Set the following options:

  Attribute Name to **customAge**;

  Data Type to **Float**;

  Attribute Type to **Per Particle (Array)**;

  Add Initial State Attribute to **On**.
- Press **OK**.

Adding customAge as a Float Array attribute

7 Assign values to customAge with a Runtime Expression

Now that you've added the attribute, you need to assign values to it for each particle. Since age changes over time, you will use a Runtime Expression instead of a Creation Expression.

- **RMB** on the *customAge* field and select **Runtime Expression**.

- Enter the following Runtime Expression in the Expression Editor:

```
if (particleId == 0)

    customAge = age;

else if (particleId == 1)

    customAge = age * 0.5;


else if ((particleId % 2 == 0) && (particleId % 3 == 0))

    customAge = age * 0.25 * particleId / 4;


else if (particleId % 2 == 0)

    customAge = age * 0.4 * particleId / 4;


else if (particleId % 3 == 0)

    customAge = age * 0.35 *particleId / 4;
```

```
else
    customAge = age * 0.2 * (particleId) / 4;
```

This expression assigns a different value to *customAge* based on multiplication of the *particleId*. Since these particles are not being emitted, they have the same age. To get around this, age is multiplied by a decimal value which was arbitrarily selected to provide variation in age for each particle. This value is then multiplied by the particleId which is, again, another unique value. The particleId is divided by 4 to keep the values small. If this division wasn't done, the values in *customAge* would get large quickly and cause the cycle to occur too quickly.

8 Set particle render type to numeric

To get a better idea of which portion of the expression is controlling which particles, you can use the Numeric Render Type.

- Select *butterflyParticles*.

- Set **Particle Render Type** to **Numeric.**

By default, the Numeric Render Type displays the *particleId* attribute for each particle. This makes it easier for you to see which particle will be affected by which portion of the expression. For example, *particleId 12* is evenly divisible by both 3 and 2 so it will therefore be set by this portion of the expression:

```
else if ((particleId % 2 == 0) && (particleId % 3 == 0))
    customAge = age * 0.25 * particleId / 4;
```

for the evaluation of *customAge*.

Tip: You can change which attribute the numeric render type displays by pressing the Current Render Type button in the Attribute Editor, then typing in the new attribute name in the field provided. Attributes such as rgbPP and Mass are other useful attributes to view in numeric mode.

---

9 Set the Cycle Options, Age attribute to customAge

- In the Instancer (Geometry Replacement) section of *butterflyParticles*, choose **customAge** from the **Cycle Options →
Age** pull-down menu.

10 Add a Float Array attribute to control the starting object index

Currently, all butterflies begin their sequence from object index 0 (position1). They all cycle through the instanced object list starting from *position1* and ending at *position8*, then repeating.

You can change the object index the sequence starts on by setting the **CycleStartObject** attribute in the Instancer. In this case, you will create another custom attribute called *startPick* to control **CycleStartObject** on a per particle basis, similar to the way you setup *customAge*.

- Add a custom Float Array attribute to *butterflyParticles* called *startPick*.

- Add the following **Creation Expression** to *startPick*. The value chosen for *startPick* here will determine which butterfly the Instancer chooses to begin the cycle on.

```
if (particleId == 0)
    {
    startPick = 0;
    }
else if (particleId == 1)
    {
    startPick = 1;
    }
else if ((particleId % 2 == 0) && (particleId % 3 == 0))
    {
    startPick = 2;
    }
else if (particleId % 2 == 0)
    {
    startPick = 3;
    }
else if (particleId % 3 == 0)
    {
    startPick = 4;
    }
else
    {
    startPick = 5;}
```

11 Set the Cycle Options, cycleStartObject attribute to startPick

- In the Instancer (Geometry Replacement) section of *butterflyParticles*, choose **startPick** from the **Cycle Options** → **cycleStartObject** pull-down menu.

Tip: The above method shows you a customized approach to selecting a starting object. A similar result can be achieved simply by setting cycleStartObject to particleId.

---

12 Add uniform and radial fields to move the particles

You can add fields or expressions to control the motion of the individual particles as desired.

Planning, optimizing, and rendering considerations

Now you have used the Instancer with an animated object and a cycled sequence of "snapshots". There are advantages and disadvantages to both methods. Using an animated object allows you to use 2D and 3D motion blur when rendering. Motion blur is not available when cycling through a sequence of instanced objects. Therefore, it is best to consider rendering requirements when setting up shots requiring instancing.

It is also important to keep your geometry as simple as possible. Making your surfaces single-sided and keeping NURBS patches low (or poly count low), makes a big difference.

One advantage to using a sequence of "snapshots" is that you have control over the duration of each snapshot and also the starting point of the cycle.

Tip: You can also instance Maya Paint Effects™ strokes to particles.

Hardware Sprite Render Type

The Sprite Render Type is used for displaying 2D file texture images on particles.

- The scene file *snowSpriteHW.mb* illustrates a simple application of hardware sprites. Open this file and playback the animation.

  A phongE shading group with a file texture of a snowflake with an alpha channel is assigned to the particles.

If you tumble the camera, the sprite images will always aim at the camera. This is a built-in feature of hardware sprites. You cannot make the hardware sprite type aim at some other object or direction.

Creating Software Sprites with the Instancer

The Hardware Sprite Render Type is only available for rendering using the Hardware Render Buffer. Therefore, you cannot render 3D motion blur, reflections, refractions, or shadows like you can when using software rendering. Here, we'll discuss a method for creating software renderable particle "sprites" using the Instancer node. This will allow you to take advantage of these important software rendering features while maintaining the core functionality that the hardware sprite render type provides.

Setup: Software Sprite camera setup (optional)

Since sprites should always face directly at the camera, you will need to setup your camera so there is some information available to tell the sprites what to point at. You will eventually use a polygon plane, particles, and the Instancer node to make the software "sprite" objects.

1 Create a new scene file

- Select **File** → **New Scene**.

2 Create a camera at the origin

- Select **Create** → **Camera**.

  For this example, you will use a single node camera with the default options.

- Rename the new camera *spriteCam*.

3 Create a locator at the origin and make it a child of spriteCam

- Select **Create** → **Locator**.

- Rename this locator *camLocal*.

- Parent the locator under *SpriteCam*.

  camLocal represents the local coordinate system of *spriteCam* at the back of the lens of the camera.

4 Duplicate the camLocal locator

- Duplicate the *camLocal* locator.

- Rename the new locator *camUpLocal*.

- Move it up one or two units so that it is directly above *camLocal*.

The locator *camUpLocal* will be used to find out which direction is up for *spriteCam* within its own local coordinate system.

5 Create another locator at the origin

- Create another locator at the origin.

- Rename this locator *camWorld.*

- This locator should *not* be placed within the *spriteCam* hierarchy.

  camWorld will be used to find out what world space coordinate the center of the camera lens is at.

6 Duplicate the camWorld locator

- Duplicate the *camWorld* locator.

- Rename this locator *camUpWorld.*

  camUpWorld will be used to find out what world space coordinate is considered up for the camera.

7 Point Constrain camWorld to camLocal

Point constraining *camWorld* to *camLocal* will cause *camWorld* to always follow the position but not the rotational orientation of *camLocal.*

- **Shift-select** *camLocal* then *camWorld.*

- Select **Constrain** → **Point**.

8 Point Constrain camUpWorld to camUpLocal

Point constraining *camUpWorld* to *camUpLocal* will cause *camUpWorld* to always follow the position but not the rotational orientation of *camUpLocal.*

- **Shift-select** *camUpLocal* then *camUpWorld.*

- Select **Constrain** → **Point**.

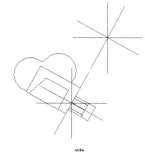

Side view of spriteCam With locators for World and Local Axes

Instancing setup

Now, you will add custom attributes to the particle object. These custom attributes will later be selected as options in the pop-up menus of the Instancer.

1 Create particles and a default polygon plane

- Select **Create** → **Polygon Primitives** → **Plane - ❑**.
- Press **Reset** then **Create**.
- Rename the plane *spritePlane.*
- Use the Particle Tool to make a cloud of particles.

2 Add vector Array attributes to particleShape1

- Open the Attribute Editor for the particles.
- Press **General** under Add Dynamic Attributes.
- Add four **Vector Array** attributes named as follows:

    spriteWorldUp;

    spriteAimPos;

    spriteAimAxis;

    spriteAimUpAxis.

3 Add a Creation Expression to particleShape1

- **RMB** select **Creation Expression** in the *spriteWorldUp* attribute field.
- Enter the following expressions:

```
spriteAimAxis = << 0, 1, 0 >>;
spriteAimUpAxis = << 0, 0, 1 >>;
vector $camPos =
<<camWorld.tx,camWorld.ty,camWorld.tz>>;
vector $camUp =
<<camUpWorld.tx,camUpWorld.ty,camUpWorld.tz>>;
vector $upDir = $camUp - $camPos;
spriteWorldUp= $upDir;
```

4 Add a Runtime Expression to particleShape added attributes

- Enter the following as a Runtime Expression on the *particleShape* node:

```
spriteAimPos = <<spriteCam.tx, spriteCam.ty,
spriteCam.tz >>;
```

```
vector $camPos =
<<camWorld.tx,camWorld.ty,camWorld.tz>>;

vector $camUp =
<<camUpWorld.tx,camUpWorld.ty,camUpWorld.tz>>;

vector $upDir = $camUp - $camPos;

spriteWorldUp = $upDir;
```

5 Create Particle Instancer for the plane object

- Select the *spritePlane* object.

- Select **Particle → Instancer (Replacement)**.

6 Set Instancer options

You have put all the pieces in place. You will now hook the particle attributes up to the Instancer.

- In the *particleShape1* Attribute Editor, open the **Particle Instancer** section, and set the following options:

  General Options:

  > **Position** to **WorldPosition**.

  Rotation Options:

  > **AimPosition** to **spriteAimPos**;

  > **AimAxis** to **spriteAimAxis**;

  > **AimUpAxis** to **spriteAimUpAxis**;

  > **AimWorldUp** to **spriteWorldUp**.

Note: If None is selected for AimDirection, a default value of <<1,0,0>> will be used. If None is selected for AimPosition, <<0,0,0>> is used. If None is selected for AimAxis, <<1,0,0>> is used. If None is selected for AimUpAxis, <<0,1,0>> is used.

---

7 Test the particle instancing

- A good test is to turn your **Particle Render Type** to **Sprite**.

  You should see that the instanced plane matches perfectly.

How do these expressions work?

- Determining the `spriteWorldUp` vector:

```
vector $camPos =
<<camWorld.tx,camWorld.ty,camWorld.tz>>;
```

```
vector $camUp =
<<camUpWorld.tx,camUpWorld.ty,camUpWorld.tz>>;
```

- $camPos is determined from the current camera position in world space. The expression gets this value from the point constrained locator camWorld. This is a vector value.

- $camUp is determined from the current position of the camUpWorld locator that is offset from the camWorld locator.

```
vector $upDir = $camUp - $camPos;
spriteWorldUp = $upDir;
```

- $upDir is determined from the difference between *camWorld* and *camUpWorld*. This is a vector value.

- spriteWorldUp is given this difference.

As the camera moves and rotates in world space, spriteWorldUp is reduced to a single vector that is used to compute each instanced object's current reference point for what is straight up. Since the camera may have rotated, what is straight up to the camera is not the same as what is straight up to the rest of the Maya world. Without this information, the Instancer would just assume that world up is the same as the Y up presented by the Maya world up setting, and the sprites would orient themselves to the wrong up reference point.

8 Ready for rendering

- Now that you have established the control of the software sprites, they are ready for software rendering. You can apply shaders and render with shadows, raytracing, motion blur, etc.

Extra: swSprite.mel

The *swSprite.mel* script in your scripts directory will automatically setup the above steps for you. Create a new scene, create a cloud of particles, select them, then type *swSprites* in the Script Editor to test it out. Raytracing will be needed in order to get shadows cast through the snowflakes. The file *snowSpriteSW.mb* was created using this script.

Exercises

- Combine the butterflies and the dragonflies together into one scene using two separate Instancer nodes.

- Create a custom attribute called customScale to control a random proportional scale of each butterfly.

- Create a cloud of particles and give them random swarming motion using an acceleration rule. Instance these swarming particles to another group of moving particles to make several collections of swarming particles.

- Make the butterflies randomly flutter, then glide for a few frames

Questions to test your understanding

- What is particle instancing?
- What is an object index?
- What happens if you increase the Cycle Step Size?
- What does the Allow All Data Types option do?
- Explain why butterflies instanced to a higher particleId flap their wings faster then those instanced to a lower particleId. How can you speed up the flapping of the butterflies instanced to lower particleIds?

TIPS AND TRAPS

- Dragonflies may disappear when the scene is rewound. This happens if the Initial State isn't set after the expression has evaluated once, or if you have not set the scale pop-up menu to *bugScaler* in the Instancer section of the *particleShape* node.

  Make sure the Initial State is set immediately after the Creation Expression is evaluated once. If you cannot get your dragonflies to come back, delete the Creation Expression and try entering a Runtime Expression like this:

  ```
  bugScaler0=<<1,1,1>>;
  ```

  Playback to see if the dragonflies reappear but don't rewind. If they do appear, set the Initial State and delete the Runtime Expression. Now you are back where you started before the problem arose and you can add the Creation Expression back in. Press Edit and Delete the Creation Expression and Set Initial State one final time. (Or you could just start the file again from scratch which may be easier!)

- If nothing happens after the expressions are entered, it's usually because you forgot to hook up the Custom attribute from within pop-up menus of the Instancing section of the Attribute Editor.

- If the Custom attribute you created doesn't show up in the pop-up menus, you likely created the Custom attribute as a different data type than what that pop-up menu expects. Turning on **Allow All Data Types** refreshes the menus and allows the attribute to show up. The better solution is to recreate the attribute as the correct data type (float for object index numbers and vector for nearly all other Instancer attributes).

- A very quick way to make each particle start on a different butterfly is to set *CycleStartObject* to *particleId*. This is faster than typing in the expression and gets the same basic results. It is still good, however, to understand the expression.

- The file *instancedArrows.mb* in the **demo** directory is good for illustrating how to make an object align to its velocity (aim direction to velocity).

- If the file texture *snowflake_wAlpha.rgb* does not appear on the hardware sprites when the scene file *snowSpriteHW.mb* is opened, reassign the file texture to the color input attribute of the *phongE1* material shader. Go to:

  ```
  support_files\maya\projects\Dynamics\sourceimages\
  snowflake_wAlpha.rgb.
  ```

- The *swSprites.mel* script does the setup automatically (camera, instancing and shader setup). It is normal for you to have to rewind and playback to get the sprites to align. Also, the "sprites" may not align on the first frame until the expressions are evaluated. This is normal. One limitation here is that you cannot play different sequences of images on the sw sprites. To do this would require a script that would create one animated shader for each polygon plane. In addition, each poly plane would need to be a duplicate rather than an instance so the current setup would not suffice.

- People often ask if there is a way to fade the instanced objects out based on the opacityPP of the particle it is instanced to. Currently, this is a limitation of instancing. There is currently no direct connection between shading attributes of the particles and the objects that are instanced to them.

- The different aim attributes on the Particle Instancer can be confusing. Here's a quick breakdown:

  AimPosition - Where the polygon plane will point at.

  AixAxis - Determines which axis of the polygon plane will point at the AimPosition

  AimUpAxis - Determines which axis of the polygon plane is considered the up axis.

  AimWorldUp - Determines which axis of the polygon plane is considered up in world space.

- Sprite Wizard option is a script that automatically sets up animation of file textures on sprite particles.

- One trick for keeping particles away from each other is to use each particle as an individual radial field.

  With nothing selected, create a radial field with Attenuation 0 and Volume Shape set to none.

  Select the particles, then the field, and choose **Fields → Affect Selected Object as Source of Field.**

  Connect the radial field up to the particles using the Dynamic Relationships Editor.

  Select the radial field and turn on **Apply per vertex** in the Attribute Editor (under the Special Effects section).

  Now each particle is a small repelling field. You don't have control over the individual field magnitudes for each particle but this is at least a start in keeping all the particles pushing away from each other. You can experiment with Max Distance settings, attenuation and magnitude settings for better results.

SUMMARY

Particle Instancing is a built-in way to move geometry around using particles. Although the geometry will not detect the other instanced geometry, you can still come up with some pretty cool effects using Particle Instancing. The fact that each parameter of the Instancer is open to Maya's MEL scripting language is a big benefit for customizing the parameters you use for your instanced animations.

13 Rendering Particles

This chapter covers rendering techniques for particles and dynamic objects.

In this chapter you will learn about the following:

- Hardware particle rendering types;
- Software particle rendering types;
- Particle caching (memory and disk);
- Particle Sampler Info Utility node;
- Particle cloud rendering.

Smoke being emitted from a cigarette

Particle Render Types

Maya provides two types of rendering for particles: hardware and software.

Hardware rendering uses the graphics buffer and graphics memory of your computer to draw the image to the display and then takes a snapshot of this image. This snapshot is then written to a file as a rendered image. This technique of using the hardware rendering capabilities of your computer has the advantage of being very fast but also the limitation of few rendering advantages such as shadows, reflections, and post-process effects like glow. Often particles are rendered only for the positional and matte or alpha information using the hardware renderer. The actual look of the particle effect is obtained by adding color, shadows, reflections, or environment lighting in the compositing stage of production. Again, speed and flexibility for aesthetic change of mind is behind this pipeline of image creation.

The hardware render types in Maya are the Point, Streak, Sphere, Sprite, and Numeric render types. As a subset of these types, there are also two versions of point and streak that utilize multi-pass rendering. These are the MultiPoint and Multi-Streak particle render types. It is probably safe to say that these two are the most commonly used hardware render types for most of the particular type of effects you create. Sprite comes in at a close second. As seen in the chapter on Particle Instancing, the sprite render type is used for displaying 2D images on particles. The sphere and point render type are more commonly used just to visualize where the particles are in space. The point render type is the simplest and one that the display draws the quickest.

The software render types in Maya are the Blobby Surface, Cloud, and Tube render types. These render types allow for various combinations of surface and volumetric shading techniques which will be discussed in an upcoming section of this book. Their shaders are constructed from the similar shading nodes that are applied to geometry and lights.

When you software render, any hardware render type particles are skipped. When you hardware render, software render type particles are rendered as their respective hardware display appearance and filled circles.

HARDWARE RENDERING

Since version 5, Maya has two hardware renderers. The Hardware Render Buffer is the original hardware renderer, the Maya Hardware Renderer is new. In this chapter you will be using the Hardware Render Buffer.

The Hardware Render Buffer

The Hardware Render window can be found under **Window → Rendering Editors → Hardware Render Buffer...** This window is a free floating window that will assume the size of the selected resolution format. It is recommended to make sure there are no windows beneath or in front of this window when you are rendering to it. It is also suggested to use an absolute black desktop background if you are going to be doing a lot of hardware rendering. Also, shut off your screen saver. The Hardware Render Buffer simply snapshots what is on the screen, therefore, you should avoid moving the window around during rendering.

Hardware rendering can also be used as a quick animation test. Geometry can be hardware rendered with lighting and textures but without shadows or advanced lighting effects. There are also many options that allow geometry matting to be generated to aid in the compositing process.

The Maya Hardware Renderer

The Maya Hardware renderer is one of the renderers listed in the Render Globals under Render Using. While it doesn't provide all the same options that the Hardware Render Buffer has, it has significant advantages. Most importantly, it can render depth mapped shadows for the Particle Hardware Render types. The exception is the Sprite render type, sprites cannot cast shadows. A workaround for rendering sprites that cast shadows is to use instanced geometry.

Starting and stopping a hardware render

You invoke a render in the hardware render buffer using **Render → Render Sequence** or by pressing the test button in the bottom center of the window to test a single frame. You can cancel a render by pressing and holding the **Esc** key or by clicking the mouse inside the Hardware Render Buffer window.

Multipass Hardware Rendering

Multipass Hardware Rendering creates a softer rendered look for your particles. It can also anti-alias your geometry that is being hardware rendered. Multipass rendering requires you to use multipass render type as your particle render type. You have the choice of MultiPoint or Multi-Streak.

For each of these render types, you will have several particle attributes that control the multi-pass effect:

> **Multi Count** - Controls the number of added and offset pseudo-particles that Maya will distribute around the original particle.

Multi Radius - Controls how far away from the actual particle that the additional pseudo-particles get drawn.

Hardware Render attributes:

Render Passes - Controls the number of times that a render is averaged.

Edge Smoothing - Controls anti-aliasing of geometry.

Motion blur - Controls samples of time taken to blur particles and geometry. Values and approach differ from Maya software motion blur.

Motion blur and caching

Motion blur allows you to average the look of the particles over time. To use motion blur it is strongly recommended that you cache your particle motion. Otherwise, you will often get strange and unpredictable results.

Note: Some hardware configurations have known problems using hardware Multi-pass motion blur.

Smoke being emitted from a cigarette

Cigarette smoke

In this example, you will create and render particles for cigarette smoke using hardware rendering techniques. The file *cigSmoke.mb* contains props and dynamic elements ready for particle rendering. The animation of this setup is interesting as well. The main trick to the particle movement is two turbulence fields that have their phase animated with a simple sin expression. The only difference between the two fields is that the second turbulence field has a slightly slower frequency. These two fields work to reinforce each other while moving the particles. Rotation is obtained with a vortex field.

1 Open the scene file

This scene file consists of a cigarette and an ashtray and several fields.

- Open the file *cigSmoke.mb.*

    There is a parented emitter under the cigarette group. You will use this emitter as your source for the particle smoke.

    Playback the scene to get an idea of how the particles are moving.

2 Open the hardware render window

The Hardware Render Buffer is the name of this window. This window cannot be minimized.

- Select **Window → Rendering Editors → Hardware Render Buffer...**

3 Set hardware render attributes

In the Hardware Render Buffer window, Select **Render → Attributes...** and set the following:

    In the Image Output Files section:

        Filename to **cigSmokeTest**;

        Extension to **name.0001.ext**;

        Start Frame to **1**;

        End Frame to **100**;

        By Frame to **1**;

        Alpha Source to **Luminance**.

    In the Render Modes section:

        Lighting Mode to **All Lights** (Hardware Rendering has a maximum limit of eight lights);

        Draw Style to **Smooth Shaded**;

        Texturing to **On**;

        Line Smoothing to **On**.

        The Line Smoothing helps smooth out the tails when rendering streak and Multi-Streak particles.

In the Mult-Pass Options section:

Multi Pass Rendering to **On**;

Anti-Alias Polygons to **On**;

Edge Smoothing to **1**;

Render Passes to **9**;

Motion Blur to **4**.

Description of additional options:

Full Image Resolution - Turn this **On** if you are rendering at resolution larger than screen resolution (for example, if you are rendering for film). The render will split the image into tiles, render each tile, then sew the tiles together into one image.

Geometry Mask - If turned **On**, you will only get particles in the final rendered image; no geometry is included.This can be useful when rendering a particle pass that will be composited over a separately rendered geometry pass. When this is on, the geometry will not be rendered into the hardware rendered image. However, the geometry will "cut out" (mask) the appropriate particles so that layering occurs correctly during the compositing stage.

You should be aware that geometry masking is not perfect. For example, if you are layering your particles over a software rendered geometry pass and that geometry pass has software motion blur, it is unlikely that the hardware particle pass' geometry masking will match the motion blurred alpha channel from the software render. This is because the software renderer is much more accurate than the hardware renderer. Changing your object's tessellation will not necessarily increase the quality of the geometry masking. Also, the geometry masking is not anti-aliased. Often you will need to use matte creation or modification tools in your compositing software to adjust how the particles will layer over the geometry.

Display Shadows - Some graphics cards support hardware shadowing. If your graphics card supports this feature, enabling this option will allow you to render shadows into your hardware rendered images.

4 Set Particle Render Type to Multi-Streak

This render type will provide streaking and multiple "jittered" pseudo-particles.

- Select the *particleShape.*

- Change the **Particle Render Type** to **Multi-Streak**.

- Press **Add Attributes For Current Render Type** and set the following:

    Depth Sort to **On**;

    Color Accum to **On**;

    Line Width to **1**;

    Multi Count to **5**;

    Multi Radius to **0.100**;

    Normal Dir to **2**;

    Tail Fade to **-0.500**;

    Tail Size to **0.750**;

    Use Lighting to **On**.

5 Fine-tune lighting of particles

For hardware rendering, you will find that lighting values are often different than what is appropriate for software rendering. You may want to use separate lights for hardware rendering and separate lights for software rendering.

- Select each light in the scene and duplicate it.

- Rename the light to a hardware designation.

- Link the hardware lights to the particles and unlink the software lights to the particles.

- Light the particles with the hardware lights. Test render to the Hardware Render Buffer.

- Toggle **Color Accum** (Color Accumulation) to see the effect that it has on the particle rendering.

    Color Accumulation: When transparent particles are in front of one another they can either render the nearest particle or add the overlapping particle's colors. By using color accumulation, you can more closely simulate transparent particle effects.

    Color Accumulation also works to hide orphaned particles that are not contributing to the overall smoke trail. This adds to the smooth look the smoke has. Note that color accumulation does not currently work with the sprite render type.

    Normal Dir: This is an attribute available on many of the hardware render types. Press Current Render Type in the particle's Attribute Editor to access it. Normal Dir affects how particles are lit. Usually you won't need to adjust this unless your particles are moving in and out of lighting. The online Dynamics documentation explains what each of the three settings specifically does so we won't repeat that here. Essentially, Normal Dir controls how the particles are lit based on the relationship of the particles to the location of the light. In practice, if your particles do not appear to be responding as you expected to the lighting in your scene, try adjusting this attribute for better results.

Caching particles

In order to apply hardware motion blur to a sequence of rendered images, you will need to cache the simulation. Motion blur requires knowing where the particle is and was, in order to determine the correct motion of the particle and determine the correct Tail Shape. Because future particle position is evaluated as the dynamic simulation calculates each frame, Maya will not be able to predetermine the motion blur future frames unless the calculations have already been performed and stored in memory or on disk. Caching also makes it easier to evaluate timing since you can scrub in the timeline once the particles have been cached.

Memory caching vs. Disk caching

You have two choices for caching particles in Maya: **Memory caching** and **Disk caching**. Memory caching for particles works very much like memory caching of rigid bodies. You select the particle objects you want to cache and enable caching via a menu. The particle information is stored in RAM the first time. Subsequent playbacks are read from the RAM making evaluation much faster. The steps below outline how to use memory caching with the cigarette smoke. For reference, the workflow of both Memory and Disk caching is outlined here. For this exercise, you should choose only one method.

Memory caching workflow

Memory caching is good to use when you have a short simulation that doesn't have a huge number of particles. It is also useful when you know you will not be using distributed rendering across multiple computers. Currently, hardware rendering cannot be distributed in this manner but software rendering can. Memory caching provides a quick way of caching your particles without having to keep track of cache data files on your hard disk. However, memory caching can quickly eat up your computer's available RAM so be aware of that before using it. The steps for enabling particle memory caching are as follows:

- Select the particle object(s).

- Select **Solvers** → **Memory Caching** → **Enable**.

  The *particleShape* will now show **Cache Data** attribute as **Enabled**.

  To disable caching for a particular particle, you can deselect this attribute.

Note: Each time you make a change to your scene, either to field values or *particleShape* attributes, you will need to delete the cache. To delete the cache, you will need to select each affected particle and select **Solvers** → **Memory Caching** → **Delete**.

Disk caching workflow

Disk caching creates files (*.pdc) on your hard drive containing all the particle attribute information in your scene. One .pdc file is written for each particle object on each frame of playback. These files can be read very quickly by Maya so near real time scrubbing is still possible. You are only limited by available disk space instead of available RAM. The .pdc files can be transferred to other machines if necessary or accessed remotely, such as when using distributed rendering.

- Save the file.
- **Solvers** → **Create Particle Disk Cache - ❒**.
- Read the dialog description, then press **Create**.

  Maya will not draw the particles on the screen but will record all their attribute information to disk.

- Save the file again (this is so Maya knows this file contains a disk cache with it).
- To temporarily disable the cache, select **Solvers** → **Edit Oversampling or Cache Settings,** then disable the **Use Particle Disk Cache** option.
- To permanently remove the disk caching, you need to locate the *particles* directory in your current Maya project using your operating system. The directories inside the particles contain all the .pdc files for the various particle objects you have cached.

Tip: For more specific control of which particle attributes will be written to disk cache, refer to the dynExport command in the MEL documentation

6 Adjust the motion blur

Now that you have cached the particles, experiment with different values of hardware motion blur.

- Open the Hardware Render Globals window.
- In the Multi-Pass Render Options section, set **Motion Blur** to values between **5** and **6**.

  What do you notice about tail size and particle blending?

Note: Some older hardware graphics configurations do not support hardware motion blur.

---

7 Adjust opacity over lifespan

The opacity of the particles should thin out as they get older.

- Add **opacityPP** attribute and apply an opacity expression that is a function of age (or apply a ramp to opacityPP).

Graininess is OK

Graininess is to be expected in your final smoke renders. This will be smoothed and blurred during the compositing stage so you should not work too hard to get rid of it. Anticipate that the small particles that are orphaned or not contributing greatly will also get removed during blurring and softening that takes place in your compositing software.

Using low opacity values with a lot of particles can really help your hardware renders look less "flat" and computer generated. Also, you can simulate self shadowing in hardware rendered smoke by using expressions to randomly assign gray values to the particles at creation time.

What about hardware glowing and incandescence?

People often ask if you can make hardware particles glow or produce self-illumination. Color Accumulation is the closest thing, currently. This task is much better suited for compositing effects that let you make this adjustment very quickly. Even the most basic compositing packages generally have some nice tools for adding in incandescence and glowing effects. For hardware rendering, focus more on the motion and shadowing qualities inside of Maya. Sweetening effects like blurs, halos, glows, etc. are traditionally easier to add during compositing.

Optional exercises

- Render the fireworks from the emit lesson.

■ Render the magic wand from the particle expressions lesson.

The emit lesson contains a very good fireworks simulation that needs some attention for rendering. Use the *emitFinal.mb* scene to work on using **MultiPoint** and **Multi-Streak** with motion blur.

The *magicWand.mb* scene is another scene that could use some fine-tuning for hardware render.

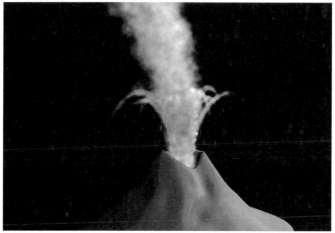

A volcano erupting

SOFTWARE RENDERING

Software rendering of particles will allow you to do post-process effects such as glow and incandescence as well as interactive effects of reflection, object occlusion, and shadows. The price for this functionality is time.

There are three types of software particle render types. They each serve a separate purpose but can be combined as well.

Blobby particles

Blobby particles depend on each other to form blobs or connected shapes based on their radius and proximity to each other. There are two attributes related to the blobby particle object that controls this behavior.

> **Radius** - Sets the diameter of the blob.
>
> **Threshold** - Sets the amount of flow between adjacent particles. The resultant blobbiness is a function of the particle radius, threshold and distance between particles. A setting of 0 generally means no blending. Values closer to 1 will normally produce

more blending (assuming that there are particles close to each other). All of these factors are interdependent so experimentation is almost always necessary.

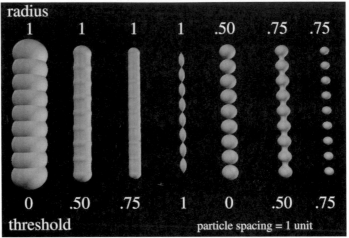

Blobby particle comparison of Radius vs. Threshold

To see a comparison of **Radius** vs. **Threshold**, open the scene file *blobCompare.mb*. Note that Threshold values that are much larger then the **Radius** may result in invisible particles.

Blobby particles are also the only render type to which you can assign shading groups and render in the same way you would assign shading groups to geometry.

It is generally recommended that you avoid depending on 2D mapping on blobby particles as blobbies use an averaging of UV space to calculate their respective mapping coordinates. This can result in artifacts or incorrect mapping of the Blobby Surface. 3D mapping works the same as you would expect for any surface. It is often best to keyframe your 3D texture placement nodes to approximate the motion of your particles, as this helps to reduce the appearance of texture swimming during rendering. However, it can be difficult to totally eliminate the appearance of swimming when rendering blobbies using 3D textures, since particles may be moving at different speeds.

Bump mapping can be used with Blobby Surfaces, but displacement mapping doesn't work as you might expect.

Motion blur is not currently supported for any software render types.

Cloud particles

Cloud particle render type, as its name implies, is designed to create volumetric rendering effects. It has an additional attribute called Surface Shading which controls how much blob the cloud will have.

Radius - Works much like the Blobby Surface attribute.

Threshold - Works much like the Blobby Surface attribute.

Surface Shading - Adjusts the degree of Surface Shading applied to the *particleCloud* shader via the Surface Shader input on the Shading Group.

Tube particles

Tube particles are the software counterpart to the hardware streak particle render type. The tube particle has attributes to control the size of either end of the particle as well as tube length. The tube particle type does not have the Surface Shading capability that the cloud and blobby type have. The tube particle is velocity dependent like the hardware streak types. The Tail Length and Direction is dependent on the velocity and direction of the particle.

Radius0 - Controls the tail size.

Radius1 - Controls the head size.

Tail Size - Controls the tail length but is also proportional to the particle velocity.

Note: Radius0 and Radius1 are per object attributes only.

Shading group organization

The Maya rendering engine accepts three basic types of shader information: Surface, Volumetric, and Displacement. These three types of rendering information are passed to the Rendering Partition through the Shading Group node. The Shading Group node acts as a place holder that tells the Rendering Partition what will be rendered and which shaders are to be used on which objects. The Light Linking Partition also looks to the Shading Group to determine which lights will work with which shaders and/or objects.

Software Particle rendering makes use of the Surface and Volume shader inputs to the Shading Group node. You connect Surface shaders (materials) and Volumetric shaders (*particleCloud*) to the three different types of particle render types via the *particleCloud* Shading Group (*particleCloudSG*). Surface shading is plugged into the Surface Material input of the Shading Group and Volumetric shading (*particleCloud*) is plugged into the Volume Material input.

Blobby particles make use of the standard surface material shaders such as Anisotropic, Phong, Lambert, Blinn, etc.

Cloud particles make use of the surface materials and the volumetric *particleCloud* shader by plugging materials into the Surface Material input of the Shading Group, and the *particleCloud* shader is plugged into the Volume Material input.

Tube particles make use of the volumetric shader *particleCloud* only. *ParticleCloud* shader is plugged into the Volume Material input of the Shading Group.

Blobby particles with Environment Reflection Map

A space blob

In this example, you will create a very simple blobby rendering. This will give you a chance to experiment with the blobby attributes and the shading parameters.

1 Open scene file

- Open the file *spaceBlobStart.mb.*

  This scene consists of particles orbiting via a Newton field.

2 Set the Particle Render Type

- Set the **Particle Render Type** to **Blobby Surface**.

- **Add Attributes** for **Current Render Type**.

3 Apply Phong shader to the blobby particles

You will use a PhongE material as the basis for the blobby particle shader. From this material, you will add other rendering nodes to control color, reflection, and specularity.

- In the Hypershade window, **RMB** select **Create** → **Materials** → **PhongE**.

- **LMB** to deposit the node in the workspace of the Hypershade window.

- **Shift-select** the particles, then the PhongE node and **RMB** on the PhongE node to select **Assign Material To Selection**.

4 Create the color and specular map

Because you want the blob to mimic clear water-like material, it will get most of its color from its environment. But you will still want some method to control the color and specularity. The 3D texture, Marble, makes a good sky texture.

- Press the square **Map** button for **Color** in the Attribute Editor.

- In the Create Render Node window, press **Marble** under the 3D Textures section. Below are some appropriate values:

Marble render node settings

- Rename the marble node to *skyMarble*.

- **MMB-drag** *skyMarble* from the Hypershade window to the **Specular Color** input on the PhongE Attribute Editor.

5 Add environment map to the reflected color of the Phong

Environment maps are a quick method to mimic raytraced reflections and refraction.

- Set the following values for the PhongE material node:

PhongE node settings

- Map the **Reflected Color** attribute with an **Env Chrome** Environment texture.

- Set the following light values for the chromeEnv node to **0**:

Settings for the envChrome node

- Set the **Grid Placement** attributes to **0**.

▾	**Grid Placement**				
	Grid Width	0.000			
	Grid Width Gain	0.000			
	Grid Width Offset	0.000			
	Grid Depth	0.000			
	Grid Depth Gain	0.000			
	Grid Depth Offset	0.000			

Grid settings

6 Map 3D textures into the chromeEnvironment inputs

The Chrome Environment map has several inputs for Sky and Floor color values. You will create a new texture for the floor.

- **Map** the **Floor Color** with a **3D Rock** texture.

- Set **Color** values to approximate what your ground will look like:

▾	**Rock Attributes**				
	Color1				
	Color2				
	Grain Size	0.042			
	Diffusion	2.000			
	Mix Ratio	0.621			

Rock color

- From the Hypershade window, **MMB-drag** the *skyMarble* texture onto the **Horizon Color** input of the *envChrome* node.

Your shading network will look something like this:

Blobby Environment shader network

7 Create a stand in sphere to IPR render with

IPR is a very quick way to fine-tune a shader. Maya's IPR rendering workflow does not incorporate particles, but you can create a Stand In object to apply the shader to. After, you will apply this shader to the blobby particles.

8 Adjust values

- Experiment with **Radius** and **Threshold** settings for the particles. Also experiment with lighting and texture parameters to see how they effect the look of the render.

The particleCloud Shader and Particle Sampler Info node

The *particleCloud* shader provides tools for many particle rendering effects. This is the most flexible shader mechanism for software particle rendering in Maya. The *particleCloud* shader provides volumetric density control and surface material attributes like color, transparency, glow, and incandescence. You can create a new *particleCloud* shader in the Hypershade window using: **Create → Materials → Volumetric → Particle Cloud**.

This section discusses some of the most important *particleCloud* and particle sampler info node attributes, so you can learn their function before putting them to work in a practical application.

Note: The *particleCloud* material works with Cloud and Tube Particle Render Types only.

Density and Transparency

Density is closely related to transparency and will interact with the method you choose to drive the particle opacity. The **Density** attributes allow you to control how a particle will look at its edges and where it overlaps with other particles. Density can be thought of as the **Volume transparency** or as another series of inputs that add greater control over several aspects of shader transparency. It is important to understand how Density works as the **Transparency** attribute alone will only get you part of the look you may be looking for. The Transparency attribute will work as the base of particle transparency whereas the Density attributes apply to the volumetric portion of the shading. The third component is the **Blob Map**, which allows a texture to be added to the internal structure of the particles appearance. Typically, the less Blob Map is applied, the less of the particle surface outline is visible. The Blob Map will also affect how the shapes of the individual clouds are drawn in the render.

Density - This attribute controls how dense the particle shading appears inside the Volume. This attribute is also necessary for example, to "beef up" the shading if there is a lot of noise. Or, if you are using the transparency attribute to drive the surface shading, you may find that the Density attribute can control the Volume portion independently. Typical values between (0-1) control slight density but values up to 10 can create interesting internal density for a very transparent particle. Also, keep in mind that the number of overlapping particles is going to affect the range of the Density attribute. If you have a lot of particles overlapping, then density values can be set lower.

Noise - This attribute controls the amount of random noise applied to the modification of the density. Noise can give you control of how extreme the density will diffuse across the particle. Typical values range from 0 to 4 but will also depend on how much density is being used and again, on the number of particles and the specific effect.

Noise Freq - This attribute controls how large or small the spacing of the Noise maps across the particle. Typical values can be quite small (.01–.1) for low frequency noise.

Noise Aspect - This attribute controls at what angle or "shear" the noise will appear to exist in the volume. Typical values of (-1– 2) will change the noise direction from horizontal to vertical.

Blob Map - This attribute controls the mixture of surface shading and volume shading independent of the presence of a Surface Material. Surface shading is controlled by the Surface Shading Properties, in particular the Diffuse Coefficient. Blob Map can have a texture applied through it to create more interesting internal structure to the particle appearance. It will interact with the overall density and transparency. If you turn this value very low you may need to increase the density and/or noise, and/or transparency to see the Cloud particles. A minimum value above 0 for Blob Map is necessary for particles being rendered with no Surface Material Shading. Otherwise, they will be invisible. Blob Map is a scaling factor for density. You can think of it as volume transparency. To see how this works, try mapping a 3D Cloud texture to the default *particleCloud* shader and then render some Cloud particles.

Life mapping and The Particle Sampler Info node

Life mapping is the process used by the renderer to map attributes from the *particleCloud* shader to the particles with respect to each particle's age. In the particle introduction chapter of this book, you learned about normalized age. So far, we have been dealing strictly with hardware rendered particles. Now you will learn how to accomplish the same thing (and more) using software rendering.

The **Particle Sampler Info** node is a utility node designed specifically for controlling software rendering of particles. It is an essential part of the life mapping process. In addition, this node lets you use particle attributes (ramps and expressions) to drive software shader attributes on a per particle basis. For example, you could use it to make the velocity of a particle affect its transparency or noise value when software rendered. Or you could make the age of a particle control the color of the particle, similar to what you did with the fountain example with hardware rendered particles earlier in this book.

The following example shows you how life mapping works and introduces you to the Particle Sampler Info node.

1 Open the scene file

- Open the file *particleSampInfo_Start.mb.*

  This file contains a directional emitter emitting Cloud particles with a predefined lifespan.

2 Map a ramp to Color and test render

- Apply a ramp to the *newCloud* shader's color channel.
- Playback until particles begin to die, then test render a frame.

  Notice the ramp pattern is applied across each particle and the mapping begins from the center of the particle. Also, note that there is no relationship between the age of the particles and the mapping in the rendered image at this point.

3 Disconnect and map the ramp to life color instead

- Break the connection between the ramp and the *newCloud* attribute in Hypershade by selecting the connection, then pressing **Delete**.
- In the Hypershade, **MMB-drag** the ramp onto the *newCloud* shader and connect it to **Life Color**.
- Playback until the particles begin to die, then render a frame.

  When you made the connection to **Life Color**, a *particleSamplerInfo* (PSI) node was automatically created and connected as an input to the texture placement node of the ramp. This PSI node is what keeps track of how old each particle is and what corresponding color along the V direction of the ramp will be assigned to the particle. In this case, and by default, the **Normalized Age** (age/lifespan) is used to look up a value on the ramp.

4 Experiment with Particle Sampler Info node settings

Changes you make to the *particleSamplerInfo* node are only visible when you render. Below are some attributes to change and explanations of what those attributes do.

- Switch **Out UV Type** to **Absolute Age**.

  When absolute age is enabled, the actual age (not normalized against lifespan) of each particle is used to determine what color on the ramp will be assigned to it. By default, the bottom of the ramp is 0 and the top is 1. Age is in seconds and is a per particle attribute. Therefore, after a particle has aged one second (30 frames at 30fps), it will have been assigned every color from the bottom to the top of the ramp.

- Set **Normalization Method** to **Oscillate** first, then **Clamp**.

  Normalization method determines what happens when the age of the particle reaches a value of 1 (the top of the ramp). If Oscillate is selected, a "wrap around" will occur and the particle will "travel through" the ramp starting at the bottom again. This wrap around will continue indefinitely until the particle dies.

  If clamp is selected, no wrap around will occur. Instead, the color at the top of the ramp will remain assigned to the particle after the particle has reached an age of 1.

- Adjust the **Normalization Value**.

  Perhaps you don't want the top of the ramp to correspond to one second of age but instead five seconds of age. In other words, you want the particles to take five seconds to "travel through" all colors of the ramp. Setting normalization value to 5 will accomplish this. To verify this, set normalization value to 5, then play to frame 150 and render. Then go to frame 200 and render.

- Toggle the **Inverse OutUV** option.

  This reverses the direction that the particles "travel through" the ramp over age. For example, if the ramp originally goes from red to green to blue, then so will the particles as they age. If Inverse OutUV is enabled, then the particles will be colored from blue to green to red as they age without having to change the original ramp.

> **Note:** The *particleSamplerInfo* node should not be confused with the
> *samplerInfo* node which is commonly used to obtain point on surface
> shading information with respect to the camera.

Self Shadowing

Self Shadowing is an important part of getting realistic cloud-like particle
rendering. To receive self shadowing on particles you must:

- Enable **Raytracing** in the Render Globals.

- The appropriate lights must be set to cast **Ray Trace shadows**.

- Enable the *particleShape* attributes for **Better Illumination** and under
  Render Stats, **Casts Shadows** should be turned **On**.

Better Illumination is not required for shadowing, however, it will produce a
higher quality image and higher quality shadowing. Better Illumination will
increase the number of lighting samples the renderer is using. It is best to
leave this option off until you are at the final tweaking stages of rendering or
if you are ready to do a final render.

A volcano erupting

A volcano

1 Open the scene file

This scene consists of a mountain with a hole in the top. Particles are emitting from the crater. There are three groups of particles - Cloud particles, ejecta particles, and thick Cloud particles.

- Open the file *volcanoStart.mb*.

  The separate particle elements have been put on separate layers to facilitate their visibility and selection. Use these layers to operate on only one particle layer at a time. Otherwise, this can be a large and unmanageable scene due to the large number of particles. Also, keep track of the Render Globals to keep render times down.

2 Set Particle Shading passes to 1

- Open the Render Globals window and then open the **Anti-aliasing Quality** section.

- In the **Number of Samples** section, set **Particles** to **1**.

- In the **Raytracing Quality** section, turn on **Raytracing**.

- Open the Attribute Editor for the *cloudParticleShape* and *ThickSmokeShape*.

- Toggle off **Better Illumination** in the **Render Attributes** section for each Cloud particle object during rough initial testing.

  Raytracing should be done from the beginning because lighting and illumination are considerably different from non-raytraced rendering. For this reason, it is recommended to find as many ways as possible to reduce the load on the renderer using layers to control visible geometry during testing.

  Raytracing provides the best self shadowing of particles. To speed rendering during testing, use only the most coarse values for shadow quality. The default values should be adequate for this.

3 Position the Lights and turn on cast shadows

- Open the Attribute Editor for **backLight** and turn on Use Ray Traced Shadows.

- Repeat for keyLight.

- Select **keyLight** select **Panels → Look through Selected**.

- Position **keyLight** with the tumble, track and dolly Camera Tools. Make sure the light can see all of the smoke.

  ▪ Repeat for **frontWideFill**.

4 Create the Cloud material for the Cloud particles

  ▪ In the Hypershade, select **Create** → **Volumetric Materials** → **Particle Cloud.**

  ▪ Rename the *particleCloud* material and its shading group to *cloudShader* and *cloudSG*, respectively.

  Note that the *cloudSG* has *cloudShader* as its Volume Material input.

Note: **With Shading Group** should be **On** in the Create Render Node window. This automatically creates a shading group when a material is created.

---

5 Assign the Cloud shader to the Cloud particles

  ▪ **Shift-select** the *cloudParticle* in the viewport and the *cloudShader* material in the Hypershade window.

  ▪ **RMB** over the material node in the Hypershade, select **Assign Material to Selection** from the pop-up menu.

6 Map Solid Fractal textures to color and transparency

  ▪ Map the *cloudShader* **Color** attribute with a **Solid Fractal** 3D Texture.

  ▪ Repeat this procedure for the *cloudShader* **Transparency** attribute.

  ▪ Rename these textures as *colorFractal* and *transFractal*.

7 Adjust Fractal texture parameters

The Solid Fractal textures will need the attributes set to create the correct scale of smoke. The *colorFractal* and the *transFractal* will need to be adjusted equally so that they track with each other. Color Gain attributes on the textures will control much of the strength of the Brightness and Transparency.

Solid Fractal Attributes

Threshold	0.000	
Amplitude	0.700	
Ratio	0.900	
Frequency Ratio	2.000	
Ripples	1.000	1.000	1.000

Depth 0.000 4.000

Bias 0.000
☐ Inflection ☐ Animated
Time 0.000
Time Ratio 2.000

Color Balance

Default Color
Color Gain
Color Offset
Alpha Gain 1.000
Alpha Offset 0.000
☐ Alpha Is Luminance

Color Fractal settings

Solid Fractal Attributes

Threshold	0.000	
Amplitude	0.700	
Ratio	0.800	
Frequency Ratio	2.000	
Ripples	1.000	1.000	1.000

Depth 0.000 4.000

Bias 0.000
☐ Inflection ☐ Animated
Time 0.000
Time Ratio 2.000

Color Balance

Default Color
Color Gain
Color Offset
Alpha Gain 1.000
Alpha Offset 0.000
☐ Alpha Is Luminance

Transparency Fractal settings

Tip: For attributes like Ripples that you will want to track equally on the two Fractal textures, you can connect them to each other with the Connection Editor. This way, when you change one texture the other will follow.

8 Adjust cloudShader attributes to achieve a smoke-like appearance

Transparency and **Density** are the most important parts of getting a soft voluminous look. This also requires the most tweaking. Use the values below as a starting point. Note how low the **Blob Map** is set.

cloudShader attribute settings

9 Use a Reverse Utility node to invert the Fractal Transparency

You may find that the *transFractal* is not tracking the way you expect it to. As you increase its buildup of luminance to match the *colorFractal*, the *transFractal* will create more transparency. By using a Reverse Utility node between the *transFractal* and the *cloudShader* transparency input, you will get the effect of more luminance and less transparency, like you see in real clouds.

- Display the *cloudShader* network in the Hypershade window.

- **RMB-select Create** → **General Utilities** → **Reverse** then **LMB** in the Hypershade window to deposit the *Reverse* node.

- Connect the **OutColor** of the *TransFractal* texture to the Input of the *Reverse* node. Connect the Output of the *Reverse* node to the **Transparency** input of the *cloudShader*.

Tip: You could also use the "invert" attribute in the effects section of the fractal instead of using the Reverse Utility node.

Graph of cloudShader network

10 Create the thick Cloud shader for the thick cloud particles

Create the thick Cloud shader from the *cloudShader* you just created. For this shader you will simply modify the attributes to create a thicker and more turbulent look.

- Select the *cloudShaderSG* shading group in the Hypershade window.

- Select **Edit → Duplicate → Shading Network**.

  This will duplicate the input nodes and connections as well as the selected shading group.

- Rename these nodes with the *"thick"* prefix.

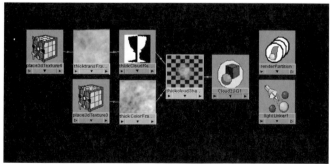

Hypershade of thickCloud shader

- Apply this material to the *thickCloud* particles.

- Use the following diagrams as guides for setting the Fractal and Material attributes.

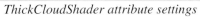

ThickCloudShader attribute settings

ThickColorFractal texture attribute settings

ThickTranFractal texture attribute settings

11 Create the ejecta shader for the tube particles

For the streaks of red hot rock being ejected from the crater, you will use the **Tube** particle type.

- In the Hypershade window, **RMB** select **Create** → **Volumetric Materials** → **Particle Cloud**.

- Rename this material and shading group as *ejectaCloud* and *ejectaTubeSG*.

- Assign this shader to the *ejecta* particles.

12 Create a Life Color Ramp texture

- Press the **Map** button for **Life Color** for the *ejectaCloud* material.

- Press **Ramp** from the Create Render Node window.

  Because there is a lifespan attribute associated with the ejecta particles, this ramp texture will now control what the particle color is throughout its life. A *particleSamplerInfo* node has been created feeding into the 2D texture placement node. This node will convert the age of the particle into a value that is referenced against the V direction of the Ramp texture. The color found at that value is then fed to the color input of the particle cloud material, thus determining the particles' color at that moment.

- Use the following illustrations as a guide for setting attributes on the *ejectaCloud* material and the *ejectaLifeColor* ramp.

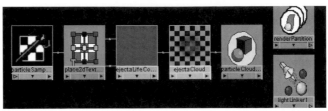

Graph of ejecta particle shader with Life Color Ramp and PSI node

Ejecta particle shader settings

EjectaLifeColor ramp settings

Exercises

- Add a smoke trail to the ejecta particles.

- Use flow and blobby particles to add lava pouring down the edge of the volcano.

- Use the particle sampler info node to change a particle's transparency or color based on its parentUV value or its velocity.

TIPS AND TRAPS

- When fading particles out, it is usually a good idea to fade them all the way out before they die, otherwise you will notice popping in your renders. If you are using opacity or transparency to fade them out, move the top handle of the ramp down from the top a little bit. You may want to do the same thing for particles fading in to avoid popping.

- You can control the shading samples rendered for particles by changing the number in the "particles" field in the render globals. This is listed under Anti-alias Quality/Number of Samples. Increasing this may increase image quality, but will slow your rendering down so only increase it if you cannot get rid of aliasing using other methods.

- Motion blur and IPR are currently not supported for software rendering of particles.

- The resolution of sphere particles is constant; you cannot change the detail of the sphere. Also, you cannot define particle collisions to occur at the edge of a sphere particle or at the edges of sprite particles. As shown in the Instancing chapter, if you need to change the resolution of the sphere render type, try instancing geometric spheres to point particles as a workaround.

- Some additional undocumented files related to rendering that are included with this data are *blobbyBlended.mb* and *blobbyFadeOut.mb*. The *blobbyBlended.mb* file shows how to mix colors between blobby particles that are intersecting. The file blobbyFadeOut shows how to fade the transparency of blobby particles over with respect to age.

SUMMARY

This chapter has introduced you to some ideas and processes involving particle rendering in Maya. Now, you may begin to understand the difference between hardware and software methods and have learned some of the advantages of each method. Remember the importance of color, lighting, and shadow in your imagery. Often, it is these elements that make the biggest difference. The upcoming chapter on compositing will also introduce some other methods for getting your imagery to look better. In this chapter, the following topics have been discussed:

- Hardware Rendered Particle Types:

    Point;

    MultiPoint;

    Streak;

    Multi-Streak;

    sphere;

    sprite.

- Cigarette smoke technique using motion blur.

- Caching (Disk based vs. memory caching).

- Software Rendered Particle Types:

    Blobby;

    Cloud;

    Tube.

- Shading Group organization:

    Surface Material;

    Volume Material;

    Displacement Material.

- Blobby particle techniques.

- Environment Mapping.

- Particle Cloud Shader and Particle Sampler Info.

- Smoke and Cloud Techniques (Volcano).

- Density and Transparency.

- Fractal 3D Texture.

14 Compositing Dynamics

This chapter covers rendering strategies for compositing dynamic effects.

In this chapter you will learn about the following:

- Layers;
- Rendering options for compositing;
- UseBackGround shader;
- Shadow passes;
- Geometry masking.

Gunbot

Compositing is a time saver

One such method of optimizing your production time is to always plan and prepare your project around compositing. Compositing has been an integral part of image creation since artists first began committing their images to some form of media. Film making pioneers were quick to grasp the power of combining image elements into a seamless sandwich of layers to produce final projected images that would not be possible otherwise.

CGI is no different and, in fact, has been a prime beneficiary of this process.

Separating your image elements into distinct rendered passes has the following advantages:

- Faster render times;
- Flexibility of version injection and artistic control;
- Faster and more precise color matching;
- Sweetening processes and post process effects;
- Lower resolution demands for inserted elements;
- Hardware particle rendering.

Larger and more elaborate concepts are made possible by compositing. For this reason, all major studios have centered their image creation pipeline around the compositing process. The compositing station is the hub that all elements are fed into.

Maya provides tools to aid the process of image creation for compositing:

- Layer management
- Shading options for Matte Opacity, BlackHole, UseBackground;
- Geometry masking;
- Z-depth and Alpha/Matte rendering;
- Object visibility;
- Shadow Pass Rendering/ Shadow Catching.

Bye-bye Gunbot

Bye-bye Gunbot

This example utilizes much of what you have learned and applies it to a scene that is in the process of layer creation and manipulation for the compositing process.

In this shot, you have a mechanical biped that is to lose its upper torso in a most violent manner. Although the scene file has been broken down into layers for easy display management, some of the actual rendered layers are derived from set management/rendering flags as well.

Layer1: gunbotPieces

These are the upper torso pieces that are shattering and flying away. They are rigid bodies that have been animated with various dynamic fields.

Layer2: Ground

This is the ground plane. It is a Passive Rigid Body.

Layer3: Legs

This is the Gunbot without the upper torso.

Layer4: blastWave

This is a sphere that is animated to mimic the initial shock wave and act as a guide for pyro timing.

Layer5: gunBotBody

This is the upper torso intact. We will swap this object for the pieces objects at go time.

Layer6: GutsLeaders

This is a particle layer that consists of leading particle emitters.

Layer7: GutsSmoke

This layer is made up of the particles emitted from the GutsLeaders. They are software rendered clouds.

Layer8: ChunkSparks

This is a layer of particles that have been emitted from the surface of the gunbotPieces.

Layer9: MattePieces

Layer10: MatteLegs

Layer11: MatteGround

These last three layers are of duplicated geometry that is parented to the gunbot and ground surfaces. These objects have useBackground shaders applied to them for use in creating mattes and holdouts of render passes.

Layers breakdown

Now let's talk about the individual rendering passes and how they fit together. Typical effects shots are likely much more complex. The emphasis here is on how the rendering passes were conceived, not on the steps involved in actual compositing.

Layer1 movie: pieces

The gunbotPieces are a layer of *rigidBody* NURBS surfaces. They were derived from detached surfaces obtained from the original gunbot body. The gunpods are included as children of standIn spheres that make up the actual Active Rigid Bodies.

These pieces were animated using a radial field and gravity. The radial field attributes as well as the *rigidBodies* have keyframes on several attributes to add control to the accelerations.

These objects were rendered in software by themselves with the ground visibility turned **Off** via its layer. The ground still acts as a Passive Rigid Body collision for the gunbotPieces when hidden.

These objects are also rendered with Z-depth to aid in compositing. But, this is a technique that you do not want to rely on as it can lead to accuracy problems for objects that overlap or are very close. Z-depth is only an 8-bit channel so you don't have a lot of detail to rely on if using Z-depth as a compositing aid.

Layer2 movie: ground and groundPreComp

This is simply the ground plane software rendered. The ground shadow pass is derived from this layer by applying the useBackground to the ground object then rendering with primary visibility turned **Off** on all of the gunbot objects (gunbotPieces and legs).

Layer3 movie: shock

This layer is an animated NURBS sphere. It is software rendered with an X-ray or ghost shader applied. This shader creates the soft edge effect by using the Facing Ratio of the *SamplerInfo* Utility node to drive the transparency of the material. This layer is useful for first timing the rate of explosion and helps to coordinate all the elements of the explosion.

Layer5 movie: smoke

These particles are emitted from the guts particles and have only a slight amount of InheritVelocity. They also have their own gravity which is very slight. The intended effect is that they are trailing smoke. These are rendered in software. The geometry of the gunbot and ground are masked by using the useBackGround shader with matte opacity set to "blackHole".

Layer6 movie: Sparks and particlePreComp

This layer of particles are surface emitted from the rigid body pieces. They have had the pixie dust treatment done to them so that they sparkle and flash. They collide with the ground and the gunbot. They have a collision event that emits other sparks at the point of collision. They are hardware rendered.

Layer7: FireBall

Stock footage of a fireball explosion was inserted into the composite. Because these images did not contain Z-depth information, a move3D event is applied to scale, position, and add Z-depth information inside the compositing application. A TimeWarp event was also used to sync the timing and duration for this effect.

Layer8: Shadow Passes

A few different shadow pass sequences were rendered separately, then composited into the final movie. You can see the floor shadow pass in the movie called *floorShadows*. The shadow pass layers were created using the "useBackground" shader on the gunbot and the ground. With their

Primary Visibility set **Off**, the geometry acts as shadow catchers. This information is only visible in the matte channel. To see your matte information when test rendering, select **Display**→ **Alpha Channel** from the Render View window. Use a compositor to manipulate this information further by using it as a mask input channel to a "Brightness" event, for example, thus recreating the shadows as darker areas on the Brightness events applied images. Using this technique, you can also render the shadows at a lower quality and then blur and add color to them in compositing. This can significantly shave time off from rendering large scenes.

Compositing

As the layers or passes are rendered, they are tested together in your compositing application.

Images that have been rendered in Maya are brought into the Compositing application as references only. As subsequent improvements or versions are created, they can directly replace referenced images in the compositing "script".

Images can undergo drastic manipulation during compositing with much less rendering time. Lighting effects and manipulation of shadow, color, and intensity as well as softness are a prime example. Rendering shadows separately and with coarse resolution with the intention of softening during composition can be a huge time and effort saver in itself.

Color correction and contrast balance as well as edge contouring (pseudo-anti aliasing), film grain, camera shake, and lighting effects such as glow and lens flare are some of the popular effects achieved during compositing, all with very fast rendering updates.

Compositing is also where elements created in other applications are brought together. These packages are also a great front end to bring in external plates or video source footage for interaction as rotoscoping or image plane/texture elements in Maya.

Maya has render layer management that can be used to organize your rendered images into separate color and shadow passes automatically. Render layers can be setup inside Maya's render globals (**Window** → **Render Globals** → **Render Layer / Pass Control**).

SUMMARY

Compositing is an important part of pulling your scene elements together. It is an especially common part of the process for dealing with the look and integration of particle rendering. The movies and descriptions in this chapter hopefully have given you some idea of what is going on at the compositing stage and will have shown you some ideas of how you can construct your scenes for this process. Taking advantage of the additional speed and flexibility that compositing offers you will expand not only the options you have to affect the look of your imagery, but also will help you organize and make changes to your work much more efficiently.

Some Compositing advantages are:

- Combining software and hardware rendered particles;
- Object and material options for visibility and lighting;
- Duplicating and parenting of child matte objects;
- Integration of shadow and glowing effects;
- Control of timing and editing.

A **Expression Appendix**

This appendix provides a more in-depth discussion of the expressions and steps used to build the examples contained in the file *expressionExamples.mb*. You can use this to walk you through how each example in that file was built and get a description of how the expressions work. This section also discusses the *order of evaluation* for the various elements in Maya's dynamics.

MOVING PARTICLES WITH EXPRESSIONS

We have been dealing primarily with using expressions to control rendering attributes such as color or opacity. We can apply similar methods to position, velocity, or acceleration to dynamically control the motion of the particles.

Write a simple expression to control position

1 Create a particle in the scene

- Use the Particle Tool to create a single particle near the origin.

- Set **Particle Render Type** to **Spheres**.

2 Add a Runtime Expression

- Add the following to Runtime Expression to **position**:

```
position = <<0, time, 0 >>;
```

3 Test the results

- Set the frame range to start at **1** and end at **300**.

- Rewind and playback.

The particle moves up in Y as time increases. As the animation plays back, *time* is a constantly changing value determined using the following relationship:

```
Time = Current Frame Number / Frames Per Second
```

Expressions for creating random motion

- Create a cloud of **100** particles.
- Try each of the following by itself in the Runtime Expression to see the interesting effects they produce:

```
velocity = dnoise (position);

acceleration = dnoise (position);

velocity = sphrand(10);

acceleration = sphrand(10);

position = position + dnoise(position);
```

An acceleration rule that uses variables and magnitude

1 Create a new scene file with a cloud of particles in it

- Select **File** → **New Scene**.
- Create a cloud of **50** particles using the Particle Tool.
- Set **Particle Render Type** to **Spheres**.
- Set **Radius** to **0.3**.

2 Add a Runtime Expression to acceleration

- Enter the following in the Runtime Expression for **acceleration**:

```
int $frequency = 65;

float $distance = mag (position);

int $limit = 3;

if ($distance > $limit)

acceleration = acceleration - (position * $frequency);
```

- Click **Create** in the Expression Editor.

3 Playback the animation

The particles move in a swarming pattern. Watch one particle to see what it is doing. It is swinging between a range in 3D space defined by $limit. When the **Magnitude** of the position is greater than that limit, the expression begins subtracting acceleration from the particle which increases its acceleration in the opposite direction.

If this is unclear to you, try the same expression on a single particle instead of a cloud. Also, try changing the values used for frequency and limit.

You can also try this same effect with emitted particles.

A position rule that uses noise and a custom attribute

1 Create a new scene with a grid of particles

- Use the Particle Tool to create a grid of particles that has some particles in all four quadrants of the grid
- Set **Particle Render Type** to **Spheres**.
- Set **Radius** to **0.3**.

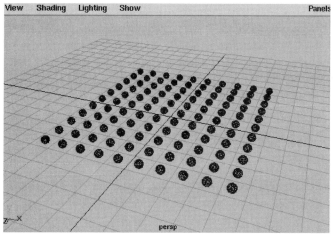

A grid of particles in all four quadrants

2 Make a custom vector attribute to store original position

Adding a custom vector attribute will give us a place to store the original position of each particle.

- Select *particleShape1*.
- In the **Add Dynamics Attributes** in **General**:

    Attribute Name to **origPos**;

    Data Type to **Vector**;

    Attribute Type to **Array**;

    Add Initial State Attribute to **On**.

- Press **OK**.

An *origPos* field is added to the Per Particle (Array) attributes section of the Attribute Editor.

Since the **Attribute Type** was set to **Array**, you just made your own custom per particle attribute.

3 Add a Creation Expression for origPos

- Add the following Creation Expression to *origPos* to store the position of each particle at the initial frame:

```
origPos = position;
```

4 Add a Runtime Expression to position

- Click the runtime radio button in the Expression Editor.

- Enter the following Runtime Expression to control **position**:

```
position = origPos + <<0, 0.8 * noise (origPos *
3+time*<<0,1,2>>),0>>
```

5 Test the results

- Rewind and playback.

Each particle moves in a wave-like fashion up and down along only the Y axis. The above expression is just adding a vector to origPos. The Y component of that vector is a statement that generates a random stream. **0.8** controls the amplitude of that stream, **3** controls the frequency, and **<<0,1,2>>** controls the direction of the phase.

The `noise` function produces a smoother random number stream than the previously discussed `rand` function.

Notice how you are setting a value for origPos in the creation, then modifying that value again in the Runtime Expression. This is a very common technique for working with particle expressions.

6 Save the file

- Save the file as *waveExpression.ma.*

Change Color based on Position

- Create an Omni Directional emitter with the default options.

- Add an **rgbPP** attribute.

- Add the following Runtime Expression to position:

```
vector $pos = position;
if ($pos.y >=0)
```

```
rgbPP = <<1,0,0>>;
else
rgbPP = <<0,0,1>>;
```

- Rewind and playback.

  This expression stores the position for each particle in a vector variable called $pos. The `if` statement checks the Y component of that vector to see if it is above or below the Y axis. If the particle is above, it is red, otherwise it is blue.

  You can try the same idea with acceleration or velocity instead of position.

Tip: The individual elements of a vector (i.e. <<x, y, z>>) are called components.

Emitter examples

Although emitters are closely related to particles, they **do not** use creation and Runtime Expressions. Below are two examples that show you some ideas you can build upon when working with emitters.

Varying the emission rate

The following example is good for obtaining a randomized emission rate that can be used to simulate an eruption, geyser, or puffing smoke effect:

1 Start with an empty scene file

- Select **File** → **New Scene**.

2 Create a directional emitter emitting particles in Y

> **Speed** to **5**;
>
> **Direction** to **0, 1, 0** for **X, Y,** and **Z**, respectively;
>
> **Particle Render Type** to **Clouds (s/w)**;
>
> **Radius** to **0.2**.

3 Add gravity to the particles

- Select the particles, then select **Fields**→ **Gravity**.

4 Add an expression to control rate

- Select **emitter1**.

- Open the Expression Editor and enter the following expression

emitter1.rate = 100*noise (time*1000);

This expression uses noise as opposed to dnoise since rate is a scalar quantity. You would only use dnoise if you were working with a vector quantity such as position or color. We multiply noise and time by 1000 to increase the amplitude and frequency of the noise values since they are far too small without these multipliers.

PARTICLE ID

Just as each building on a street has its own address number, each particle in a particle object has its own unique numerical identity called the **particleId**. ParticleId is an integer value ranging from **0** to **count - 1**. The particleId attribute makes it easier to control attributes of specific particles independently of other particles within the same particle object. This is especially useful for adding variation to attributes of a particle object.

Control color based on particleId

1 Create a new scene file

- Select **File** → **New Scene**.

2 Create an Omni emitter with default values

- Select **Particles** → **Create Emitter**.
- Set **Emitter Type** to **Omni**.

3 Add an rgbPP attribute to particleShape1

4 Add a Runtime Expression to rgbPP

- Add the following to the Runtime Expression for *particleShape1:*

```
if (particleId==10)
rgbPP = <<0,1,0>>;
```

- Press **Create** in the Expression Editor.
- Rewind and play the animation.

The first particle in a particle object is always particleId **0**. Therefore, the 9th particle emitted into *particleShape2* is particleId **10** and is colored green due to the **if** conditional statement in the expression. Below is another particleId example you can add as runtime or Creation Expression for rgbPP to produce some interesting results.

```
if (particleId % 10 == 0)
```

```
rgbPP = sphrand(1);
```

The % symbol stands for the **modulus operation** which is the remainder produced when two numbers are divided. The above expression divides the particleId by 10, if the **remainder** of that division is 0 then the **sphrand** function picks a random vector value between <<0,0,0>> and <<1,1,1>>. In other words, every 10th particle will get a random color assigned.

ORDER OF EVALUATION

The following is a breakdown of the order in which Maya evaluates the various dynamic elements in a simulation.

- First, the **acceleration** is cleared at the beginning of each frame or evaluation.

- **Particle Runtime Expressions before Dynamics** are evaluated secondly. The expressions can get, set, or add to the current values of the particle's attributes.

- Next, the **forces** are computed. Forces include **fields, springs,** and **goals**. These forces are added to whatever is currently in the acceleration which includes whatever a particle expression may have put there.

- The **velocity** is computed from the acceleration. This also just adds to whatever value is currently in the velocity which may have previously been set in an expression.

- The **positions** are computed from the velocity. Just as with acceleration and velocity, position is added to whatever is currently stored in position from expressions or forces computed above.

- Finally, the **Runtime Expressions after Dynamics** are evaluated.

The expressions do not override the dynamics. The dynamics happen after the expressions are evaluated, and their results are added together. It is possible to have expressions calculated before dynamics on a per object basis by disabling the **Expressions After Dynamics** checkbox of the particleShape object.

B Emit Appendix

This appendix provides detailed descriptions of the expressions used in the Emit function lesson.

Fireworks1 Expression

Below is the Runtime Expression used for *fireworksShape1*. The short command flags have been replaced with the long flag names for additional clarity. A detailed description is provided after the expression.

```
if ($vel.y < 0)
{//opening bracket for the if statement
fireworksShape1.lifespanPP = 0;
float $antiGrav = launcher.antiGrav;
int $upperCount = launcher.showerUpper;
int $lowerCount = launcher.showerLower;
int $upperLife = launcher.streamUpper;
int $lowerLife = launcher.streamLower;
int $numPars = rand($lowerCount, $upperCount);

string $emitCmd = "emit -object fireworksShape2
";

for ($i=1; $i<=$numPars; $i++)
 {//opening bracket for the for loop
    $emitCmd += "-position " + $pos + " ";
    vector $vrand = sphrand(10);
    $vrand = <<$vrand.x, $vrand.y + $antiGrav,
$vrand.z>>;
    $emitCmd += "-attribute velocity ";
    $emitCmd += "-vectorValue " + $vrand + " ";
    float $lsrand = rand($lowerLife,
$upperLife);
    $emitCmd += "-attribute lifespanPP ";
```

```
        $emitCmd += "-floatValue " + $lsrand + " ";
} //closing bracket for the for loop


 eval($emitCmd);
} //closing bracket for the if statement
```

Step-by-step explanation

```
float $antiGrav = launcher.antiGrav;
```

- Store the value for *antiGrav* into a float (decimal) variable called **$antiGrav**. *AntiGrav* is one of the **custom** attributes previously added to *launcher*.

  The **$antiGrav** variable will be used later in this expression to add or remove velocity in the Y direction as particles fall. This provides a way to add to or counteract the effect of gravity.

```
int $upperCount = launcher.showerUpper;
int $lowerCount = launcher.showerLower;
```

- *showerLower* and *showerUpper* are two of the **Custom** attributes previously added to *launcher*.

- These attributes define a range (lower and upper bound) out of which a random number will be picked later in the expression.

- That random number will be used to control the **number of particles** emitted into **fireworks2**.

```
int $upperLife = launcher.streamUpper;
int $lowerLife = launcher.streamLower;
```

- *streamUpper* and *streamLower* are two more of the **custom** attributes previously added to *launcher*.

- These attributes define a range (lower and upper bound) out of which a random number will be chosen later in the expression.

- That random number will be used to control the **Lifespan** of particles emitted into **fireworks2**.

```
int $numPars = rand($lowerCount, $upperCount);
```

- Choose a random integer number from within the range of values defined by **$lowerCount** and **$upperCount**.

- Assign that random value to **$numPars**.

- **$numPars** will be used later in this expression to control the **number of times** the commands within a loop will be executed.

```
string $emitCmd = "emit -object fireworks2Shape ";
```

- The remaining portion of the expression is designed to piece together the emit function and execute it once it has been fully assembled.

- Each particle created in *fireworksShape2* will be the result of using the same basic syntax framework for the emit function. The only difference will be substituting in different attribute values (position, velocity, etc.) for each particle.

- **$emitCmd** stores the emit command while it is being constructed in the expression. The bold text above is the first piece of the emit function. The remaining elements will be constructed using the following looping structure.

```
for ($i=1; $i<=$numPars; $i++)
```

- This is a looping structure (for loop) that will execute the commands following it that are enclosed by curly brackets.

- The number of times those commands are executed is controlled by the random value assigned to **$numParts**.

- The basic syntax of a **for loop** is:

```
for (startValue; endValue; increment).
{
statements;
}
```

  In the expression's loop, **$I** is the **startValue** and represents how many times you've cycled through the loop.

  The first time through the loop, **$i** is the **startValue** (1).

  Then, **$i** is incremented by **1** (this is what **i++** in the increment does).

  Therefore, the second time through the loop **$i =2**.

  As long as the condition defined by **endValue** ($i<=$numPars) is true, **$i** will be incremented and the loop will continue.

  When the **endValue** condition is false, the loop is exited and the next line in the expression is evaluated.

```
$emitCmd += "-position " + $pos + " ";
  vector $vrand = sphrand(10);
  $vrand = <<$vrand.x, $vrand.y + $antiGrav, $vrand.z>>;
  $emitCmd += "-attribute velocity ";
  $emitCmd += "-vectorValue " + $vrand + " ";
  float $lsrand = rand($lowerLife, $upperLife);
```

```
$emitCmd += "-attribute lifespanPP ";

$emitCmd += "-floatValue " + $lsrand + " ";
```

- In this case, the syntax convention **+=** means "take what is currently stored in **$emitCmd** and append what is on the right side of the symbol to the end of **$emitCmd**."

- In the first exercise of the emit function lesson, you constructed three emit statements to add three individual particles to a particle object. The contents of the for loop listed here does the same thing many times. Each line above is executed once for each iteration of the for loop.

- $vrand uses the **sphrand** function to select a random vector value between <<0,0,0>> and <<10,10,10>>. This provides a random value to use for velocity.

- The expression constantly appends to **$emitCmd**. Each line is setting a different attribute for the emit command.

```
eval($emitCmd);
```

- The `eval` command is a MEL command that functions much like the = button on a calculator. However, in this case we are "inputting" letters and numbers instead of only numbers.

- The for loop is like entering all the values in the calculator to construct the **$emitCmd** variable.

- After the loop has been finished, the expression evaluates the contents of **$emitCmd** to actually place the particle in the correct locations and assign them the correct attribute values.

INDEX

NUMERICS

R

V

Variable 140
Vector 140
Velocity 141
view panels 8
volcanoStart.mb 277
Vortex Field 83, 160

W

Windy City 70

NOTES

NOTES

Novice/New to 3D

Looking for a better understanding of 3D space and the concepts and theory behind working in Maya? Want a highly visual tour through 3D space? Try *The Art of Maya*, a full-color illustrated guide to working in 3D or get hands-on experience through one of our Maya Beginner's Guide DVDs. The Maya Beginner's Guides provide you with a step-by-step, highly visual guided learning experience to help you understand how to animate, render and create dynamic effects in Maya.

Intermediate

Transitioning to Maya from another 3D package? Looking to improve your general skills when using Maya? Choose from our Learning Maya family of books. Explore Maya through theoretical discussions, step-by-step instructions and with helpful instructor-led chapter overviews - the Learning Maya books are must-have reference materials for any Maya user. Delve deeply into *Character Rigging, Modeling, Rendering, Dynamics, MEL,* and *Maya Unlimited Features*.

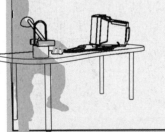

Step 1

Step 2

Want to Learn More?
Visit
www.alias.com/store
and check out our books and training materials.

Step 3

Advanced

Are you a seasoned Maya user looking for time and money saving tips and techniques? Want to understand how your industry peers have successfully solved their production problems? Select from our extensive selection of Maya Techniques™ DVDs and learn from pros like Jason Schleifer (Weta Digital, Dreamworks/PDI); Tom Kluyskens (Weta Digital); Erick Miller (Digital Domain); Paul Thuriot (Tippett Studio) and more.

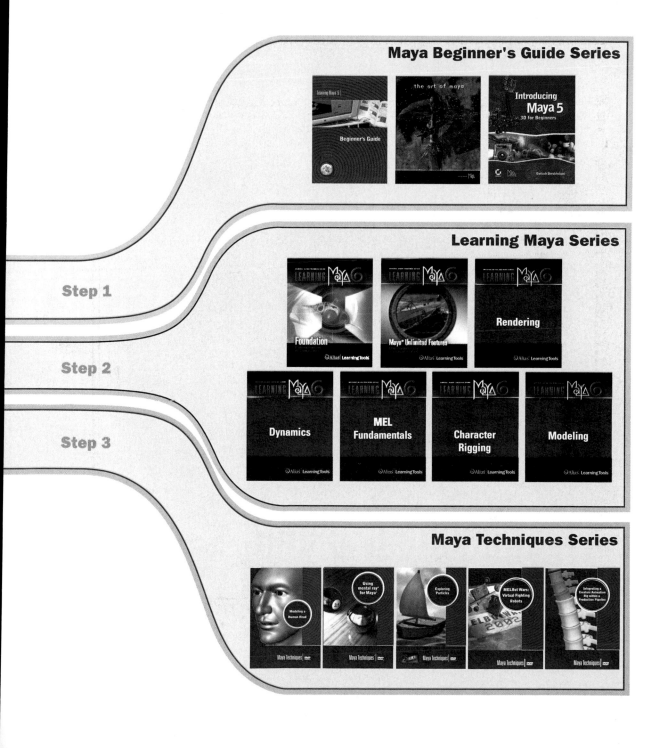